Construction of American

FURNITURE TREASURES

Construction of American
FURNITURE
TREASURES

MEASURED DRAWINGS OF SELECTED MUSEUM PIECES WITH COMPLETE

INFORMATION ON THEIR CONSTRUCTION AND REPRODUCTION . . .

38 FULL-PAGE PLATES, 344 DETAIL DRAWINGS AND MORE

THAN 40 PHOTOGRAPHS OF THE WORK OF THE MOST

FAMOUS EARLY AMERICAN CABINETMAKERS

By LESTER MARGON, A. I. D.

DOVER PUBLICATIONS, INC., NEW YORK

This Dover edition, first published in 1975, is an unabridged and corrected republication of the work first published in 1949 by the Home Craftsman Publishing Corporation. A Brief Summary of Early American Furniture Styles has been prepared especially for this edition by the author.

International Standard Book Number: 0-486-23056-2
Library of Congress Catalog Card Number 74-79937

Manufactured in the United States of America
Dover Publications, Inc.
180 Varick Street
New York, N. Y. 10014

BRIEF SUMMARY
of
EARLY AMERICAN FURNITURE STYLES

IT HAS LONG BEEN SAID THAT A HISTORY OF FURNITURE IS THE HISTORY OF A CIVILIZATION. THIS IS ESPECIALLY TRUE IN A HISTORY OF EARLY AMERICAN FURNITURE WHERE THE GRADUAL PROGRESS OF FURNITURE development from the very primitive to the elaborate Federal period parallels the progress of the Colonists from the earliest settlements to the development of the new nation.

William Penn encouraged people from the Rhineland to come to America with promises of freedom of religious expression. The Pennsylvania Dutch founded their homes near Philadelphia. Rich burghers settled in New York; the militant French Huguenots favored the South. These early settlers were soon followed by the Scandinavian peasants and the persistent Irish. All of these colonists brought with them from their homelands ideas and traditions that influenced their architecture and furniture design.

In the early years sparsely furnished multipurpose rooms served the settlers for cooking, eating and sleeping. Little furniture made before 1650 has survived in America. Later, most of the furniture was styled in England, and the colonial cabinetmakers tried to copy European designs. Lacking tools, material and knowledge, much of the output of the early cabinetmakers was heavy and crude. The furniture was made of oak and consisted mainly of cupboards to supply space for everything. There were also various types of tables, but chairs were a rarity. If there was one chair in a household it was reserved for the master or for a favored guest. Other members of the family either sat on benches or remained standing. The court cupboard remained the sole decorative object in the room.

The expansion of the American economy at the beginning of the eighteenth century ushered in a period of development and change as the affluent began to acquire a taste for more elegance in home furnishings. The style of William and Mary (1700-1725) and Continental tastes in architecture and furniture designs became popular. Tall chests of drawers with desk compartments were favored. Lowboys and highboys, often painted in gray, called "grisaille," were featured. Velvets, damasks, and crewel embroidery were used for upholstery. With the introduction of marquetry the period soon became known as the "Age of Walnut."

Later (1725-1760) the Queen Anne style found favor in the Colonies. The main feature of this period was the introduction of the curvilinear line. The cabriole leg was universally favored, and lowboys and highboys were enhanced by various shapings of the skirtings. A sense of movement was produced by the innovation of "bonnet" tops on highboys. Rooms increased in number and became larger with higher ceilings. Wall panellings with pilasters and other architectural ornaments were featured.

In London in 1754, Thomas Chippendale, the famous cabinetmaker, published his *Gentleman and Cabinet-Maker's Director*. By 1760 copies of this volume had reached America, and its influence was tremendous. Chippendale was not an innovator; he used many styles in his work including Georgian, French, Chinese, Gothic and Classic. It was a period that knew no bounds and was more prolific in adaptation than invention. Especially excellent were Chippendale's designs of chairs featuring pierced back slats and ribbon-back patterns. Mahogany with fine carving as decoration became the favored wood.

The Federal period in American furniture (1785-1840) was named after the form of government. Designers welcomed the neo-classical art forms popularized by Robert Adam in England after his studies of the excavations then being conducted in Pompeii and Herculaneum. The American eagle became the foremost motif in design and decoration. Graceful line, applied carvings, painted decoration and architectural details were prominent. In America, Duncan Phyfe became the most prominent cabinetmaker. His work embodied eloquence with artistry. He supplied the affluent leading citizenry of New York with an array of furniture of distinction at high prices. His chairs were particularly magnificent as were his carved settees with caned panels, reed arms and fluted carved legs. Other pieces of furniture popular at this time were tables, global stands, tip-top tables and credenzas. Crystal chandeliers and Aubusson rugs completed the elegant assemblage. To this day the name of Duncan Phyfe is magic. Examples of his work may be seen in most museum furniture collections. Besides being an accomplished artisan he proved to be an astute businessman who succeeded in manipulating his output to suit the changing times.

Although England and France played important roles in influencing funiture design in early America, and while a goodly number of imports found their way here, it should be clearly understood that these influences were minimal. The cabinetmakers in America acquired the skills and the initiative to design furniture that best suited the needs of the new country. No longer did they merely attempt to copy foreign products. This was a growing country, free and uninhibited, and much of the work done here was superior to and of better design than the European output.

LESTER MARGON, A.I.D.

INTRODUCTION

IF YOU HAVE SEEN EVEN A SMALL PROPORTION OF THE RARE AND VERY BEAUTIFUL PIECES OF AMERICAN FURNITURE ILLUSTRATED ON THE FOLLOWING PAGES, YOU ARE FORTUNATE INDEED. They are treasured heritages of a rich past which are now housed in museums and historic shrines. Only a few persons who have the leisure and means to travel extensively have visited all the collections from which these masterpieces have been selected, and even they probably did not appreciate the designs or understand the construction as well as you will when you have studied the magnificent pencil drawings of Mr. Margon. It is as if he were taking you on a personally conducted tour to see each piece. You can imagine him to be saying:

"Here are the significant features of the design as they appear to me. Note these proportions . . . this characteristic molding . . . this skillful bit of carving . . . the refinement of these lines."

He does even more than that, because he then takes the piece apart for you, as it were, and reveals every detail of the cabinetmaker's art—how the stock was laid out and cut, the joints made, the molding, shaping, carving and inlaying done, and the whole assembled.

It would be a stimulating experience to have so great a furniture expert as Mr. Margon explain all this, and yet that is exactly what he does in this book through his inimitable pencil drawings—among the finest furniture plates ever produced—and the numerous construction detail drawings, most of which are in perspective for easy understanding.

To this work Mr. Margon brings a lifetime's experience. A native of New York City, Mr. Margon's accomplishments in architecture and interior decoration at Cooper Union won the attention of Mr. Wilson Hungate, then head of the design department of the great furniture establishment of W. and J. Sloane, who invited him to join the staff. Beginning as an apprentice, Mr. Margon developed into one of the designer-decorators of the organization, where he worked for seven years. At that time the leading Grand Rapids furniture factories had Sloane-trained designers. Mr. Albert Stickley — another famous name in American furniture—invited Mr. Margon to go to Grand Rapids, which was the furniture capital of America. There he served several of the largest factories and was sent to the Exposition des Arts Decoratifs in 1925.

Upon his return from abroad, he joined the

staff of The Hampton Shops in New York, and later Schmieg-Hungate-Kotzian, possibly the finest cabinetmakers in America. During this period he continued his studies. He took the Beaux Arts course at New York University, where he won a First Medal and a Second Medal in national competitions.

Several years of free-lance furniture designing followed, including five study-tours in Europe. Traveling from Naples to northerly Trondjhem, he visited innumerable places and made some 500 measured drawings of furniture in public and private collections in Italy, France, Germany, Belgium, Denmark, Czechoslovakia, England, Norway, Sweden and Switzerland. This is perhaps the largest group of furniture drawings of this kind.

Upon his return from his last trip, Mr. Margon opened his own studio in New York, where he now specializes in the design of modern stores and their furnishings and equipment. Furniture design is still an important part of his work, and he is a regular contributor to the Home Craftsman Magazine. This volume contains the first series of his American furniture drawings to be published in book form.

We know of no one who has the good taste and excellent technique, which enables him to express in simple line the characteristics and individuality of each piece of furniture selected. He will spend a year searching for a particular piece and then travel a thousand miles to sketch it.

It will be noted that only once did Mr. Margon find a model outside of the United States. During a visit to Montreal, his eye was attracted by an especially fine cradle of the Pilgrim type. He thought this might well be included because of its typically American character.

As an experienced interior decorator, he feels that fine furniture of the type he describes should be seen in an appropriate setting. For this reason—and merely as a suggestion—he has included measured drawings of a pine-paneled wall from a room now in the Brooklyn Museum.

All lovers of fine furniture, students, craftsmen, cabinetmakers, interior decorators, architects and collectors should find in this book a wealth of material. There is no better way to learn to understand and appreciate the design of museum pieces than to see, not only the full-page plates and the photographs, but the actual, intimate details of construction. This information can only be obtained by personal study in museums. Even then, the hidden construction is often difficult to figure out.

For the craftsman who wishes to build reproductions of any of these pieces, the information given is perhaps the most complete and exhaustive that has ever been published in book form.

HARRY J. HOBBS

TABLE OF CONTENTS

Pennsylvania Provincial Dower Chest

This highly decorative chest provides drawer space and a blanket compartment. It is made of pine and poplar with painted ornamentation that looks intricate but is not hard to copy. The piece is used by courtesy of the Metropolitan Museum of Art.

NO STUDY of Pennsylvania Provincial furniture would be adequate without the inclusion of one example of painted furniture. A lively sense of design and a fondness for gay and robust coloring distinguished the work of these early craftsmen. Chief among the motifs used were the tulip, carnation and fuchsia, chosen no doubt as representations of the colorful gardens which the builders remembered from the Fatherland. An unusually fine sense of color made these bits of painted furniture real treasures within the family, and make them so highly regarded today as to be worthy of reproduction.

The painted dower-chests from Berks County, of which the one chosen for study and illustration is possibly the finest, invariably used unicorns from medieval times as the guardians of fair maidenhood. The turtledoves

portrayed in thrush-like posture sang the love songs in the imagined courtship. The cavaliers in the side panels portrayed the suitor on his way to plead his case for the hand of a lovely maiden. On the illustrated chest he is

portrayed almost like a hunter, which is perhaps just as well. On woods like pine and poplar the polychrome decoration was used lavishly but with an excellent sense of black and white as can be clearly seen in the photograph.

This particular chest is painted all black with three white panels on the front and two white panels on the top. The effect is most dramatic. The colors used are all "earth colors", red that is almost vermilion, terra-cotta brown, a deeper brown more on the sepia tone, a mouse gray and a golden light tan. These shades with black and white also used in the decoration form the color scheme.

The accompanying chart designating the colors used on the original chest will be found useful, but the craftsman who likes to paint and has had a little experience will want to use his own imagination.

It should be noted that the chest is made up of solid panels ranging in widths from $16\frac{1}{4}$" to $24\frac{1}{4}$". While it is possible to obtain stock as wide as this in some localities, it may be necessary to glue up several narrower pieces to obtain panels of the widths required. If it is necessary to do this, each panel should be made up a little wider and longer than required so that it can be

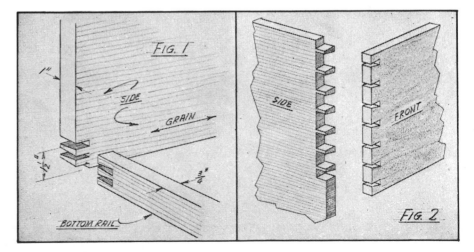

A · PAINTED · & · DECORATED · CHEST·

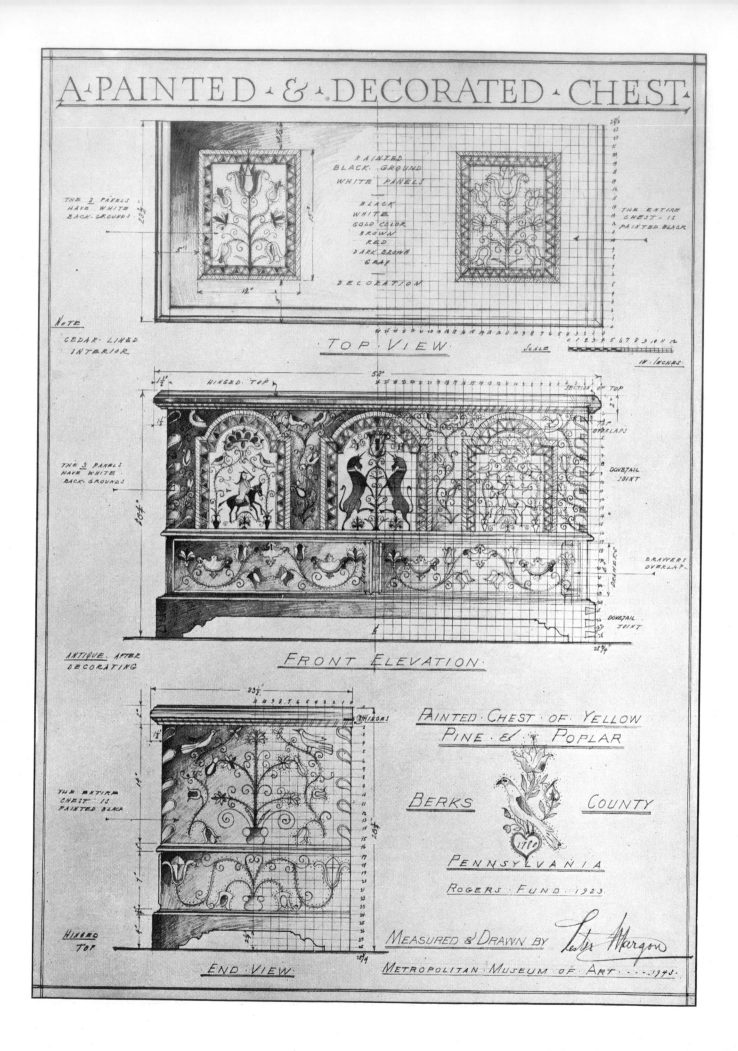

THE 2 PANELS
HAVE WHITE
BACK-GROUNDS

PAINTED
BLACK · GROUND
WHITE · PANELS

BLACK
WHITE
GOLD COLOR
BROWN
RED
DARK BROWN
GRAY

DECORATION

THE ENTIRE
CHEST · IS
PAINTED BLACK

NOTE
CEDAR · LINED
INTERIOR

TOP · VIEW

SCALE

IN · INCHES

HINGED · TOP

SECTION OF TOP

TOP
OVERLAPS

DOVETAIL
JOINT

THE 3 PANELS
HAVE WHITE
BACK-GROUNDS

DRAWERS
OVERLAP.

DRAWERS

DOVETAIL
JOINT

ANTIQUE · AFTER
DECORATING

FRONT · ELEVATION·

HINGES

PAINTED · CHEST · OF · YELLOW
PINE · & · POPLAR

THE ENTIRE
CHEST · IS
PAINTED BLACK

BERKS   COUNTY

PENNSYLVANIA

ROGERS · FUND · 1923

HINGED
TOP

MEASURED & DRAWN BY   Lester Margon

END · VIEW·

METROPOLITAN · MUSEUM · OF · ART · · · · 1945·

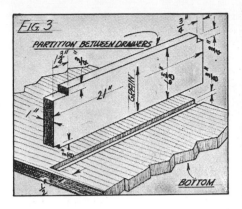

FIG 3

PARTITION BETWEEN DRAWERS

GRAIN

21"

BOTTOM

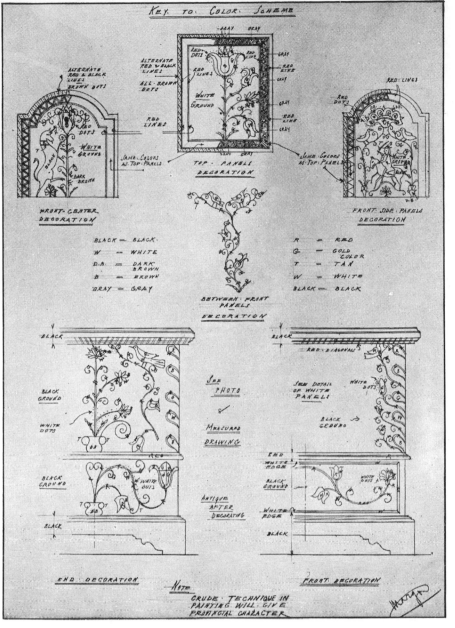

KEY TO COLOR SCHEME

FRONT CENTER DECORATION

TOP PANELS DECORATION

FRONT SIDE PANELS DECORATION

BLACK — BLACK.
W — WHITE
D.B. — DARK BROWN
B — BROWN
GRAY — GRAY

R — RED
G — GOLD COLOR
T — TAN
W — WHITE
BLACK — BLACK

BETWEEN FRONT PANELS DECORATION

END DECORATION

See Photo

Measured Drawing

Antique After Decorating

FRONT DECORATION

Note

CRUDE TECHNIQUE IN PAINTING WILL GIVE PROVINCIAL CHARACTER

squared to the proper size later. Butting edges of each piece making up a panel must be squared by means of a hand plane, preferably the size of a jointer plane. If the jointing of the edges is done properly the use of dowels will be unnecessary. A good grade of glue should be used and the stock should be left in clamps until the glue is completely dry.

The sides are made of two pieces of 1" stock 24¼" wide and 22" long. The back is made of 1" stock 24¼" wide and 49" long. The front panel is made of 1" stock 16¼" wide and 49" long. The bottom rail is ¾" x 1½" x 49". After these pieces have been squared to the proper sizes, the work of laying the dovetail joints can be started.

The front panel has seven dovetail sockets laid out at each end as shown in Fig. 2. These are cut out with the aid of a dovetail saw or back saw and a chisel. The dovetail pins on the forward end of each side member are located and marked by placing the front member on the end of the side

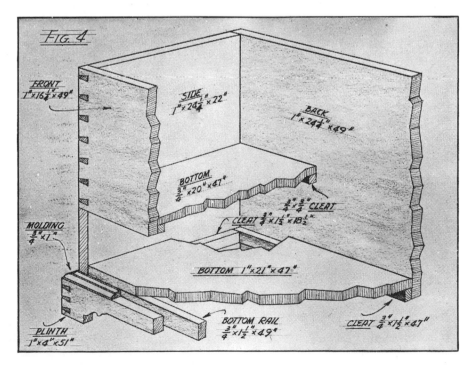

FIG. 4

FRONT 1"x16¼"x49"

SIDE 1"x24¼"x22"

BACK 1"x24¼"x49"

BOTTOM ¾"x20"x47"

½"x½" CLEAT

CLEAT ¾"x1½"x18½"

BOTTOM 1"x21"x47"

MOLDING ¾"x1"

BOTTOM RAIL ¾"x1½"x49"

CLEAT ¾"x1½"x47"

PLINTH 1"x4"x51"

member and outlining the dovetail sockets with a knife. When the pins are being formed it is best not to cut directly on the lines. Allow a little for trimming and fitting in order to produce tight joints. The bottom rail has two sockets laid out and cut at each end as shown in Fig. 1. The outline of the pins on the end of the side member that are to fit in the sockets is done in the same manner as described above.

The back panel is joined to the side members in the same manner as the front panel. The sockets are laid out and cut first, then the pins are fitted to them. With the completion of the dovetail joints the members are assembled temporarily to check the work and to make certain that all joints fit tightly. The work is taken apart and glue is applied to all joining surfaces.

Clamps should be applied between the front and back panels to force out the surplus glue and to bring the butting surfaces of the panels in close contact. It is important to check the corners of the cabinet in order to have them square. This can be done with a large try square or framing square or it may be done by checking the diagonal measurements. If the case should be out of square it must be forced back into place then held there by means of diagonal braces fastened to the top and bottom edges of the side and front members or the side and back members.

The lower bottom is a piece of 1″ stock 21″ side and 47″ long while the chest compartment bottom is made of ¾″ stock 20″ x 47″ as shown in Fig. 4. Between these two members the drawers are fitted. The drawer compartments are separated by means of a partition as shown in Fig. 3. This partition is made of 1″ stock 21″ wide and ⅝″ long. The lower bottom has a stopped dado or gain cut across the face to take this partition as shown in Fig. 3. The gain, measuring 1″ wide and ⅜″ deep, is cut to within ½″ of the forward edge. The partition is cut to fit this gain.

Cleats are cut and fastened to the sides, back and front to take these two bottom panels as shown in Fig. 4. The lower bottom is fastened in place first, then the partition is glued in the gain. The chest compartment bottom is set in place last. Screws driven through the bottoms and into the cleats are used to fasten these members.

The plinth is made of 1″ stock 4″

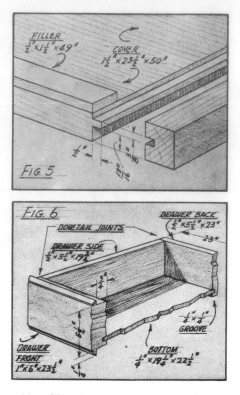

Fig. 5

Fig. 6

wide. The front member is 51″ long while the two side members are 23″ long. They are joined together by means of dovetail joints, with sockets cut on the front member and pins on the side members. These pieces have the lower edge shaped as shown in the drawing. A full-size pattern must be drawn and traced on the stock as a guide for band saw or jig saw. The plinth members are glued up and fastened to the chest with wood screws. The ¾″ x 1″ molding as shown in Fig. 4 is cut to size and fastened to the upper edge of the plinth with 1″ brads.

The top is made of 1½″ stock

23½″ wide and 50″ long. A tongue is cut on each end as shown in Fig. 5. The two battens are made of 2″ stock 1½″ wide and 23½″ long. A groove is cut in one edge of each batten to take the tongue on the end of the top member. These are glued in place, then a filler made of ½″ stock 1½″ wide is fastened to the face of the top member between the projecting surfaces of the battens as shown in Fig. 5. After these pieces have been glued up, the front edge and the two ends of the chest cover are molded as shown in the drawing. Three hinges are set in place as shown in the end view.

The two drawers are made of two pieces 1″ x 6″ x 23½″ for the fronts, four pieces ½″ x 5½″ x 19¾″ for the sides, two pieces ½″ x 5½″ x 23″ for the backs and two pieces ¼″ x 19¼″ x 22½″ for the bottoms. The front pieces have a ¼″ x ¾″ rabbet cut on all four sides as shown in Fig. 6. The sides are joined to the front and back by means of dovetail joints. The sockets are cut in the side members while the pins are to be cut in the front and back members. All four members of each drawer are grooved to take the bottom panel. These grooves are ¼″ x ¼″ and are placed ¼″ above the lower edge. The outside face of each drawer front is molded as shown in the drawing.

The original chest contained locks for the drawers as well as for the cover. These can be installed if desired. The drawer pulls as well as the lock escutcheons should be of similar design to those shown in the drawing.

Colonial Corner Cupboard in Walnut

*Dating from about 1745, this distinctive piece is from
the American Wing of the Metropolitan Museum of Art*

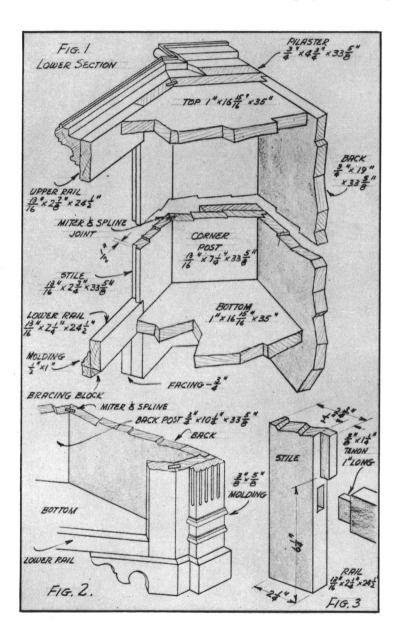

THE CORNER cupboard has remarkable utility as a piece of furniture, but its contribution goes much further. It actually becomes part of the architectural setting of a room and in this capacity lends dignity and eloquent style to surroundings. The cupboard selected for reproduction was made of walnut, but the same design could be worked out in any hardwood. The interior may be painted; in fact, the entire piece could be painted to match the woodwork of the room.

The cupboard is built as two separate units which are placed one on the other. Construction should be started with the bottom unit. It requires two back pieces, a back post and two corner posts, the sizes of which are shown in Figs. 1 and 2. The door

AMERICAN·COLONIAL·CORNER·CUPBOARD
·1745·

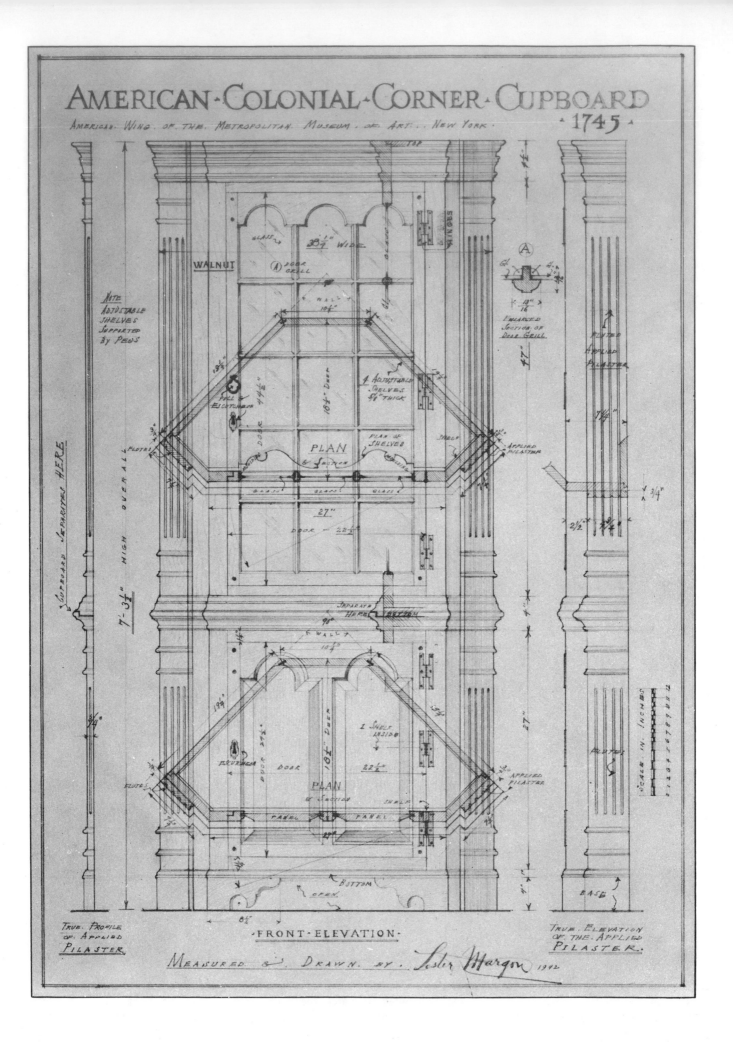

NOTE
ADJUSTABLE
SHELVES
SUPPORTED
BY PEGS

WALNUT

GLASS

DOOR
GRILL

ENLARGED
SECTION OF
DOOR GRILL

FLUTED
APPLIED
PILASTER

CUPBOARD SEPARATES HERE

7'-3½" HIGH OVERALL

PLAN
& SECTION

PLAN OF
SHELVES

4 ADJUSTABLE
SHELVES
⅝" THICK

APPLIED
PILASTER

WINGS

27"

DOOR - 22½"

SEPARATE
HERE   BOTTOM

PLAN
& SECTION

2 SHELF
INSIDE

22½"

PANEL   PANEL

APPLIED
PILASTER

BASE

BOTTOM
OPEN

TRUE·PROFILE
OF·APPLIED
PILASTER.

·FRONT·ELEVATION·

TRUE·ELEVATION
OF·THE·APPLIED
PILASTER.

MEASURED & DRAWN BY Lester Margon 1942

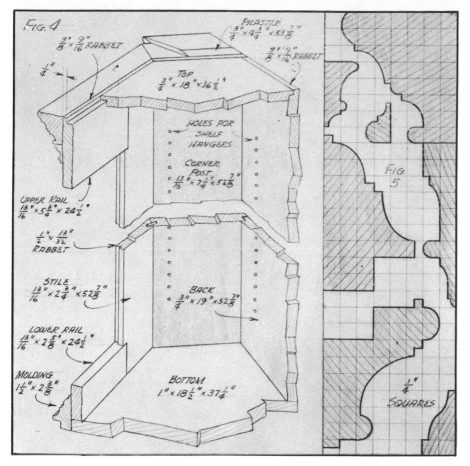

Fig. 4

frame, which also forms the front of the lower unit, is made of two stiles and a lower and upper rail. The back post is joined to the back members by means of a miter-and-spline joint. Butting edges are cut at 67½ degrees and grooved for the spline. The two back panels are rabbeted along the front edge as shown in Figs. 1 and 2. The corner posts are likewise rabbeted to join these back panels.

The door frame is made next. The wide stile is rabbeted as shown in Fig. 3 to form the door stop. The rails are joined to the stiles by means of mortise and tenon joints as shown in

Fig. 3. The frame is assembled with glue. After clamps are removed the edges of stiles, and corner post edges that butt against this frame, are joined by means of a miter-and-spline joint. The miter is cut at 67½ degrees, then the grooves for the splines are cut. The bottom unit is now ready for assembling with glue together with 2″ brads used to fasten the back to the corner post after glue has been applied to the rabbets.

Top and bottom panels are made up and fitted in place as shown in Fig. 1 then fastened with 1½″ No. 8 flathead screws driven through the back

post, corner post and door frame rails. The two pilasters are made up to dimensions given in Fig. 1. They are then fluted as shown in the drawing and fastened to the case with glue and 1¼″ No. 8 flathead screws.

The base blocks are made of stock which is mitered and fitted to the lower end of the case as shown in Fig. 2. The scrollwork on the two front members is laid out and cut after the pieces have been fitted. Scrolled parts are fastened in place with glue and 1½″ brads. The various moldings which are to be applied to this lower section are made up next. Fig. 5 gives these moldings in graph squares.

The door is made up of two stiles, a mullion, bottom and top rails and two fielded panels. The rails and stiles are made up and joined together by mortise and tenon joints as shown in Figs. 6, 7, and 8. The detail of the fielded panels is shown in Fig. 9.

The upper unit is constructed in the same manner as was the lower section. The necessary dimensions for the members that make up this unit are given in Fig. 4. Top and bottom panels are of different construction, but application of the pilasters and moldings is identical to the lower unit.

The glazed door has the rails and muntins mortised into the stiles. The vertical muntins are also mortised into the rails. Fig. 10 shows the top rail, while Fig. 11 shows the cross section of the stiles. The muntins are crosslapped as shown in Figs. 12 and 13, then coped to fit against the rails and stiles. The door is fastened to the frame with "H" hinges. The glass is held in place by molding as in Detail A. The shelves have scrolled edges, inherited from earlier cupboards in which tall objects were stored.

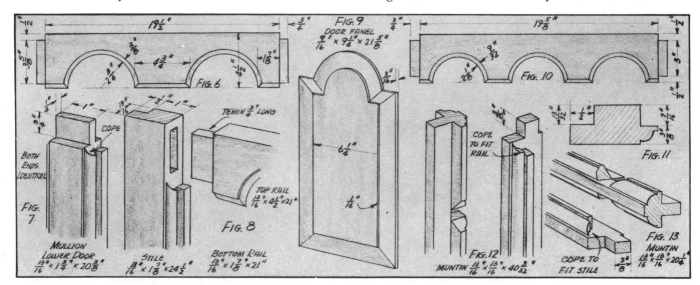

Historic Desk of Drop-Front Design

MEASURED DRAWINGS ENABLE CRAFTSMEN TO REPRODUCE COLONIAL DESK DATED 1730

The desk on which George Washington is said to have signed Major Andre's death warrant. It is presented by courtesy of the New York Historical Society.

ONE OF the finest desks for craftsmen who are adding reproductions of American furniture to their homes is this commodious drop-front desk dating back to about 1730. Aside from the dignity and service it brings to any room, this particular desk has an interesting legend. It is said that on this desk George Washington signed the death warrant of Major John Andre, English spy, while occupying the De Windt House in New York at Tappan in September of 1780.

Although the general style is Chippendale it is so thoroughly American in its details and adaptation that it may rightfully be called American Colonial in character. It is made of mahogany throughout. Construction involves dovetail joints on the drawers, carving on the two front feet and scroll saw work in the desk compartments. Drawer fronts overlap rails and desk sides. All of these features add to the task of making the desk, but they should be followed to make an accurate reproduction and to produce a piece that will be a lasting tribute to the builder.

When considered separately the various members that make up the desk are not beyond the skill of the average craftsman. The claw-and-ball feet are bandsawed to shape on two sides. Carving the foot from here on is not too difficult. The case is made as another unit. The interior compartments are little more than a series of pigeon holes adorned with scrolled overlays at the pilasters and topped with a scrolled band. These parts are assembled in one piece and slipped

as a unit into the complete desk.

Construction of this desk is started by making the two side members. Two pieces of $1\frac{3}{16}''$ stock 21" wide and $36\frac{3}{4}''$ long are required for these members. It may be necessary to glue up two or three pieces of stock to obtain a panel of the width required. The panel should be made wider and longer than is required for the finished size so that it may be squared properly after it has been glued up. Half-inch diameter dowels are used for joining. The dowels should be so located that they will not come within the areas which are to be dadoed to take the various drawer runners and bearer rails. The location of the dadoes as given in Fig. 1 will aid in placing the dowels so that they will not interfere.

SIDE PANELS DADOED FOR RAILS

After the panels have been finished to the required dimensions, the dadoes and the rabbet at the lower end should be located as shown in Fig. 1. All of these dadoes stop within $\frac{3}{8}''$ of the front edge. They may be cut by hand with a back saw, hand router and chisel or they may be cut on the bench saw with the aid of a dado head. If the latter method is used the cut will have to be stopped $\frac{3}{8}''$ from the front edge and the forward corners of the dadoes and rabbet squared with a chisel. A $\frac{3}{8}'' \times \frac{1}{2}''$ rabbet is cut along the back edge on the inside face to take the $\frac{3}{8}''$ back panel. This rabbet is open at the lower end but stops within $\frac{7}{16}''$ of the upper end. The upper front corners of these side members are cut at an angle to take the drop front as shown in the main drawing as well as in Fig. 1. The two side members should now be sandpapered first with No. 1 sandpaper and with finer grades down through No. 00 for final smoothing. This completes these two members.

The front and back bearer rails are made of six pieces of $\frac{7}{8}''$ stock $2\frac{1}{2}''$ wide and $35\frac{3}{8}''$ long. The bottom bearer rails require two pieces of $1\frac{3}{4}''$ stock, the same

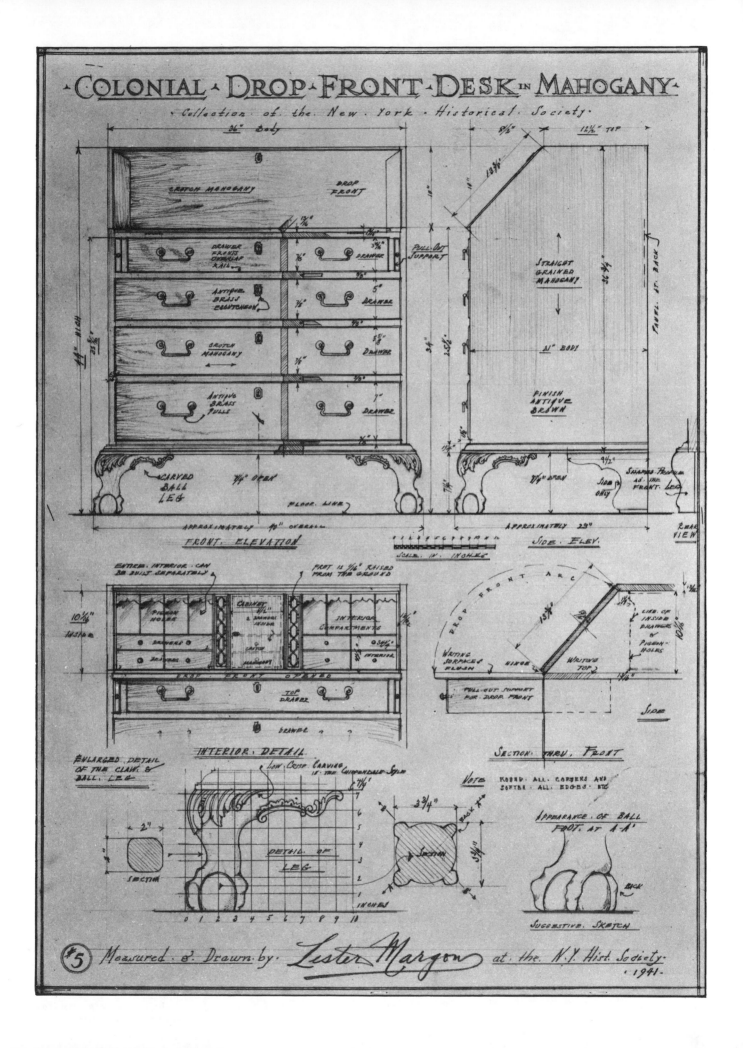

COLONIAL · DROP · FRONT · DESK in MAHOGANY ·

· Collection · of · the · New · York · Historical · Society ·

FRONT · ELEVATION

SIDE · ELEV.

SCALE · IN · INCHES

INTERIOR · DETAIL

SECTION · THRU · FRONT

ENLARGED · DETAIL OF THE CLAW & BALL · LEG

DETAIL · OF LEG

APPEARANCE · OF · BALL FOOT · AT · A-A'

SUGGESTIVE · SKETCH

#5 Measured & Drawn by Lester Margon at the N.Y. Hist. Society · 1941 ·

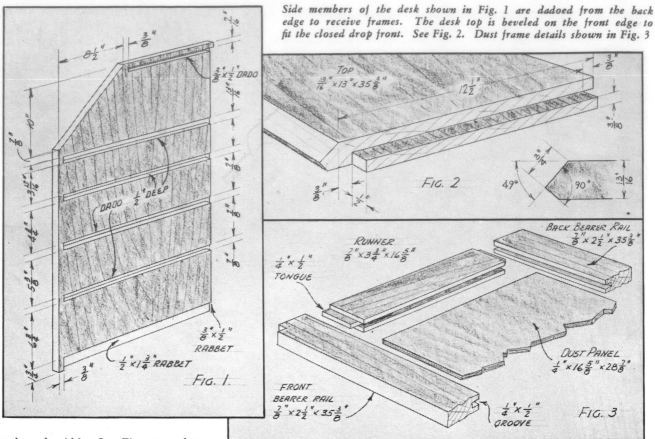

FIG. 1

FIG. 2

FIG. 3

length and width. See Figs. 3 and 5. The drawer runners are made of six pieces of $\frac{7}{8}''$ stock $3\frac{3}{4}''$ wide and $16\frac{5}{8}''$ long, except for the bottom runners which require two pieces of $1\frac{3}{4}''$ stock of the same length and width. Four dust panels made of $\frac{1}{4}''$ stock $16\frac{5}{8}''$ wide and $28\frac{7}{8}''$ long will be needed for the four frames which carry the drawers. The bearer rails and drawer runners have a $\frac{1}{4}'' \times \frac{1}{2}''$ groove cut along the inside edge to take the dust panel. On each rail this groove should be placed $\frac{1}{4}''$ below the upper face. A dado head set up in the bench saw will do this work quickly. The ends of each runner have a tongue cut on them as shown in Fig. 3 to fit in the groove cut along the edge of the bearer rails. The four frames should be assembled with glue, and the dust panels should be inserted as the work of assembling progresses. As soon as clamps are applied each frame should be checked with a try square to make certain that it is square. While the frames are set aside to allow the glue to set, work on the writing top can be undertaken.

The panel for the writing top is made of $1\frac{3}{16}''$ material and should measure $20\frac{5}{8}''$ wide and $35\frac{3}{8}''$ long. As with the side members, it may be necessary to glue up two or three narrow pieces of stock to obtain a panel of the required width. After the writing top has been cut to the proper size, it is trial fitted in the dado already cut in the side members. In order to fit it in place properly

the front corners must be notched. The stock which is to be cut out should be marked off and the cutting done on the bench saw to insure square shoulders. Each of the four frames which carry the drawers must be handled in the same manner.

The support members for the drop front travel in a pocket formed by a partition extending between the writing top and the drawer support frame as shown in Figs. 4 and 5. The partitions are made of two pieces of $\frac{7}{8}''$ stock $20\frac{5}{8}''$ wide and $4\frac{9}{16}''$ long; the grain runs vertically. These partitions are set into a groove cut in the upper face of the

drawer support frame and in the underside of the writing top. The location of the groove in these members is shown in Fig. 4. They can be cut by hand or with the aid of a dado head on the bench saw. These cuts stop within $\frac{3}{8}''$ of the front edge of the frame and writing top, making it necessary to complete the cutting by hand. The partitions are cut to fit in the groove and dado.

The support for the drop front must be provided with a stop to prevent it from being pulled out entirely. Part of this stop consists of a dado $\frac{9}{16}''$ wide and $\frac{1}{2}''$ deep cut across the face of these partition members. The dado should be

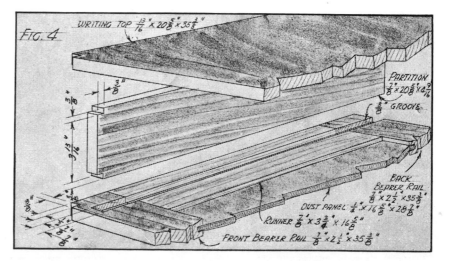

FIG. 4

Partitions placed between the upper bearer rails and the writing top form long pockets in which the support strips for the lowered drop front can travel

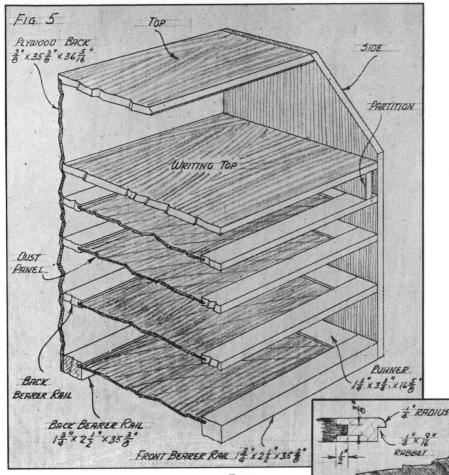

Fig. 5
PLYWOOD BACK $\frac{3}{8}'' \times 35\frac{3}{8}'' \times 36\frac{5}{16}''$
TOP
SIDE
PARTITION
WRITING TOP
DUST PANEL
BACK BEARER RAIL
BACK BEARER RAIL $1\frac{3}{4}'' \times 2\frac{1}{2}'' \times 35\frac{3}{8}''$
RUNNER $1\frac{3}{4}'' \times 3\frac{3}{4}'' \times 16\frac{5}{8}''$
FRONT BEARER RAIL $1\frac{3}{4}'' \times 2\frac{1}{2}'' \times 35\frac{3}{8}''$

the corners finished off at a radius of $\frac{1}{8}''$. The $\frac{1}{2}''$ dowel which is to act as a stop is located and set in place. The completed supports are placed in position from the back of the desk. The back panel which is made of $\frac{3}{8}''$ plywood faced with mahogany is cut to size and fastened in place with $1\frac{1}{4}''$ brads. See Fig. 5 for dimensions.

The drop front is made of a piece of $1\frac{3}{16}''$ stock $13\frac{3}{8}''$ wide and $34\frac{7}{8}''$ long. Two battens $1\frac{3}{16}'' \times 2'' \times 13\frac{3}{8}''$ will also be required. The battens are joined to the front member as shown in Fig. 6. After they have been glued in place, a $\frac{1}{4}'' \times \frac{9}{16}''$ rabbet is cut along the side and top edges of the drop front. These edges are then finished off at a radius of $\frac{1}{4}''$ as shown in Fig. 6.

The molding around the lower end of the case is cut from $1\frac{1}{8}'' \times 1\frac{1}{4}''$ strips of mahogany. Corners are mitered and the molding is applied with glue and brads.

The two front legs are carved in claw-and-ball style after several pieces of stock have been glued together. The

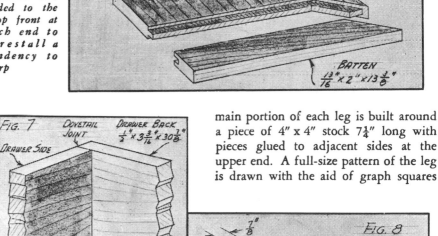

Fig. 6
$\frac{1}{4}''$ RADIUS
$\frac{1}{4}'' \times \frac{9}{16}''$ RABBET
DROP FRONT $\frac{13}{16}'' \times 13\frac{3}{8}'' \times 34\frac{7}{8}''$
BATTEN $\frac{13}{16}'' \times 2'' \times 13\frac{3}{8}''$

Battens are added to the drop front at each end to forestall a tendency to warp

placed in the center and should extend from the back edge to within 1" of the front. The other part of the stop will consist of a $\frac{1}{2}''$ dowel placed in the face of the support member and allowed to project $\frac{3}{8}''$ beyond the face. This dowel is located $7\frac{1}{2}''$ from the back end of the support.

The desk top shown in Fig. 2 is made of a piece of $1\frac{1}{8}''$ stock 13" wide and $35\frac{3}{8}''$ long. A tenon is cut on each end of this piece to fit the dadoes that were cut in the side members. A $\frac{3}{8}'' \times \frac{3}{8}''$ rabbet is cut along the underside of the back edge to take the back panel. The front edge of the top member is beveled to conform with the slope of the drop front.

The top, writing top, partitions and drawer support frames should be sandpapered thoroughly and made ready for assembling to the side members. The various horizontal members are glued to one of the desk sides, then the second side member is placed in position. Clamps must be used to hold these parts together. The partitions are slipped into place from the back. The completed carcass should be kept square with temporary cross braces applied to the back while the glue is given time to set.

The drop-front supports are made of two pieces of $1\frac{1}{8}''$ stock $3\frac{1}{8}''$ wide and $20\frac{3}{4}''$ long. The forward end of each has

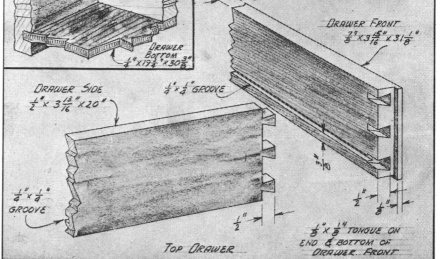

Fig. 7
DOVETAIL JOINT
DRAWER BACK $\frac{1}{2}'' \times 3\frac{3}{16}'' \times 30\frac{7}{8}''$
DRAWER SIDE
DRAWER BOTTOM $\frac{1}{4}'' \times 19\frac{3}{4}'' \times 30\frac{3}{8}''$
DRAWER SIDE $\frac{1}{2}'' \times 3\frac{13}{16}'' \times 20''$
$\frac{1}{4}'' \times \frac{1}{4}''$ GROOVE
TOP DRAWER

main portion of each leg is built around a piece of 4" x 4" stock $7\frac{1}{4}''$ long with pieces glued to adjacent sides at the upper end. A full-size pattern of the leg is drawn with the aid of graph squares

Fig. 8
DRAWER FRONT $\frac{7}{8}'' \times 3\frac{5}{16}'' \times 31\frac{1}{8}''$
$\frac{1}{4}'' \times \frac{1}{4}''$ GROOVE
$\frac{3}{8}'' \times \frac{1}{2}''$ TONGUE ON END & BOTTOM OF DRAWER FRONT

shown in the leg detail in the main drawing. The legs are cut to shape on the band saw and are then carved. Each of the two back legs is made of $2\frac{3}{4}''$ stock $7\frac{1}{4}''$ wide and $9\frac{1}{2}''$ long. They are shaped as shown in the side elevation of the main drawing. The legs are fastened to the carcass with flat head screws driven up through the brackets and into the side members and bottom frame.

Stock for the various drawer members can now be cut to size. The drawer fronts are made of $\frac{7}{8}''$ stock. The top drawer front shown in Fig. 8 is $31\frac{1}{8}''$ long, while the other three are $34\frac{5}{8}''$ long. The width of each drawer front is shown in the front elevation of the main drawing. The sides of each drawer are made of $\frac{1}{2}''$ stock $20''$ long. The widths vary in each case. The top drawer takes sides that are $3\frac{13}{16}''$ wide while all the others require side members that are $\frac{1}{4}''$ narrower than the drawer fronts. The drawer backs require $\frac{1}{2}''$ stock. The length of the top drawer back should be $30\frac{7}{8}''$, while the length of the back member for each of the other three drawers should be $34\frac{3}{8}''$. The width of each back member should be $\frac{5}{8}''$ narrower than the side member of the drawer.

The edges of the drawer fronts overlap the rails and sides of the desk. Each drawer front, therefore, must have a $\frac{1}{8}''$ x $\frac{3}{4}''$ rabbet cut along each end as shown in Fig. 8. The three lower drawer fronts have this rabbet carried along the top and bottom edges as well. The top drawer front has the lower edge rabbeted as shown in Fig. 8 with the upper edge left plain.

The drawer sides are joined to the front by means of dovetail joints. These joints should be laid out and cut with care. The drawer backs are fastened to the sides in the same way. A $\frac{1}{4}''$ x $\frac{1}{4}''$ groove is cut on the inside face of the side and front members on a line $\frac{3}{8}''$ from the lower edge. The $\frac{1}{4}''$ bottom panels, cut to the proper size for each drawer, fit in these grooves. The top drawer takes a panel $19\frac{3}{4}''$ x $30\frac{3}{8}''$ while the other three require panels $19\frac{3}{4}''$ wide and $33\frac{7}{8}''$ long. The drawer fronts have the edges and ends rounded off at a radius of $\frac{1}{8}''$. They are assembled with glue. The bottoms should be slipped in place to keep the drawers square while the glue is setting. Afterwards they are fastened in position with several $1''$ brads.

If the drawers are to be equipped with locks as shown in the drawing, these locks should be set in place and the escutcheon mounted in position. The location of the drawer pulls should be established on each drawer front and screw holes should be bored. The pulls may be attached at this time, but all hardware must be removed before the chest is stained. The two support members for the drop front have small wood knobs which act as pulls. These knobs are turned to shape on the lathe and are then glued in place. The drop front can now be hinged in place. The lock and escutcheon on the desk front is set in place to complete construction of the main portion of the desk.

The interior fittings of the desk including pigeon holes and drawers are made up as a separate unit and slid in place. The sides, top, bottom and partitions which form the center compartment, as well as the drawer fronts and the door, are made of $\frac{3}{8}''$ stock. All other members are made of $\frac{3}{16}''$ stock. The various members which go to make up the pigeon holes are cut to size and assembled. The drawers are made up to fit their respective spaces.

Since mahogany has been used in construction, the desk should be finished with a paste filler and then be stained. The tone of mahogany stain used will depend on the individual's choice. Four coats of clear varnish should be applied and each should be rubbed down with pumice stone. The last coat should be rubbed down with rottenstone and the surface may be waxed and polished.

Sawbuck Dining Table from Pennsylvania

THIS SAWBUCK TABLE MADE BY AN EARLY PENNSYLVANIA SETTLER OFFERS MORE UTILITY THAN MOST TABLES WORTH REPRODUCING

Gracefully scrolled legs and a battened table top are features that will assure long service to craftsmen who reproduce this sturdy old table from the accompanying measured drawings

THE STONE houses of Pennsylvania settlers had whitewashed interiors, relieved only by a heavy fireplace made of wood and often placed diagonally across the corner of the room. Wood baseboard, chair rail and a wood molding at the ceiling broke the otherwise ascetic simplicity of the room.

The furniture which adorned these rooms clearly expressed the character of the people who created it. Pieces were sturdy, well-built and possessed an innate sense of design and craftsmanship, as well as a strong individuality which reflected the work of the homeland. Hardwoods used in furniture construction were oak, walnut, poplar and cherry, while the softwood used was pine. Pieces made of softwood were generally over-decorated with polychrome motifs. The most popular pieces of furniture were tables, chairs, chests, cabinets, beds and corner cupboards.

Tables were often the most elaborate, fanciful and distinctive of all the furniture of this period, as the one shown here attests. This sawbuck table—named for its cross-lapped end members—is one of the finest of its type. It is large enough for dining and yet not too large for the average room. The design is traditional, yet it has the Pennsylvania sturdiness combined with a keen sense of decorative values. The original table has a top made of walnut and an understructure made of solid oak. This scheme could be carried out in reproduction or pine could be appropriately substituted for all parts.

Construction of the table can be started with the legs. These require four pieces of 1¾" stock 5" wide and 42½" long. The ends of these pieces are cut at an angle of 52°. While the height of the table and the width of the base differ ½" in the original table the error of making these cuts at 52° in a reproduction of the table is so slight as to be negligible. The dadoes that are cut at the center of each leg to produce the crosslap joint should be laid out and then cut on the bench saw equipped with a dado head, or back saw and chisel can substitute for the bench saw. When the joint is being laid out each pair of legs should be laid in sawbuck fashion on the workbench and the distance be-

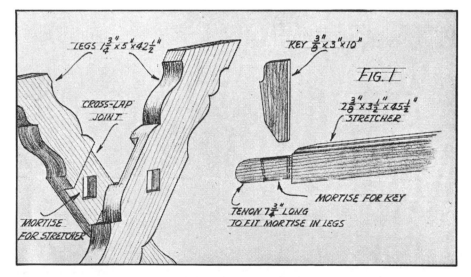

LEGS 1¾" x 5" x 42½"

CROSS-LAP JOINT

MORTISE FOR STRETCHER

KEY ⅜" x 3" x 10"

FIG. I

2⅜" x 3½" x 45½" STRETCHER

MORTISE FOR KEY

TENON 7¼" LONG TO FIT MORTISE IN LEGS

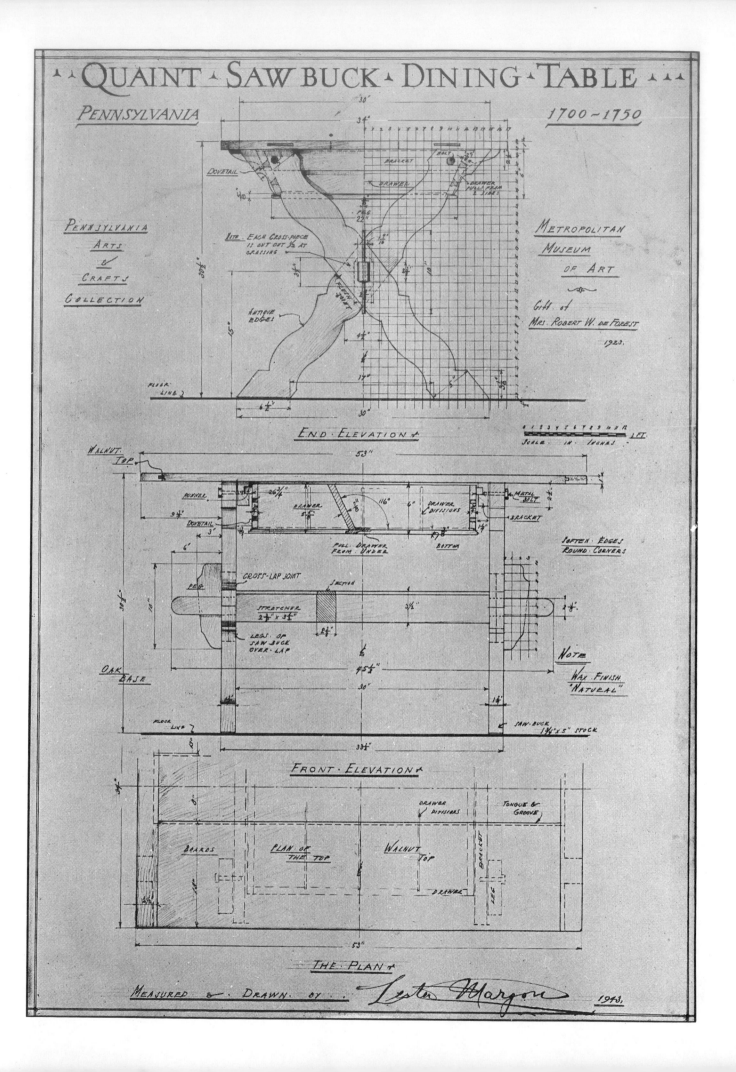

QUAINT ▲ SAW BUCK ▲ DINING ▲ TABLE

PENNSYLVANIA

1700–1750

PENNSYLVANIA
ARTS
&
CRAFTS
COLLECTION

METROPOLITAN
MUSEUM
OF ART

Gift of
Mrs. Robert W. de Forest
1923.

END ELEVATION

SCALE IN INCHES

SOFTEN EDGES
ROUND CORNERS

NOTE

WAX FINISH
"NATURAL"

FRONT ELEVATION

THE PLAN

MEASURED & DRAWN BY ___ Lester Margon ___ 1943.

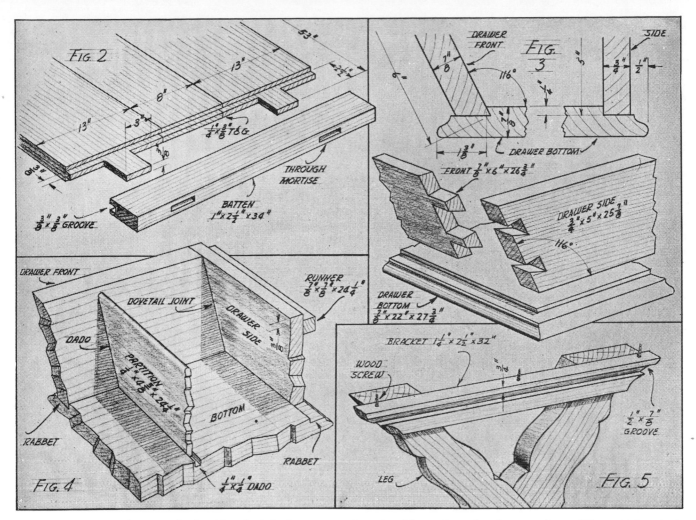

tween the upper and lower ends should be the same as shown in the end elevation. With each pair in this position, the angle at which the dadoes are to be cut can be marked off without difficulty.

A full-size pattern of the scrolled edges of the legs must be drawn and then traced on each piece of stock. The pieces are cut to shape on the band saw or jig saw; edges are finished smooth with a file and sandpaper. The two pieces that form each end unit should be glued together. After the clamps have been removed the mortises for the tenoned stretcher must be laid out. Each mortise is $1\frac{9}{16}$" wide and $2\frac{3}{8}$" long. It is located $\frac{1}{4}$" above the center as shown in the drawing. This is a through mortise and may be cut by hand with a $\frac{7}{8}$" or 1" auger bit to bore the holes and a chisel to square the mortise.

The stretcher is made of a piece of $2\frac{3}{8}$" stock $3\frac{1}{2}$" wide and $45\frac{1}{2}$" long. Tenons measuring $7\frac{3}{4}$" long by $2\frac{3}{8}$" wide and $1\frac{9}{16}$" thick are laid out and cut at each end. Trimming may be necessary to make an accurate fit with the mortise. The ends of each tenon are rounded off at a radius of $1\frac{3}{16}$".

A spokeshave serves best for this work. The key that pins the leg units to the stretcher passes through a mortise that is cut in the tenon as shown in the drawing and Fig. 1. This mortise is located $1\frac{5}{8}$" from the shoulder of the tenon and on the upper edge of the tenon is 3" long. The mortise tapers from 3" on the upper edge to $2\frac{5}{8}$" at the lower edge. The width of the mortise is $\frac{3}{8}$". The key is made of $\frac{3}{8}$" stock, 3" wide and 10" long. A pattern of this member is drawn, then traced on the stock. The graph square drawing should be followed when making this pattern if an accurate reproduction is desired. Two keys are cut to shape on the jig saw and are fin-

The sawbuck table has a place of honor in the room of Pennsylvania Arts and Crafts at the Metropolitan Museum of Art through whose courtesy this presentation is made possible

ished smooth on the edges. The upper edge of the stretcher is molded as shown in the drawing.

The brackets that act as the drawer supports and also serve for fastening the table top are shown in Fig. 5. Two pieces are required. A groove ⅞" wide and ½" deep is cut in one face of each bracket to take the drawer runners. The top of the groove is located ¾" from the upper edge as shown in Fig. 5. The ends of these brackets are shaped as shown in the main drawing. The brackets are joined to the legs by means of bolts. These bolts act as pins rather than bolts. Holes should be bored in the brackets so that the bolts will fit snugly and will have to cut their own threads as they are driven. They should be 2¼" long and ⅜" in diameter.

The top is made of three pieces of 1" stock 53" long. Widths of these boards are shown in Fig. 2. The pieces are joined together by means of tongue-and-groove joints. The glued-up panel for the top is finished to a width of 34". Two battens are made up each measuring 1" x 2½" x 34". These battens have two through mortises and also have a groove cut into one edge as shown in Fig. 2. The table top has two tenons to fit the mortised batten and a tongue to fit the finished panel. It may be fastened to the brackets with screws driven from underneath as shown in Fig. 5, or the panel may be set on the brackets and fastened from the top with 1½" screws driven into counterbored holes in the top. After the top is fastened to the brackets plugs are cut and glued in the counterbored holes to cover the screw heads.

The drawer is made of two side members, measuring ¾" x 5" x 25⅞" and a front and back member each of which measures ⅞" x 6" x 26¾". The ends of the side members are cut at an angle of 116° while the edges only, not the ends, of the front and back members are cut at the same angle. The drawer sides are joined together by means of dovetail joints as shown in Fig. 3. The drawer bottom is made of ⅞" stock 22" wide and 27¾" long. Rabbets are cut along each edge to take the front and back drawer members and along each end to take the side members. The size of these rabbets is shown in Fig. 3. The edges and ends of the drawer bottom are molded on the shaper. A ¼" x ¼" groove is cut in the drawer bottom and on the inside face of the front and back members to take the partitions. See Fig. 4. The partitions are cut to fit the drawer and are made of ¼" stock 4⅝" wide and 24¼" long. When assembling the drawer, the partitions are set in the drawer bottom before the front and back members are placed in position. The side members are set in place last. Glue should be used on all joints. The bottom is fastened to the drawer sides with 1¼" flathead screws. The drawer runners, which are made of two pieces of ⅞" square stock 24¼" long, are fastened to the drawer side with 1½" flathead screws. Recesses are cut in the underface of the drawer bottom to act as drawer pulls.

Finishing of the table depends upon the type of wood used in construction. If walnut was selected for the top, this should be treated with wood filler and protected with several coats of shellac and several well-rubbed wax coats.

Unique Scroll Arm Enriches
RARE EMPIRE CHAIR

UNDER the leadership of Duncan Phyfe, a style of furniture sometimes known as Empire, found fresh interpretation in America. Devoid of intricate and heraldic detail, the graceful style was widely copied. In this tradition the illustrated arm chair was made. Its scrolled arms mark it as the master chair of a dining set.

Reproduction of this piece by today's craftsman will yield a chair of fine background and elegant taste.

While the normal procedure in constructing a chair would be to make the leg members first, work on the Empire arm chair should be started with the arms. This departure is caused by the sweep from the top of the back uprights into the arm. At the point where the arm joins it, the back upright must be cut so that sufficient wood is left to complete the even flow of the line. If the arm is finished before the contour of the back upright is laid out a smooth sweep can be attained.

As shown in Fig. 1, each arm is made of five pieces of 1¼″ mahogany as a means of reducing short-grain stock to a minimum. After each piece has been cut to the shape indicated; tongues indicated by broken lines are cut to produce lap joints. After the joints have been cut, the pieces are arranged

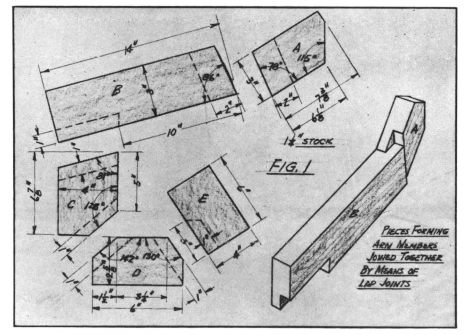

FIG. 1

PIECES FORMING ARM MEMBERS JOINED TOGETHER BY MEANS OF LAP JOINTS

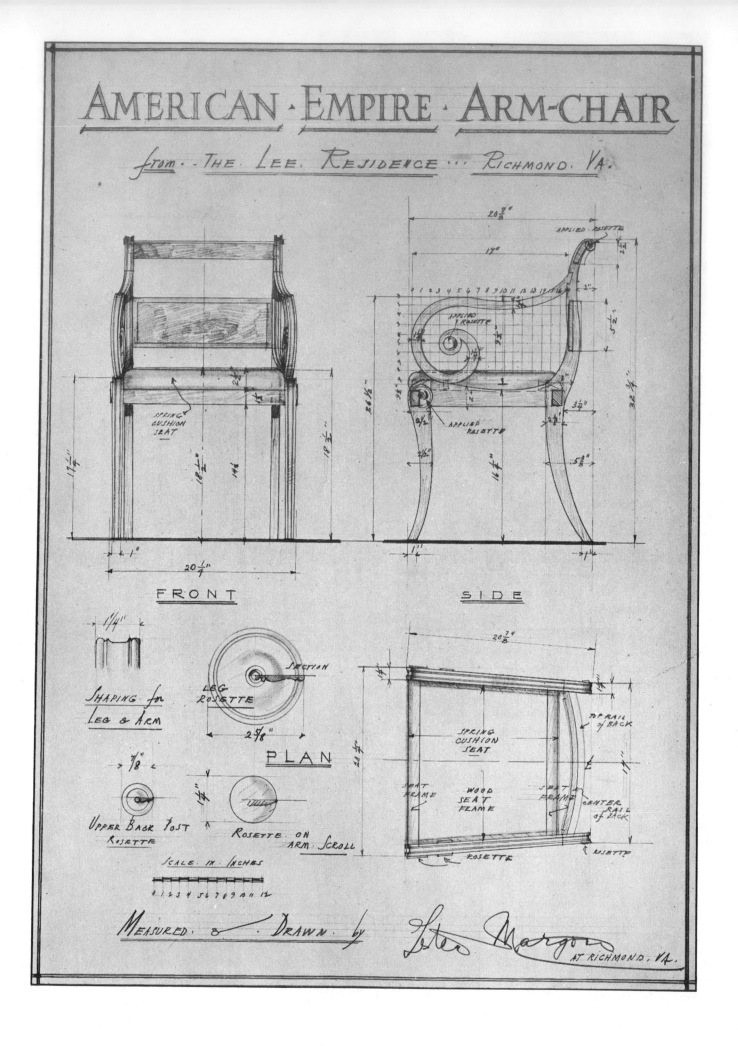

AMERICAN·EMPIRE·ARM-CHAIR

from·The·Lee·Residence···Richmond·VA·

FRONT

SIDE

SHAPING·for LEG & ARM

LEG ROSETTE

SECTION

PLAN

UPPER BACK POST ROSETTE

ROSETTE ON ARM SCROLL

SCALE·IN·INCHES

SPRING CUSHION SEAT

SPRING CUSHION SEAT

TOP RAIL of BACK

SEAT FRAME

WOOD SEAT FRAME

SEAT FRAME

CENTER RAIL of BACK

ROSETTE

ROSETTE

APPLIED ROSETTE

APPLIED ROSETTE

APPLIED ROSETTE

MEASURED·&·DRAWN·by

AT RICHMOND·VA.

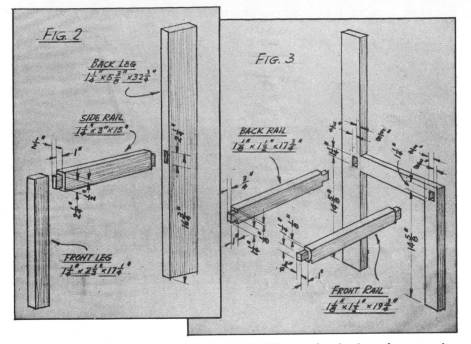

FIG. 2

BACK LEG
$1\frac{1}{4}" \times 5\frac{3}{8}" \times 32\frac{3}{4}"$

SIDE RAIL
$1\frac{1}{4}" \times 3" \times 15"$

FRONT LEG
$1\frac{1}{4}" \times 2\frac{1}{2}" \times 17\frac{1}{4}"$

FIG. 3

BACK RAIL
$1\frac{1}{4}" \times 1\frac{1}{2}" \times 17\frac{3}{4}"$

FRONT RAIL
$1\frac{1}{4}" \times 1\frac{1}{2}" \times 19\frac{3}{4}"$

for gluing. When these pieces are placed in their relative positions, the corner of piece (E) will interfere or overlap piece (C). In order to fit these together, it will be necessary to remove the section of piece (C) which interferes. When all pieces can be arranged properly, glue is spread on the joints and clamps are applied.

Preparation of a full-size pattern of the arm member can be undertaken while the stock is in clamps. If it is possible to obtain wrapping paper at least 20″ wide and 33″ long, considerable work can be eliminated by laying out a full-size pattern of the chair side while developing the full-size pattern of the arm. If the layout is made in this manner, the sweep of all curves can be kept in harmony. Utmost care is needed in laying out the dovetail and sweep at the point where the arm joins the upright. If this part of the work is done properly, no difficulty will be encountered later on in shaping and assembling the various members.

The full-size layout of the arm can be cut from the main pattern, and when the clamps have been removed from the glued-up arm members, the pattern can be traced on the stock. The arm members are cut to shape on the band saw or jig saw, and then the sawed surfaces are finished smooth with spokeshave, rasp and file. These surfaces must not be finished on a sander or with sandpaper. Sanding before carving will leave sandpaper grit in the grain and will dull the carving tools. After the arms have been shaped, work on the side units should be undertaken.

Each side unit, as shown in Fig. 2, is made of one piece of $1\frac{1}{4}" \times 2\frac{1}{2}" \times$

17¼″ stock for the front leg, one piece of $1\frac{1}{4}" \times 5\frac{3}{8}" \times 32\frac{3}{4}"$ stock for the back leg and one piece of $1\frac{1}{4}" \times 3" \times 15"$ stock for the side rail. These members are joined together by means of mortise and tenon joints. Mortises laid out on the edge of each leg are cut 1″ deep. Tenons are cut on the side rails to fit. These three members that make up the side unit can now be glued and clamped.

After the clamps have been removed, the mortises to take the front and back seat rails, as shown in Fig. 3, as well as the mortises for the center and top back rails, as shown in Fig. 4, should

be laid out on the side units but should not be cut until the full-size pattern of the legs and rail has been traced on the unit. After the pattern has been traced, the location of the mortises can be verified. It may be necessary to shift the upper rail mortises to locate them within the area of the shaped member. At this time, the arm members should be placed on the side units to verify the location of the dovetail socket that is to be cut into the back upright and to verify the sweep of the arm into the upright. When everything is satisfactory, the side units can be bandsawed. Edges are dressed with spokeshave, rasp and file. The mortises for the rails can now be cut. These mortises must be cut at an angle of 85° to allow for the difference in width between the front and back of the chair. The front legs are to be tapered from their present thickness of 1¼″ from a point ⅛″ below the front rail mortises to 1″ at the lower end. Tapering should be done on both faces by means of a smooth plane.

Carving of the molding along the arm and leg can now be undertaken. Lines are drawn along the surfaces to be molded. If suitable molding cutters for the spindle shaper are available, they may be used; otherwise the work will have to be done by hand with carving chisels. The carving of the side units should be done from the lower end of the front leg to the dovetail socket near the top of the back upright. The section of the back upright beyond

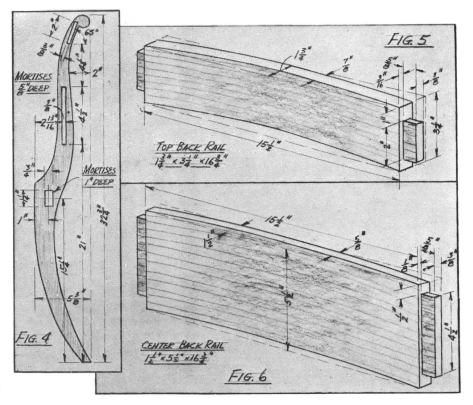

FIG. 4

MORTISES
⅝″ DEEP

MORTISES
1″ DEEP

TOP BACK RAIL
$1\frac{3}{4}" \times 3\frac{1}{4}" \times 16\frac{3}{4}"$

CENTER BACK RAIL
$1\frac{1}{4}" \times 5\frac{1}{2}" \times 16\frac{3}{4}"$

FIG. 5

FIG. 6

the dovetail socket should not be done until the arm has been set in place. The carving of the molding on the arm should be completed up to the dovetail. In order to continue the carving above the dovetail socket on the back of the uprights, the arm should now be assembled to the side units. The lower portion of the arm is joined to the rail by means of a ½" dowel 1" long. When the glue has set, the carving of the molding can be completed.

The seat rails are the next members to be prepared. The rails shown in Fig. 3 are made of 1⅛" stock, 1½" wide. The front rail has an overall length of 19¾" while the back rail measures 17¾". Tenons on each end are cut to fit mortises which have shoulders cut at 85° to conform with the slant of the side units. The outer face of the front rail is slightly rounded as in Fig. 3.

The center back rail as shown in Fig. 6 will require a piece of 1½" stock 5½" wide and 16¾" long on which a tenon is cut at each end. The curve of the rail is cut to shape on the band saw or the shaping can be done with chisel and spokeshave. In either case, the rail should be dressed smooth with the spokeshave. Mahogany veneer is applied to the concave face as shown in the front view of the main drawing.

The top back rail, as in Fig. 5, will require a piece of 1¾" x 3¼" x 16¾" stock having a tenon cut on each end. The rail is then shaped. The seat and back rails are joined to the side members with glue.

The rosettes shown in the main drawing are faceplate turnings made of thin stock. A scrap piece of ¾" softwood about 4" in diameter is attached to the faceplate. The rosette stock is glued to the softwood with a piece of heavy wrapping paper between. Paper filler allows easy removal of the turned rosettes. They are glued in place.

The seat frame consists of four pieces of 1" x 2½" stock cut to fit on the front and back rails and joined together by means of slip joints. The outer edges of the frame members are rounded. Upholstering of the seat can be turned over to the local upholsterer with the specification that the completed cushion be 2½" high.

For a fine finish the wood should be filled with paste filler or by means of a number of shellac coats, each sanded when dry. A hand-rubbed oil finish will be found suitable for this chair.

Mantel Clock Made by Aaron Willard

This fine example of American clock making is reproduced by courtesy of the Museum of Fine Arts, Boston

E VERYONE is familiar with the Grandfather's Clocks of huge dimensions and the much popularized Banjo Clocks, but the Mantel Clocks are not so well known and examples of them are rare. It was therefore of special interest to discover a fine example in the Museum of Fine Arts at Boston, the very city in which this clock was made.

This clock was made by Aaron Willard who seems to have been one of the outstanding clockmakers of his time. He opened a shop in Roxbury, a suburb of Boston, in 1780 but later moved to Washington where he opened a factory and employed from 20 to 30 men. His work is distinguished for its simplicity, refinement and elegance of line.

The decoration of the glass should not cause alarm. There is no reason to copy the design which is painted in colors on the back of the glass. This clock was evidently made for a man with nautical interests, for anchors and seaweed pattern prevail. It would be appropriate to design your own decoration and sign your name. Use the same paints and method that sign painters use on glass. Even crude technique will look pleasing through the glass. Before the case is made it is advisable to obtain the dial and works so that their dimensions may be checked with those of the case. A modern electric works is recommended.

Construction of the mantel clock should be divided into two main units, the lower case and the upper case. Each one is made independent of the other. Work should be started with the bottom unit. Two pieces of stock are required for the side members (B). The front (A) is made of one piece. Two filler strips (C) are required to fill in the space at the back of the lower case section in order to take the full-length back panel. With these five members cut to size the work of assembling can start.

The front member (A) has a $\frac{3}{8}'' \times \frac{3}{8}''$ groove cut on the inside face $\frac{5}{8}''$ from each edge as shown in the cross section through the base as well as in the detail sketch. A tongue is cut on the side members (B) to fit the groove. The side members (B) also have a $\frac{3}{8}'' \times \frac{3}{8}''$ groove cut on the inside face $\frac{3}{8}''$ from the back edge to take filler strips (C). These filler strips are rabbeted to produce a tongue that will fit the groove. The front member (A) has a crotch mahogany veneer surrounded by a $\frac{1}{16}''$ ebony line. This in turn is bordered by a cross banding of plain mahogany. This veneer facing is made of a piece of crotch mahogany veneer cut $9\frac{7}{8}''$ wide and $10\frac{5}{8}''$ long and squared accurately at all corners. The $\frac{1}{16}''$ ebony banding is now cut to the lengths required to fit around the sides of the crotch veneer; ends are mitered. The mahogany veneer which is

29

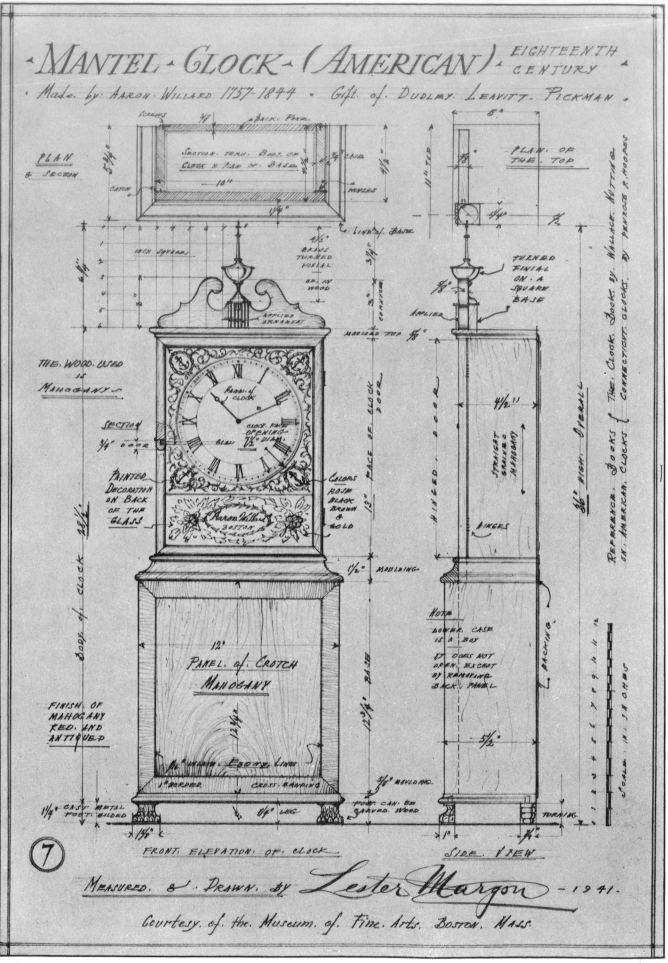

MANTEL · CLOCK · (AMERICAN) EIGHTEENTH CENTURY

· Made · by · Aaron · Willard 1757-1844 · Gift · of · Dudley · Leavitt · Pickman ·

PLAN & SECTION

SECTION · THRU · BODY · OF · CLOCK & PLAN · OF · BASE

PLAN · OF · THE · TOP

THE · WOOD · USED IS MAHOGANY

SECTION
3/4" DOOR

PAINTED DECORATION ON BACK OF THE GLASS

HANDS · OF CLOCK

CLOCK · FACE OPENING 7½" DIAM.

Aaron Willard BOSTON

COLORS ROSE BLACK BROWN & GOLD

TURNED FINIAL ON · A SQUARE BASE

STRAIGHT GRAINED MAHOGANY

4½"

HINGES

NOTE
LOWER · CASE IS A BOX
IT · DOES · NOT OPEN · EXCEPT BY · REMOVING BACK · PANEL

FINISH · OF MAHOGANY RED · AND ANTIQUED

12"
PANEL · of · CROTCH MAHOGANY

EBONY · LINE

CROSS · BANDING

CAST · METAL FOOT · GILDED

FRONT · ELEVATION · OF · CLOCK

SIDE · VIEW

REFERENCE · BOOKS { THE · CLOCK · BOOK · BY · WALLACE · NUTTING · ON · AMERICAN · CLOCKS · CONNECTICUT · CLOCKS · BY · PENROSE · R · HOOPES ·

⑦

MEASURED · & · DRAWN · BY Lester Margon — 1941 ·

Courtesy · of · the · Museum · of · Fine · Arts · Boston · Mass ·

The pediment adorning the clock is made in several pieces shown above. At right upper and lower case structure are shown

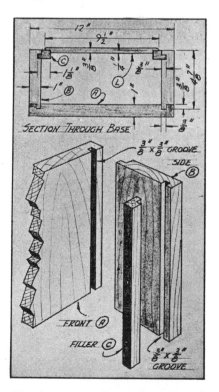

used for the outer cross banding is cut into strips $1\frac{1}{8}''$ long and wide enough to produce the border as shown in the front elevation. The cross banding may be made up of two or more pieces to produce strips wide enough to form the border, but in this case care should be taken to match the grain. The various members that make up the veneer panel should be held together with gummed paper, or wrapping paper to which glue has been applied. It will be sanded off later.

When the completed veneer is ready to be applied to the front panel, glue is spread on the face of panel (A) as well as on the back of the veneer, the back being the side opposite to that on which the gummed paper has been applied. If a veneer press is available it should be used to hold down the veneer while the glue is given time to set. In the absence of such equipment, hand screws or "C" clamps may be used with success if large pressure blocks are applied under the jaws of the clamps. It will be noted that the assembled veneer is slightly larger than the panel. This is necessary in order to make certain that the veneer will carry through to the ends and edges of the front panel. When the veneer is being placed on the panel an even border must be maintained on all four sides. After the clamps have been removed, the excess veneer can be trimmed off flush with the panel. The front and sides should be sandpapered thoroughly and made ready for assembly.

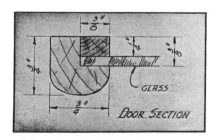

The painted glass panel fits in the door frame rabbet, is held by strips

The filler strips are glued in place with the lower end of the filler strip flush with the lower end of the side member. The sides in turn are glued to the front. Clamps are applied to hold the members together. A temporary brace should be applied between the sides at the back to keep these members properly spaced until the base is set in place.

The base (D) is made of a piece of $\frac{5}{8}''$ stock. The ends and front edge are molded on the spindle shaper to produce the ogee curve. The completed base is fastened to the front and side members with $1\frac{1}{2}''$ No. 8 flathead wood screws in holes bored and countersunk. The forward feet may be of cast metal as noted on the front elevation or they may be carved from the wood. They are held in place by means of a $\frac{3}{8}''$ dowel. The rear feet are turnings with $\frac{3}{8}''$ round pins on

the upper end. This completes the entire bottom unit and work may now be started on the upper section.

Construction of the upper unit is started with side members (F). Two pieces of $\frac{3}{4}''$ stock are required. The top (G) is made of $\frac{5}{8}''$ stock. A dado $\frac{3}{8}''$ wide and $\frac{1}{4}''$ deep is cut on the under face of the top member $1\frac{3}{8}''$ in from each end. These dadoes are $3\frac{3}{4}''$ long, starting from the back edge. Tongues are cut on one end of each side member, as shown in the detail sketch, to fit the dadoes that were cut in the top member.

The molding along the front edge and both ends of the top member is an ogee with the upper edge finished off round as shown in the front and side elevations. The ogee molding should be no deeper than $\frac{3}{8}''$. This allows for a $\frac{1}{16}''$ space between the deepest portion of the molding and the side members.

The front member (E) is fastened to the front edge of the side member with $1\frac{1}{2}''$ No. 8 flathead wood screws. Holes should be bored and countersunk in the front member to take the screws. Glue should be applied to the butting surfaces before the parts are assembled. The top member is joined to the sides with glue applied to the dadoes and tongues before assembly. Clamps should be applied to hold the top member to the sides. The completed upper unit may now be assembled to the lower section. As shown in the detail sketch this is done with $1\frac{1}{2}''$ No. 8 flathead wood screws driven through the front and side member of the upper section. The holes to take

The lower case, shown above, is made as a separate unit. Front is veneered

these screws should be bored and countersunk in the upper case.

The molding applied at the joint where the upper and lower cases join is made of stock $1\frac{1}{2}''$ x $1\frac{1}{4}''$. A piece of material 25″ long is sufficient to obtain the front and two side pieces. The molding may be cut on the shaper if the correct cutters are available, or it may be shaped by hand with the aid of carving tools and a hand beader. The molding is applied with glue and $1\frac{1}{2}''$ screws driven in from the back of the upper case.

The pediment is made of three main units with a finial and beaded ornament applied. The swan necks (J) are made of $\frac{5}{8}''$ stock. A full-size pattern of these members is drawn with the aid of graph squares as laid out in the front elevation. They are cut to shape on the jig saw and finished by hand with a file and sandpaper. The block (H) to which the finial and applied ornament is attached is made of $1\frac{1}{4}''$ square stock $1\frac{1}{2}''$ long. These three members—that is, the swan necks (J) and the block (H)—are as-sembled as a unit by means of the $\frac{1}{4}''$ dowels shown in the detail sketch. The applied ornament (I) is made of $\frac{1}{8}''$ stock $1\frac{1}{4}''$ x $1\frac{1}{2}''$ beaded as shown and fastened to block (H) with glue. The finial is a brass turning and may be made of a piece of round stock 2″ in diameter and 5″ long. A finial as shown may be purchased if the shop is not equipped to turn out this member. The pediment is fastened to the top member of the upper case with $1\frac{1}{4}''$ No. 7 flathead wood screws driven up through the top and into the swan necks.

The door frame is made of $\frac{3}{4}''$ square stock 48″ long. A $\frac{3}{8}''$ x $\frac{3}{8}''$ rabbet is cut along one edge to take the glass and stops. The front edge of this piece is rounded off at a radius $\frac{3}{8}''$ as shown in the detail sketch. After this has been done the stock can be cut to the required length and mitered to make up the door. The miters are grooved to take a spline, then the door frame is glued and assembled. The glass is cut to fit the frame and held in place with strips $\frac{1}{4}''$ x $\frac{3}{8}''$ fastened to the rabbet with $\frac{5}{8}''$ brads. The glass decoration is painted on the inside as shown in the front elevation. Two $\frac{3}{4}''$ brass butts are used to hinge the door.

The clock movement should have a face $8\frac{1}{2}''$ square. Two strips of wood $\frac{3}{4}''$ square and $8\frac{1}{2}''$ long (K) are fastened on the inside of the upper case, as shown in the detail sketch, to take the clock face. The face is fastened to these strips with wood screws.

The case back is made of a piece of $\frac{3}{8}''$ stock $9\frac{1}{2}''$ wide and 28″ long. A $\frac{1}{4}''$ x $\frac{3}{8}''$ rabbet is cut on the end and edges as shown in the plan and sections. The back is fastened in place with $\frac{3}{8}''$ No. 2 roundhead screws.

The completed case should be filled and then stained with a red mahogany stain. This treatment is followed by three coats of white shellac or clear varnish rubbed down with No. 00 steel wool or pumice stone when dry. The case is polished with a good grade of furniture wax.

Dolly Madison Table

COURTESY U. S. NATIONAL MUSEUM

each piece of stock should be at least 31⅛" long. This will allow 1" waste at each end and will provide a finished overall length of 29⅛". The lathe centers should be located with special care at the ends of each leg because the upper section of the piece is to be left square.

When the leg has been centered, the first step is to mark off the waste sections at each end so as to leave a space of 29⅛" between the marks. The next step is to mark off the 10" square section. The remaining portion of the stock can now be turned down to a finished outside diameter of 1⅞". While a gouge and skew chisel are accomplishing this work, calipers are used to check the diameter. Before the various beads and coves are marked off on the cylindrical section it is advisable to prepare a full-size layout of the turned leg as shown in the end view of the main drawing so that accuracy is assured in establishing locations and diameters of these beads and coves.

The reeded portion of each leg, as shown in the end view and section of

WHEN in company of other fine furniture, the elegance of this little table will be markedly apparent. Built of mahogany, equipped with two drop leaves, two drawers and a serviceable shelf, the table is suitable as an occasional table in hallway or living room, and it would make an excellent night table flanking a mahogany bed.

The original table illustrated was acquired during the early 19th Century by Dolly Madison, wife of U. S. President James Madison. It was later owned by Mary M. McGuire who gave it to Smithsonian Institution.

Construction of the table will require four pieces of 1⅞" square stock for the legs. Since each leg must be turned between centers on the lathe,

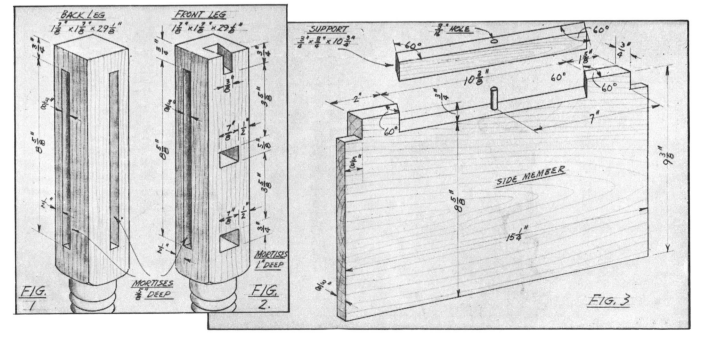

Note to Reprint Edition: This piece is now in the National Museum of History and Technology, Division of Political History.

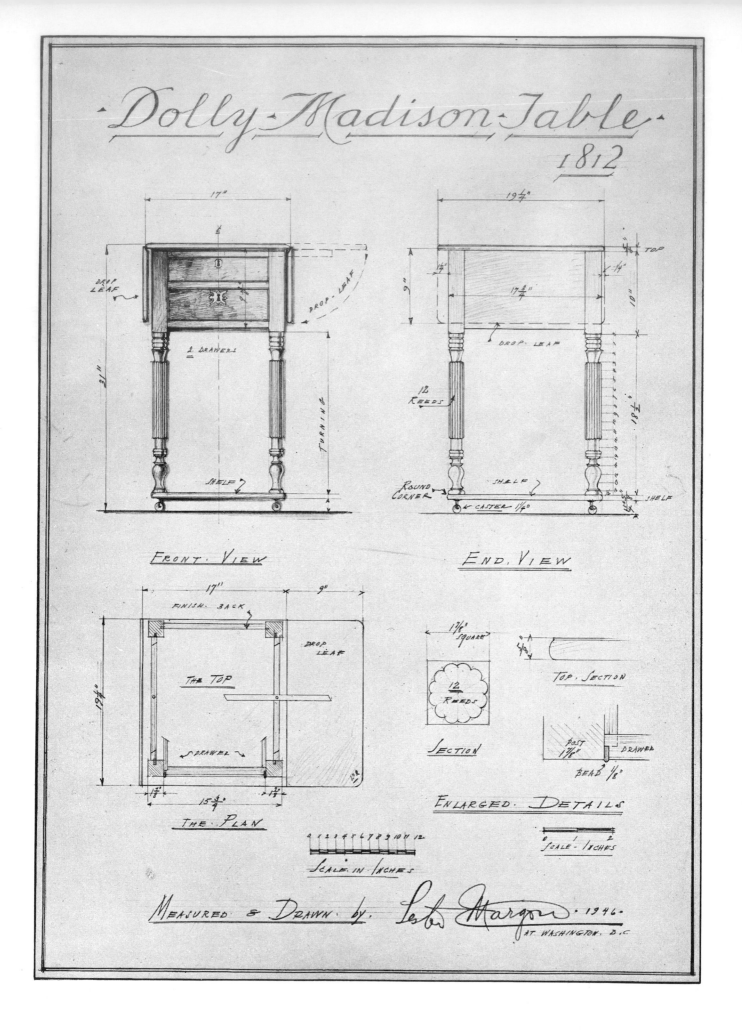

Dolly Madison Table
1812

FRONT VIEW

END VIEW

THE PLAN

SECTION

ENLARGED DETAILS

SCALE IN INCHES

SCALE IN INCHES

MEASURED & DRAWN by Lester Margon 1946

AT WASHINGTON D.C

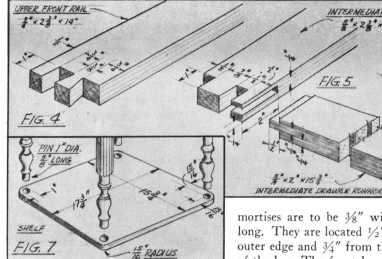

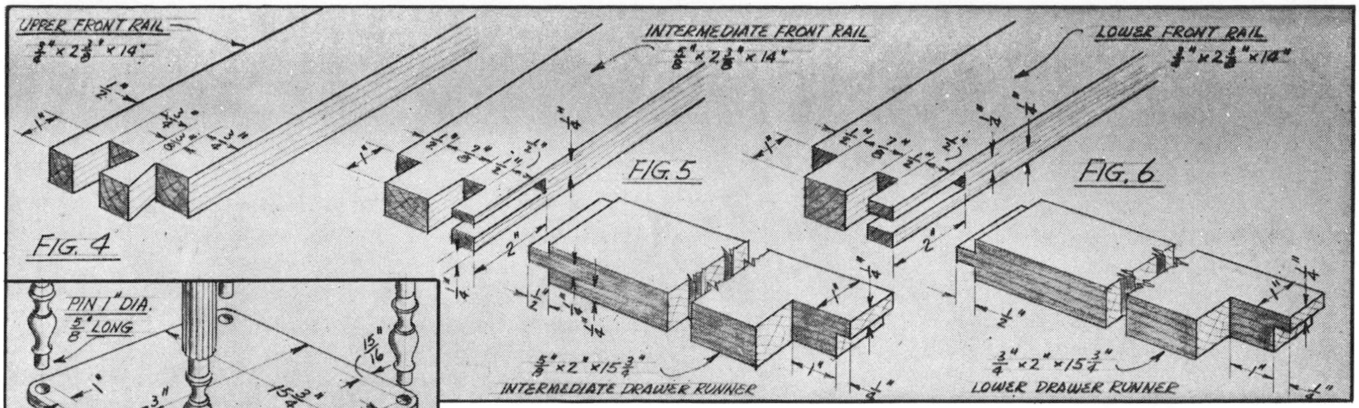

UPPER FRONT RAIL
¾" x 2⅜" x 14"

INTERMEDIATE FRONT RAIL
⅝" x 2⅜" x 14"

LOWER FRONT RAIL
¾" x 2⅜" x 14"

FIG. 4

FIG. 5

FIG. 6

INTERMEDIATE DRAWER RUNNER
⅝" x 2" x 15¾"

LOWER DRAWER RUNNER
¾" x 2" x 15¾"

PIN 1" DIA.
⅝" LONG

17¾"

15 15/16"

15/16"

15 3/4"

SHELF

FIG. 7

15/16" RADIUS

the main drawing, will require the cutting of twelve reeds. The cutting of these reeds should be done in the lathe before the waste is removed from each end. The first step in reeding is to mark off the twelve segments of the cylinder. If the lathe on which the leg has been turned is equipped with an indexing head, the dividing of the cylinder into the twelve sections will be a simple matter. In the absence of such a device the cylinder can be divided by wrapping a strip of paper around the stock and then cutting it to the exact circumference of the cylinder. The strip is removed and laid flat on the bench. The length of the strip is divided into twelve equal parts. The marked strip is replaced on the cylinder, and the divisions are carried over to the stock. When the cylinder has been marked off, lines can be drawn parallel to the axis by setting the tool rest against the turning and using the edge of the rest as a pencil guide for extending the segment marks.

The method of reeding will depend on equipment available in the shop. Reeds may be cut with a portable shaper, or they may be cut by hand with a wood carver's parting tool and gouge. Another method of reeding utilizes the services of a regular shaper or drill press set up with a suitable cutter. If the shaper or drill press is used, the stock will have to be removed from the lathe and a fixture prepared to hold the turning while the reeding is cut. After the four legs have been turned and reeded, their relative positions should be marked so the mortises and gains that are to take the various rails and panels shown in Figs. 1 and 2 can be laid out.

The back legs as shown in Fig. 1 have mortises laid out on adjacent sides to take the back and end panels. These

mortises are to be ⅜" wide and 8⅝" long. They are located ½" in from the outer edge and ¾" from the upper end of the leg. The front legs as shown in Fig. 2 have a ⅜" x 8⅝" mortise laid out on one side to take the front rails. The mortises for the end and back

panels should be cut to a depth of ⅝", while those for the front rails are cut 1" deep. If a hollow mortising attachment for the drill press is available, this unit can be used to cut the mortises. The dovetail socket at the end of the front legs should be cut by hand.

With the completion of the legs, work on the side or end members and the back member can be undertaken. These members as shown in Figs. 3 and 8 will require two pieces of ¾" stock 9⅜" x 15¼" and one piece ¾" x 9⅜" x 13¼". Each of these members has a ⅜" x ⅝" bare-faced tenon laid out and cut at each end as shown in Fig. 3 to fit the mortises in the legs. The back member as shown in Fig. 8 has mortises laid out and cut on the inside face to take the tongue on the end of each drawer runner.

The two side members must be prepared to take the drop-leaf supports as shown in Fig. 3. This will require the removal of a section along the upper edge of the side pieces. The section to be removed should be laid out on each piece according to dimensions given in

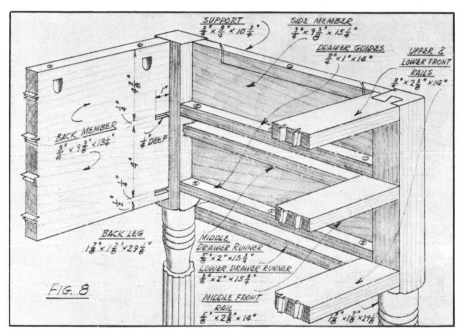

SUPPORT
¾" x ¾" x 10¾"

SIDE MEMBER
¾" x 9⅜" x 15¼"

DRAWER GUIDES
¾" x 1" x 14"

UPPER &
LOWER FRONT
RAILS
¾" x 2⅜" x 14"

BACK MEMBER
¾" x 9⅜" x 13¾"

¼" DEEP

BACK LEG
1¾" x 1¾" x 29⅝"

MIDDLE
DRAWER RUNNER
⅝" x 2" x 15¾"

LOWER DRAWER RUNNER
¾" x 2" x 15¾"

MIDDLE FRONT
RAIL
⅝" x 2⅜" x 14"

1¾" x 1¾" x 29⅝"

FIG. 8

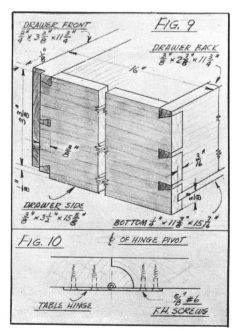

DRAWER FRONT
⅞" x 3⅜" x 11¾"

FIG. 9

DRAWER BACK
⅜" x 2⅝" x 11¾"

3/16"

⅜"

DRAWER SIDE
⅜" x 3½" x 15⅝"

BOTTOM ¼" x 11¾" x 15¼"

FIG. 10

℄ OF HINGE PIVOT

TABLE HINGE

⅝" #6
F.H. SCREWS

35

Fig. 3. The 60° angle cut at the ends of these sections may be cut on the bench saw.

The drop-leaf support is to swing on a pivot which is a $\frac{3}{16}$" dowel $1\frac{3}{4}$" long as shown in Fig. 3. To provide for this pivot, a $\frac{3}{16}$" hole is located as shown and is bored to a depth of 1". The dowel is glued in place. The side members, after being sandpapered, can be joined to the legs. After the side units have been glued and set in clamps, the work should be checked for squareness before the glue sets.

The supports shown in Figs. 3 and 8 are made of two pieces of $\frac{3}{4}$" x $\frac{3}{4}$" stock $10\frac{3}{4}$" long. The ends of these members are cut at an angle of 60° as indicated. The support has a $\frac{3}{16}$" hole bored in the center to permit its placement over the pivot set in the side member.

The front rails shown in Figs. 4, 5, and 6 are made of stock $2\frac{3}{8}$" wide and 14" long. The upper and lower rails as shown in Figs. 4 and 6 are to be $\frac{3}{4}$" thick, while the intermediate rail is to be $\frac{5}{8}$" thick. The upper rail shown in Fig. 4 is to have a dovetail pin laid out and cut at each end to fit the socket in the leg. The intermediate and lower rails in Figs. 5 and 6 are to have tenons cut on each end to fit the mortises.

Drawer runners are to be provided for the drawers. These runners are to be joined to the intermediate and lower rails by means of tongue-and-groove joints and are to be supported at the back by means of $\frac{1}{4}$" x $\frac{1}{4}$" tongues that are fitted into the mortises previously cut in the back panel as shown in Figs. 5 and 6. The runners that are to be joined to the intermediate rail are

to measure $\frac{5}{8}$" x 2" x $15\frac{3}{4}$" while those that are to be joined to the lower rail should be $\frac{3}{4}$" x 2" x $15\frac{3}{4}$". After these members have been prepared, they should be fitted together temporarily to make certain that the work has been done properly.

In the final assembly the runners are glued to the rails, and the rails and back panel are glued to one side unit. The other end of the rails and back panel can now be joined to the other side unit. Clamps should be applied and the work checked for squareness. Drawer guides as shown in Fig. 8 are made of four pieces of $\frac{3}{4}$" x 1" x 14" stock; they are secured to the drawer runners with $1\frac{1}{4}$" No. 7 flathead screws set in countersunk holes.

The shelf shown in Fig. 7 will require a piece of $\frac{5}{8}$" stock $15\frac{3}{4}$" wide and $17\frac{3}{4}$" long. It may be necessary to glue up two or more pieces of stock to produce a panel of the required width. Holes 1" in diameter are bored $1\frac{5}{16}$" from each corner as shown. These are through holes and are to take the pins turned on the lower end of each leg. The corners of the shelf are to be rounded off at a radius of $1\frac{5}{16}$". The edges of the shelf are rounded slightly. After the shelf has been sandpapered it is joined to the legs with glue.

The top is made up in three sections. The center or main section will require a piece of $\frac{5}{8}$" stock 17" x $19\frac{1}{4}$"; the two drop leaves each need a $\frac{5}{8}$" piece measuring 9" x $19\frac{1}{4}$". A rule joint as shown in Fig. 10 is cut along the butting edges of each section. Hinges are provided as indicated. These hinges can be set in place at this time

but will have to be removed in order that the corners of the drop leaves can be rounded and the edges molded as shown in the detail on the main drawing. The main section of the top is fastened to the table with flat-head wood screws driven up through the upper front rail and the back member as shown in Fig. 8.

The drawers are made as shown in Fig. 9. The drawer members are joined together by means of dovetail joints. The $\frac{1}{8}$" x $\frac{3}{8}$" rabbet along the ends of the drawer front and the $\frac{1}{8}$" x $\frac{3}{4}$" rabbet along the lower edge of the drawer front for the cock bead should be cut after the drawers have been assembled. The cock bead as shown in the enlarged detail of the main drawing should project $\frac{1}{16}$" beyond the outside face of the drawer; therefore, the beading that is applied to the upper and lower edges of the drawer front should be $1\frac{3}{16}$" wide while the beading applied to the ends should be $\frac{7}{16}$" wide. Butting ends of the beading should be mitered.

Suitable drawer pulls and escutcheon plates should be applied to the fronts but should be removed for finishing. Casters of such size as to raise the shelf $1\frac{1}{4}$" above the floor are applied to the lower end of each leg member as shown in the front and end views of the main drawing.

For a fine mahogany finish the table may be stained and filled. This treatment should be followed by several coats of white shellac, each rubbed down with fine steel wool after the shellac has set. Clear lacquer or varnish may be substituted for shellac. A coat of wax, brought to a polish with a soft cloth, will complete the work.

Selected for its unpretentious posts, free of intricate work, this canopy bed makes an ideal project for craftsmen having access to a wood-turning lathe

Early American Canopy Bed

COLONIAL atmosphere in homes of today can be achieved by no easier means than by making the canopy bed illustrated here. Replete with the traditions of Early American life this monumental piece of furniture contributes much more than it takes in the making.

While known as a canopy, this style of bed also is called a tester, and often is labeled a four-poster field bed. The term "field" bed came from the supposed resemblance of the arched framework to a field tent. Two purposes are attributed to the style: the draperies kept out the cold and provided privacy from children who often slept in the same room as evidenced by the trundle bed and cradle in the photograph.

Construction of the bed should be started with the posts. The overall finished length of these members is 64". Since the average home workshop lathe can take stock no longer than 36" or 40" it will be necessary to construct each post in two units and to join by means of a pin turned on the upper member as shown in Fig. 5. Each post is made of cherry 3" sq. x 36½" for the lower portion and a piece 3" x 3" x 30" for the upper section.

Before the pieces are turned, it is advisable to lay out and cut in the lower post sections the mortises that are to take the tenons on the rails and headboard. The location and size of each mortise is shown in Fig. 1. The mortises can be cut with a hollow mortising chisel set up in the drill press, or they can be cut by hand with auger bit and chisel. The mortises for the head and foot rails are cut 2⅜" deep as shown in Figs. 2 and 3, while those for the side rails are cut ⅝" deep. The mortises for the headboard are 1¼" deep.

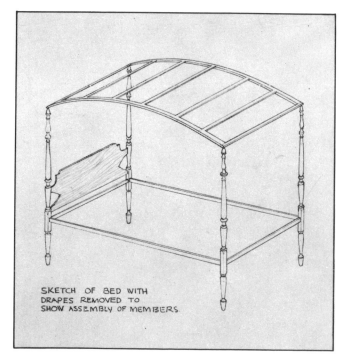

SKETCH OF BED WITH DRAPES REMOVED TO SHOW ASSEMBLY OF MEMBERS.

Within the Brooklyn Museum, parts of the old Schenck House built at Canarsie Park in 1775 have been restored to provide a natural setting for the graceful canopy bed. By courtesy of the Brooklyn Museum, shown below, and the City of New York this presentation is made

·FOUR-POSTER·FIELD·BED·

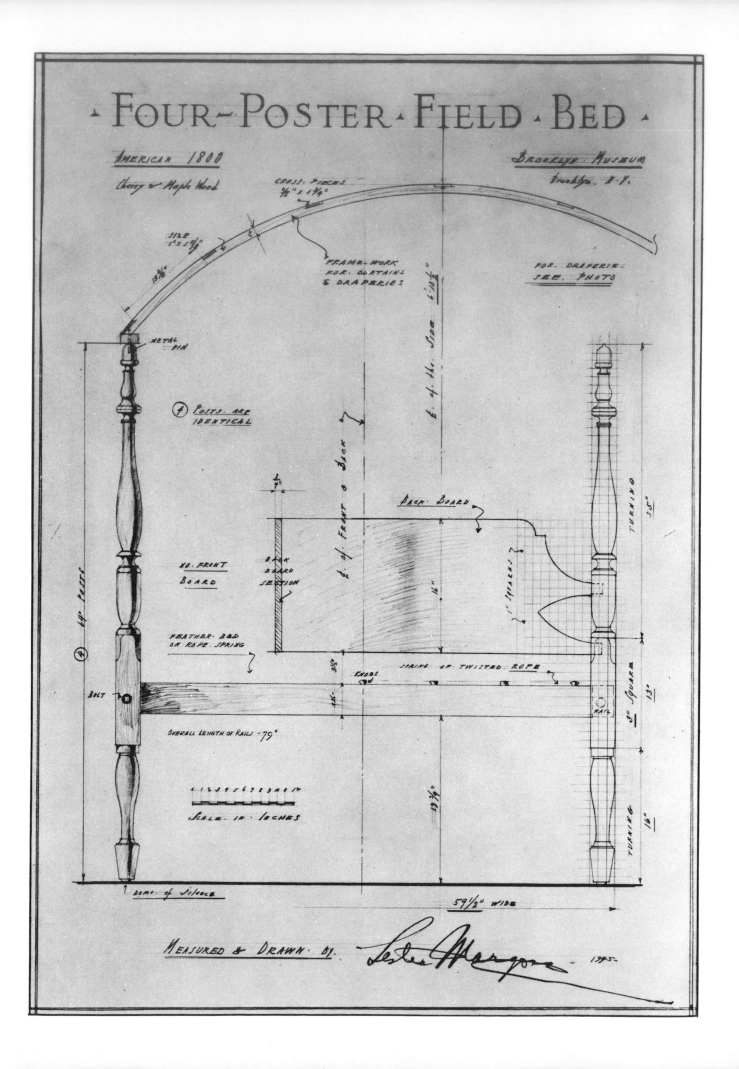

AMERICAN 1800

Cherry & Maple Wood

BROOKLYN MUSEUM
Brooklyn. N.Y.

CROSS·PIECES
3/8"x 1 1/4"

FRAME·WORK
FOR CURTAINS
& DRAPERIES

SIZE
1"x 1 5/8"

FOR DRAPERIES
SEE PHOTO

METAL PIN

4 POSTS ARE
IDENTICAL

BACK BOARD

E. of the floor 6'10 1/2"

E. of front & back

NO FRONT
BOARD

BACK
BOARD
SECTION

1" SPACES

TURNING

35"

FEATHER BED
ON ROPE SPRING

SPRING OF TWISTED ROPE

KNOBS

3" SQUARE

13"

BOLT

RAIL

OVERALL LENGTH OF RAILS - 79"

13 1/2"

· 1 2 3 4 5 6 7 8 9 10 11 12 ·
SCALE IN INCHES

TURNING

16"

DOME OF SILENCE

59 1/2" WIDE

MEASURED & DRAWN BY

1945

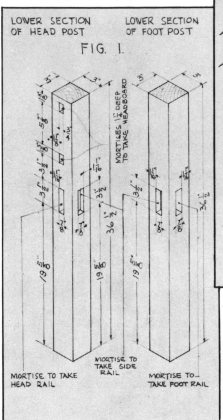

LOWER SECTION OF HEAD POST   LOWER SECTION OF FOOT POST

FIG. 1.

MORTISE TO TAKE HEAD RAIL

MORTISE TO TAKE SIDE RAIL

MORTISE TO TAKE FOOT RAIL

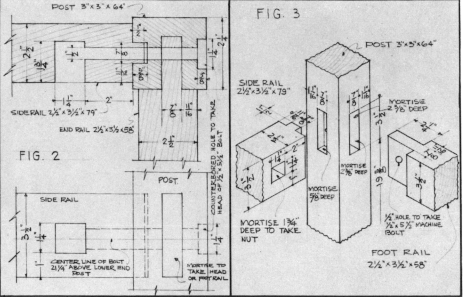

FIG. 2

FIG. 3

POST 3"x3"x64"

SIDE RAIL 2½"x3½"x79"

END RAIL 2½"x3½"x58"

POST

SIDE RAIL

CENTER LINE OF BOLT 21¼" ABOVE LOWER END POST

MORTISE TO TAKE HEAD OR FOOT RAIL

COUNTERBORED HOLE TO TAKE HEAD OF ½"x5½" BOLT

SIDE RAIL 2½"x3½"x79"

MORTISE 2⅜" DEEP

MORTISE 2⅜" DEEP

MORTISE ⅝" DEEP

MORTISE 1¾" DEEP TO TAKE NUT

½" HOLE TO TAKE ½"x5½" MACHINE BOLT

FOOT RAIL 2½"x3½"x58"

The head and foot rails will require two pieces of maple 2½" x 3½" x 58". Tenons should be laid out and cut on both ends of each member to fit the mortises in the lower post sections. These tenons should be 2¼" long, ⅞" thick and 3½" wide, as shown in Figs. 2 and 3.

The side rails will require two pieces of maple 2½" x 3½" x 79". These rails require stub tenons on each end. The tenons are made ½" long, ⅞" thick and 3½" wide as shown in Figs. 2 and 3. The side rails are secured to the posts by means of machine bolts that pass through the posts and into the ends of the rails as shown in Fig. 2. To provide space for a nut, a mortise must be cut on the inside face of the side rails near each end as shown in Figs. 2 and 3. This mortise measures 1¼" square and should be located 2" from the shoulder of the tenon. It is cut to a depth of 1¾". The boring of the ½" bolt hole through the post and rail as well as the counterboring on the outside face of the post for the bolt head can be done after the end rails have been joined to the posts.

The headboard will require a piece of ¾" cherry finished to a width of 16" and a length of 55¾". Tenons as shown in Fig. 4 are cut on each end of the headboard. After the tenons have been cut and fitted, a full-size pat-

tern of the shaped portion of the headboard should be prepared and traced on the stock for bandsawing or jigsawing. Sawed edges are smoothed with file and sandpaper. After the rails and headboard tenons have been fitted to the lower post sections, the work of shaping the posts on the lathe can be undertaken.

Each lower post section is set up in

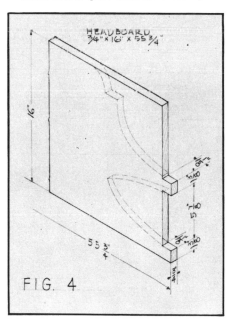

HEADBOARD 34"x16"x55¾"

FIG. 4

the lathe between centers for turning. Extreme care should be taken to locate the exact center on each end of the square stock; an error will keep the turned sections from being concentric with the square portions.

It is advisable to prepare a full-size drawing of the turned portion. The square stock, with the upper end of the live center, when set up in the lathe, should be marked off to establish the limits of the turned and square sec-

tions. The sections that are to be shaped should be turned down to a finished outside diameter of 3" by means of a gouge and a skew chisel. Next, the limits of the various curves, coves, fillets and taper are laid out and the diameters of these cuts are established with a parting tool. The shaping of the post is done with gouge, roundnose and skew chisels. The completed turning should be sandpapered while on the lathe.

After all four lower sections have been completed, a 1⅛" hole is bored in the upper end of each, to a depth of 2" as shown in Fig. 5. This operation may be done on the drill press by tilting the table to a vertical position and securing the bed post to the vertical surface of the table with a hand screw.

Each upper post section, which is

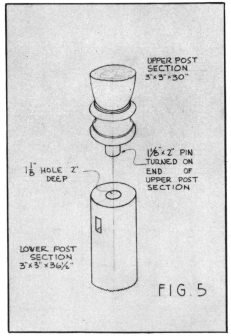

UPPER POST SECTION 3"x3"x30"

1⅛"x2" PIN TURNED ON END OF UPPER POST SECTION

1⅛" HOLE 2" DEEP

LOWER POST SECTION 3"x3"x36½"

FIG. 5

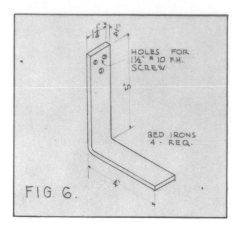

FIG. 6.

HOLES FOR 1½" #10 F.H. SCREW

BED IRONS 4 - REQ.

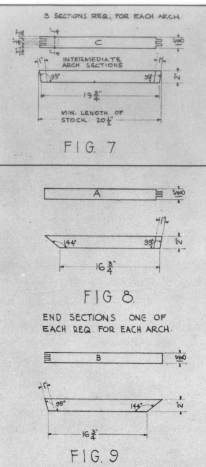

3 SECTIONS REQ. FOR EACH ARCH.

C

INTERMEDIATE ARCH SECTIONS

19¾"

MIN. LENGTH OF STOCK 20½"

FIG. 7

A

144°   99°

16¾"

FIG. 8.

END SECTIONS ONE OF EACH REQ. FOR EACH ARCH.

B

99°   144°

16¾"

FIG. 9

made of stock 30″ long, is set up between centers in the lathe. The 30″ length allows for ¾″ waste at the live center end. The square stock is first turned to a finished outside diameter of 3″. The limits of the various curves, coves, beads and fillets should be marked off and their diameters established with the aid of parting tool and calipers before the shaping is begun. The 1⅛″ x 2″ dowel pin on the lower end of these post sections should be located at the live center and should be cut after all other turning and sanding has been completed. The upper and lower sections are glued together.

Examination of the back posts will show that the pin on the upper post section extends downward into the mortise that is to take the upper tenon on the end of the headboard. It will be necessary to remove with a chisel the section of the pin that fills the mortise. The canopy framework covering the bed is supported on the ends of the posts. To secure the framework to the posts, a steel pin is used as shown in the main drawing and in Fig. 11. A ¼″ hole is bored in the upper end of each post to take the pin.

Assembly of the head and foot units is the next operation. The parts are glued together and set in clamps. Special care should be exercised to keep the foot posts parallel while in clamps.

Now that the end units have been completed they can be bored for the bolt that joins them to the side rails. As shown in Fig. 2, the center of the bolt hole is to be located 21¼″ above the lower end of the post. A 1¼″ hole is bored to a depth of ⅜″ to take the bolt head. A ½″ hole is bored in the center of this 1¼″ hole. Since the bolt must pass through the post and into the side rail, it is advisable to set the side rails into the posts and bore the ½″ hole through both members as a single operation. The hole passes into the rail mortise made for the nut.

The original bed shown in the main drawing was equipped with knobs fastened to the upper edge of the rails around which cord was passed to form

the spring. Since modern box springs are used in beds today, these knobs can be eliminated. To carry a box spring, angle irons should be formed as shown in Fig. 6 and secured to the inside face of the side rails with 2″ No. 10 flathead screws. They are placed on the side rails, 12″ from each end. Four are required.

The bows of the canopy should be made of 1″ x 1⅝″ stock, 9 ft. long. These pieces on early beds were steambent and clamped in curved forms. If

facilities are available a suitable form for bending the stock can be prepared by laying out the arc on the shop floor as shown in Fig. 10 and securing blocks of wood to the floor for shaping.

A more practical method for most craftsmen calls for bows built up of sections and cut to shape on the band saw or jig saw. Figs. 7, 8 and 9 snow the various sections that should be prepared to form the bows. The minimum length of stock required for each section is 20½″. After each section is ready, it should be placed on a full-size arc marked on the shop floor according to Fig. 10. The sections are glued together on this layout. After the glue has set, the arcs can be drawn out on the wood for guidance in bandsawing.

Dadoes are laid out and cut on the upper edge of the bows to take ⅜″ x 1¾″ slats as shown in Fig. 11 and in the main drawing. The slats are secured to the bows with ¾″ No. 7 flathead screws. The base member at each end of the bow has a ¼″ x 3″ steel pin driven through to secure the canopy assembly to the bed posts.

The completed bed may be left natural or may be stained. Several coats of shellac, clear varnish or lacquer should be applied to protect the wood. The finished surfaces should be rubbed down with No. 00 steel wool or with pumice and rottenstone.

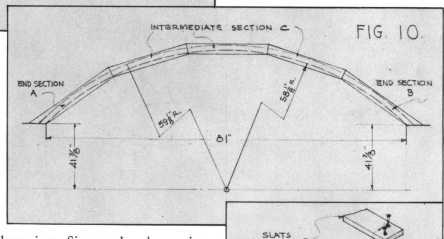

INTERMEDIATE SECTION C

END SECTION A   END SECTION B

58⅝" R.   59⅝" R.

81"

41⅛"   41⅛"

FIG. 10.

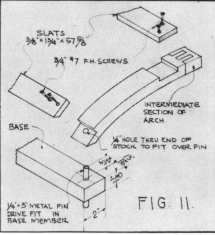

SLATS ⅜" x 1¾" x 57⅝"

¾" #7 F.H. SCREWS

INTERMEDIATE SECTION OF ARCH.

BASE

¼" HOLE THRU END OF STOCK TO FIT OVER PIN

¼" x 3" METAL PIN DRIVE FIT IN BASE MEMBER

FIG. 11.

Antique Stand Makes Excellent Magazine Rack

Originally made as a music stand with storage shelves, this distinguished piece could well be used for holding magazines. It is shown by courtesy of U. S. Dept. of the Interior

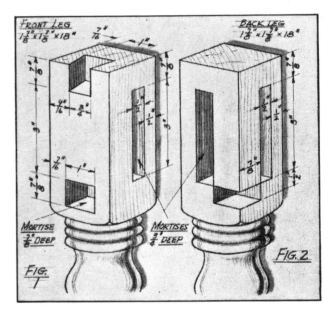

IN THE grand parlor of Lee Mansion at Arlington, Virginia, a graceful mahogany music stand occupies a focal corner of a room which is rich in crystal chandeliers and claw-footed chairs and tables characteristic of the colonial period. Though worthy of reproduction in its own right this fine piece also lends itself admirably to use in today's homes as a magazine stand.

Construction of the stand should be started with the base unit. As shown in Fig. 8 this unit consists of legs, end aprons, back apron, upper and lower front rails, drawer runners and kick rail. The table top and drawer which are parts of this unit should be made up after the carcase has been assembled.

The legs are made of four pieces of 1 7/8" square stock 18" long. No allowance for waste is necessary because the

marks left by the live and dead centers will not be seen on the completed stand. After the legs have been cut to size, the mortises, gains and dovetail sockets to take the aprons, rails and drawer runners can be laid out. If desired, the mortises for the end and back aprons may be cut before the stock is turned, but the dovetail socket, the mortise for the lower front rail and the gain for the drawer runner should not be cut until the turning has been completed.

As shown in Fig. 1, the front legs have the dovetail sockets laid out at the upper end to take the upper rail. On the same surface a mortise is laid out to take the lower front rail. The adjacent surface of each front leg has

a mortise for the end apron. The back legs shown in Fig. 2 have mortises of the same size laid out on adjacent faces to take the end and back aprons. The inside corner of each back leg has a gain to take the end of the drawer runner. After these joints have been laid out, the legs are ready for turning in the lathe.

The center of each end should be established with diagonal lines. The upper end of the leg goes against the live center, while the dead center takes the lower end of the leg. Craftsmen who are not accomplished wood turners should prepare a full-size drawing of the contour of the leg by enlarging the graph-squared drawing of the leg.

Note to Reprint Edition: Since 1971 the official name of the mansion has been Arlington House, the name used by the Custis and Lee families. Since Arlington House was completed around 1820, the furnishing emphasis is on a later period; the only colonial pieces being those typical of the kind of furniture Mr. Custis would have inherited.

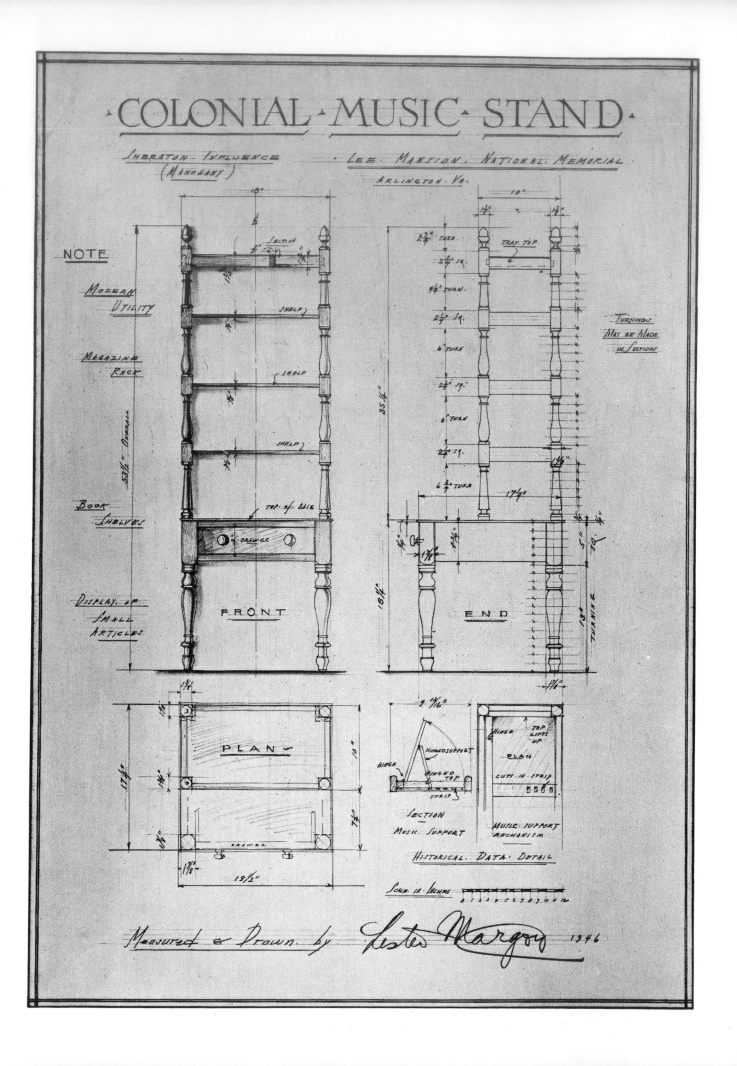

COLONIAL · MUSIC · STAND ·

Sheraton Influence (Mahogany)

Lee · Mansion · National · Memorial ·

Arlington · Va ·

NOTE

MODERN UTILITY

MAGAZINE RACK

BOOK SHELVES

DISPLAY OF SMALL ARTICLES

FRONT

END

Turnings May be Made in Sections

PLAN

Section — Music Support

Music Support Mechanism

Historical Data Detail

Scale in Inches

Measured & Drawn by Lester Margon 1946

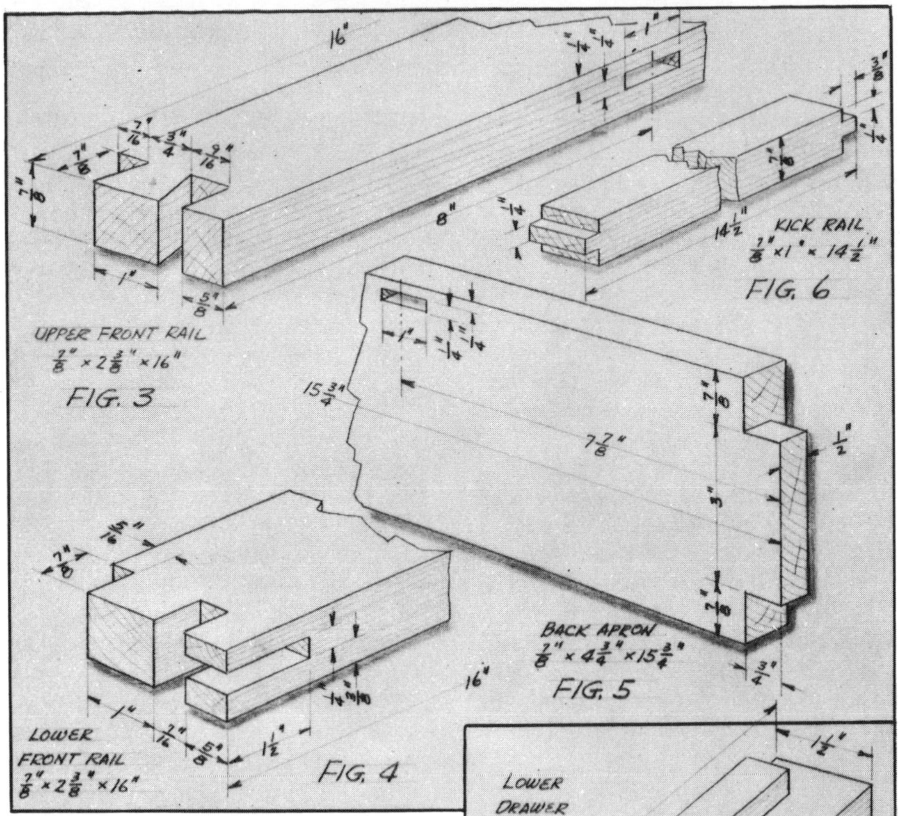
UPPER FRONT RAIL
⅞" × 2⅜" × 16"
KICK RAIL
⅞" × 1" × 14½"
BACK APRON
⅞" × 4¾" × 15¾"
LOWER
FRONT RAIL
⅞" × 2⅜" × 16"

FIG. 3 FIG. 4 FIG. 5 FIG. 6

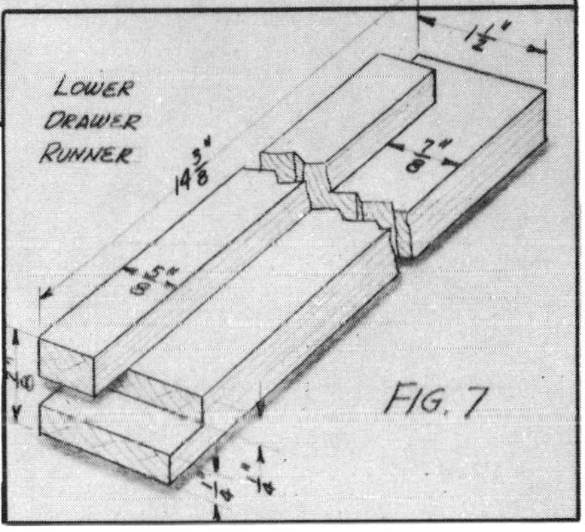
LOWER
DRAWER
RUNNER

FIG. 7

The first step in the actual turning consists of marking off the square section at the upper end of the leg and turning down the remainder of the stock to a finished outside diameter of 1⅞". Locations of the various cuts should be marked on the cylinder. The ultimate diameters of the curves should be established at these points by using calipers to measure the diameter while a parting tool is used to cut to the required size. After establishment of the various depths the work of shaping the leg is done with gouge, roundnose and skew wood-turning chisels. Each turned leg should be sanded while in the lathe.

The mortises that take the end and back aprons are cut ½" wide and ¾" deep. If a hollow mortising unit is part of the shop equipment, it can be used to speed the work. The gain in the back legs as well as the mortise to take the lower front rail can be cut with the same chisel that is used for the apron mortises. The dovetail socket is cut with back saw and chisel.

End aprons shown in Fig. 8 and back apron in Fig. 5 are the next members to be prepared. The end aprons are made of ⅞" stock 4¾" wide and 15" long, while the back apron calls for ⅞" x 4¾" x 15¾" stock. Tenons are laid out on both ends of these three pieces as shown in Fig. 5. They are cut to shape on the bench saw and are then fitted to their respective mortises. The back apron has a mortise cut on the inside face to receive the end of the kick rail.

Upper and lower front rails each require a piece of ⅞" stock 2⅜" wide and 16" long. The upper front rail, as shown in Fig. 3, has a dovetail pin laid out on each end to fit sockets previously cut in the front legs. When these pins are being cut, allowance of some stock for trimming and fitting the pin is essential. A mortise must be laid out and cut on the inside edge of this member, as shown in Fig. 3, to take the forward end of the kick rail. The lower front rail has tenons laid out and cut on each end, as shown in Fig. 4. It is important that these tenons be fitted to their respective mortises. A ¼" groove must be laid out and cut along the inside edge of the lower front rail.

Work is now started on the kick rail and drawer runners. The kick rail is made of a piece of stock ⅞" x 1" x 14½"; the drawer runners in Fig. 7 require two pieces of ⅞" stock 1½" wide and 14⅜" long. The kick rail has a ¼" x ⅜" tongue cut on each end, as shown in Fig. 6, to fit the mortises previously cut in the inside face of the back apron and on the inside edge of the upper front rail. The drawer runners have a ¼" x ⅝" tongue cut on the forward end, as shown in Fig. 7, to fit the groove in the inside edge of the lower front rail. A ⅜" x ⅞" rabbet is cut across the back end of these runners so that the runners will fit the gain in the back legs. A rabbet is cut along the inside edge to carry the drawer.

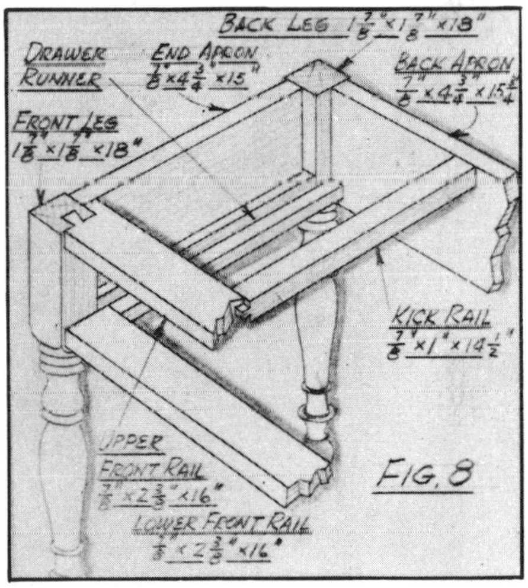
BACK LEG 1⅞" × 1⅞" × 18"
DRAWER RUNNER
END APRON ⅞" × 4¾" × 15"
BACK APRON ⅞" × 4¾" × 15¾"
FRONT LEG 1⅞" × 1⅞" × 18"
KICK RAIL ⅞" × 1" × 14½"
UPPER FRONT RAIL ⅞" × 2⅜" × 16"
LOWER FRONT RAIL ⅞" × 2⅜" × 16"

FIG. 8

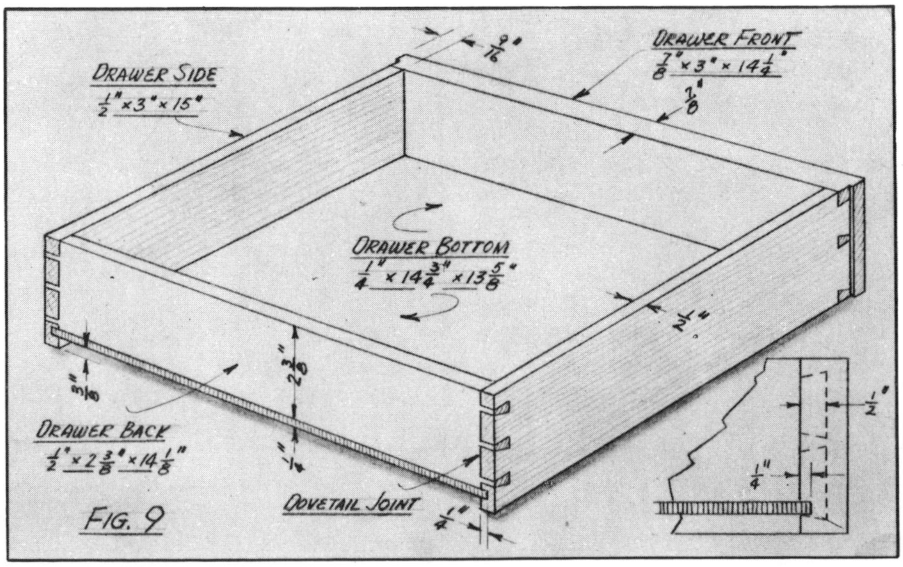
DRAWER SIDE
½" × 3" × 15"
DRAWER FRONT
⅞" × 3" × 14¼"
DRAWER BOTTOM
¼" × 14¾" × 13⅝"
DRAWER BACK
½" × 2⅜" × 14⅛"
DOVETAIL JOINT

FIG. 9

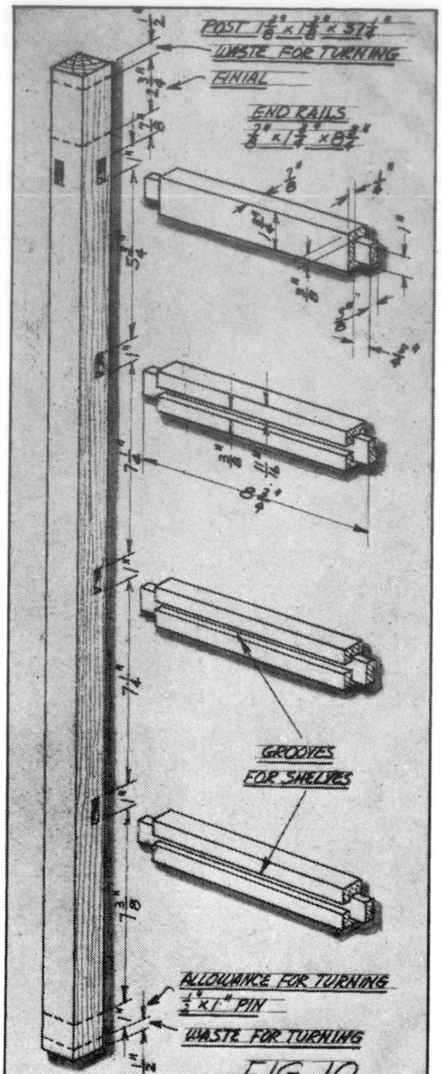
POST 1 3/8 x 1 3/8 x 37 1/4
WASTE FOR TURNING
FINIAL
END RAILS
7/8 x 1 3/4 x 8 3/4
GROOVES
FOR SHELVES
ALLOWANCE FOR TURNING
1/2 x 1 PIN
WASTE FOR TURNING
FIG. 10

Carcase members of the base unit are now ready for trial assembly so that the work can be checked before it is glued. The end aprons are set into the legs, then the drawer runners are set into the gains. The lower front rail and the back apron are set into one end unit, then the second end unit is placed on the rail and apron. The kick rail is placed in the upper front rail, and this unit is set in place. Bar clamps should be applied to tighten the assembly.

The table top is made of 1/4" stock 17 1/2" x 18 1/2". This size provides for a 1/8" overhang on the edges and ends. After half-round molding has been shaped on the edges and ends, the top is sanded and is then glued to the aprons and upper front rails.

The drawer, as shown in Fig. 9, is dovetailed. The drawer bottom, which is made of 1/4" stock, is set into grooves cut along the inside face of the front and side members. Suitable knobs may be turned in the lathe or purchased.

The upper section of the stand is made of four posts joined together with eight end rails, as shown in Fig. 10. There are three shelves, as shown in Fig. 11, and a front and back rail, as shown in Fig. 12.

Posts for the upper section, shown in Fig. 10, require four pieces of 1 3/8" square stock 37 1/4" long. This length is sufficient to make the entire turning from the adorning finial at the top to the pin at the bottom for joining the upper unit to the lower section. The first step in preparing the posts is to lay out and cut the mortises to take the rails. Each mortise should be cut to a depth of 3/4". After the mortises have been completed, the posts are turned to shape in the lathe.

End rails will require eight pieces of 7/8" x 1 3/4" x 8 3/4" stock; front and back rails call for two pieces 7/8" x 1 3/4" x 17 3/4". Tenons are laid out and cut on both ends of each rail, as shown in Fig. 10. As these tenons are being cut each one must be fitted to its respective mortise. The three lower end rails have a 3/8" x 1/4" groove cut along the face to take the shelf member. The front and back rails shown in Fig. 12 have a mortise cut on the inside face to take the cleat on which the music stand upright is to rest.

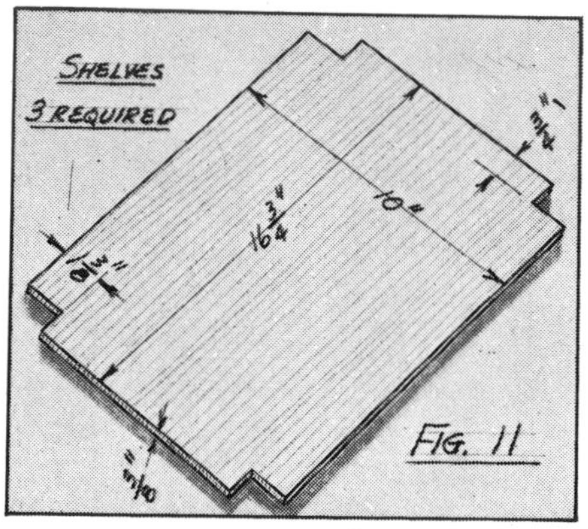
SHELVES
3 REQUIRED
10"
16 3/4"
FIG. 11

The cleat is made of 1/2" x 1" x 8 3/4" stock and has tongues cut on each end to fit the mortises. In the upper face of the cleat shallow mortises are cut to take the support. Each of the three shelves is made of 3/8" x 10" x 16 3/4" stock which is notched at each corner, as shown in Fig. 11. The completed members should be assembled for trial fitting before final assembly.

Added inside the front rail is a cleat made of 3/4" square stock 17 1/4" long with a rabbet cut at each end to fit it around the posts. See Fig. 12. It is fastened in place with flathead wood screws. The music stand requires a piece of 3/8" stock 7 3/8" wide and 16 1/4" long. The support is a piece of 1/4" x 1/2" x 4 3/8" stock hinged to the back of the music stand, as shown in Fig. 13. The music stand is attached to the rail cleat with 3/4" brass butts.

Joining the upper section to the base unit is the final step in construction. Holes are located in the top of the table unit at points determined directly from the pins on the lower end of the upper unit. After the holes have been bored with a 1/2" bit to a depth of 1 1/8" the two sections are assembled.

If mahogany has been used for construction, the completed piece should be stained, filled and given several coats of white shellac rubbed down with No. 00 steel wool. Waxing and polishing are the final operations.

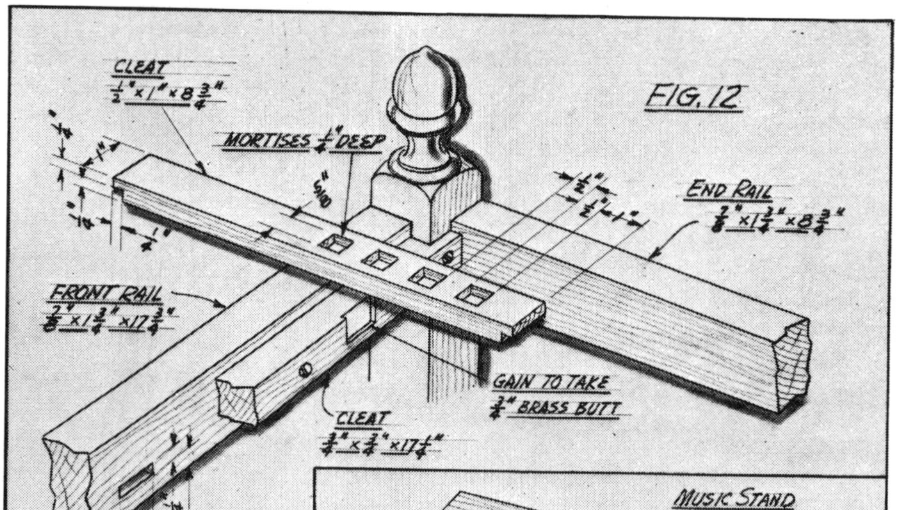
CLEAT
1/2 x 1 x 8 3/4
MORTISES 1/4" DEEP
END RAIL
7/8 x 1 3/4 x 8 3/4
FRONT RAIL
7/8 x 1 3/4 x 17 3/4
GAIN TO TAKE
3/4" BRASS BUTT
CLEAT
3/4 x 3/4 x 17 1/4
FIG. 12

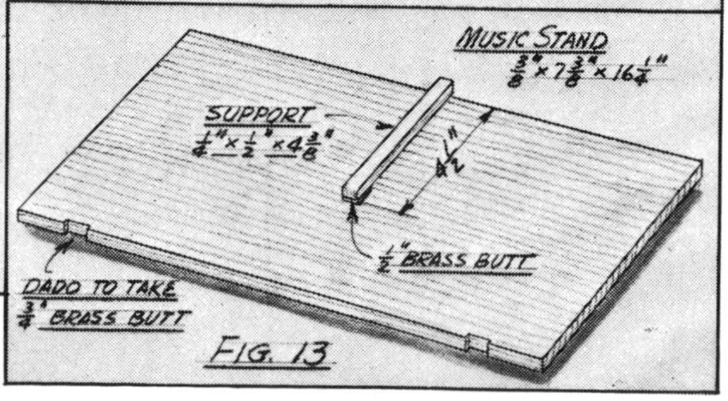
MUSIC STAND
3/8 x 7 3/8 x 16 1/4
SUPPORT
1/4 x 1/2 x 4 3/8
1/2" BRASS BUTT
DADO TO TAKE
3/4" BRASS BUTT
FIG. 13

All who like woodworking as a hobby will be quick to recognize the outstanding excellence of this antique Duncan Phyfe table. Designed by the master American cabinetmaker, it has the typical features that have been identified with his work for well over a century. The reverse curve of the legs, the crisp acanthus-leaf carving, the fluted pedestal base and the use of rich veneers all contribute to a style that is still in high favor

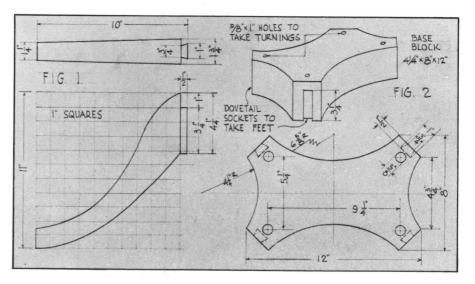

Plans for a Duncan Phyfe Drop-Leaf Table

THE ORIGINAL Duncan Phyfe drop-leaf table shown in the photograph and the main drawing is enriched with carving on the legs, on the turned pedestals and base block, but a reproduction can be made without these embellishments if carving is beyond the ability of the craftsman. Construction of the table can be broken down into two main units. These are the lower base unit which consists of the four legs and the base block as shown in Figs. 1 and 2, and the upper

unit as shown in Figs. 6 and 7. When completed, these units are joined by turned and carved pedestals.

Work on the base unit is started by preparing the base block from a piece of stock 4¼" thick, 8" wide and 12" long. After the stock has been squared to size, the four holes to take the turned pedestals should be located on one face. The holes are located from center lines as shown in Fig. 2; they are bored with a ⅝" bit to a depth of 1". The next operation is that of laying out the curved ends and edges as well as the corner cuts. The limits of the small arcs are first established on each end; the 45° angles are laid out on each corner from the limits of the small arcs. This method will automatically establish the limits of the larger arcs which can now be drawn at

a radius of 6⅝". The small arcs are drawn at a radius of 4¼". After the stock has been cut to shape on the band saw, the curved ends and edges should be dressed smooth with a spokeshave. It is not advisable to sand these curves if they are to be carved. A sanding drum is used if carving is omitted.

The next operation is that of laying out and cutting the dovetail sockets that are to take legs. These sockets are located along the center of the miter cut and extend 3¼" up from the underface of the base block as shown in Fig. 2. The sockets are cut to shape with a back saw and a chisel. If the work is to be carved, it should be done at this time. A full-size sketch of the rosette as shown in the end elevation of the main drawing must be drawn for tracing on the stock. The flutes shown in

Whitby Hall, illustrated above, is the home of the Duncan Phyfe table. This truly Colonial building erected in part in the Detroit Institute of Arts furnishes authentic background. By courtesy of the Institute this presentation of photographs and drawings was granted

45

Duncan·Phyfe·Drop-leaf·Table··

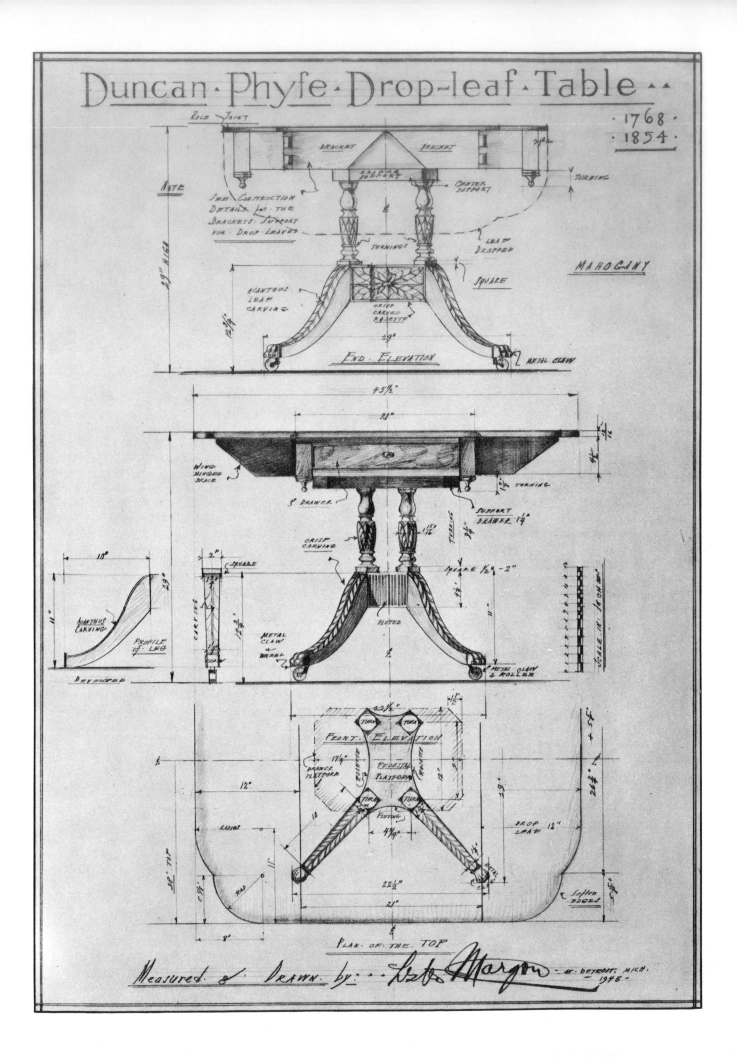

·1768·
·1854·

MAHOGANY

END·ELEVATION

PROFILE OF LEG

FRONT·ELEVATION

PLAN·OF·THE·TOP

Measured & Drawn by: ... Orb. Morgan — N. Detroit, Mich. —1945—

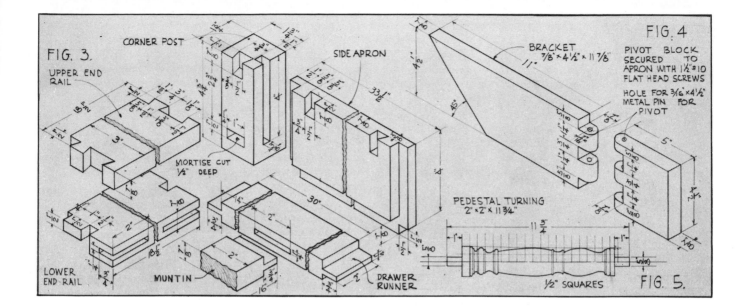

FIG. 3.

UPPER END RAIL

CORNER POST

MORTISE CUT ½" DEEP

SIDE APRON

LOWER END RAIL

MUNTIN

DRAWER RUNNER

BRACKET 7/8" × 4½" × 11 7/8"

FIG. 4

PIVOT BLOCK SECURED TO APRON WITH 1½" #10 FLAT HEAD SCREWS

HOLE FOR 3/16" × 4½" METAL PIN FOR PIVOT

PEDESTAL TURNING 2" × 2" × 11¾"

11¾"

½" SQUARES

FIG. 5.

the side elevation may be laid out directly on the work. The rosette is outlined with a parting chisel and is then modeled with carving gouges. The flutes are cut with a sharp-sweep gouge.

The legs as shown in Fig. 1 will require four pieces of 1¾" stock, 5" wide and 15" long. A full-size pattern is traced on each piece of stock. Cutting the legs to rough shape is done on the band saw or jig saw. The dovetail pin on the end of each leg should be laid out and cut to fit its respective socket. Each socket should be numbered to correspond to the pin on the leg that has been fitted to it. The sawed edges of each leg are dressed smooth with a spokeshave. As shown in the developed sketch in the main drawing and in the top view of the leg in Fig. 1, the leg tapers from 1¾" at the upper end to 1¼" at the lower end. This taper is marked for guidance in planing. It is best to fit the metal claw foot now.

The acanthus leaves which are carved on the upper edge of each leg should be laid out on paper for tracing on the

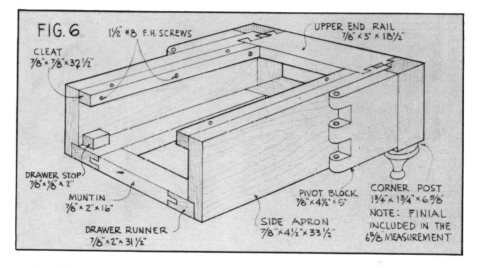

FIG. 6

1½" #8 F.H. SCREWS

CLEAT 7/8" × 7/8" × 32½"

UPPER END RAIL 7/8" × 3" × 18½"

DRAWER STOP 7/8" × 7/8" × 2"

MUNTIN 7/8" × 2" × 16"

DRAWER RUNNER 7/8" × 2" × 31½"

PIVOT BLOCK 7/8" × 4½" × 5"

SIDE APRON 7/8" × 4½" × 33½"

CORNER POST 1¾" × 1¾" × 6 5/8"

NOTE: FINIAL INCLUDED IN THE 6 5/8" MEASUREMENT

stock. The leaves are outlined with a parting tool before modeling with various gouges is undertaken.

After the carving has been completed, the legs and base block members should be sandpapered in preparation for assembly. Glue is spread in the dovetail sockets as well as on the pins; the legs are joined to the base block by sliding the pins into the sockets from

the underside of the base block. The base unit can then be set aside while work on the upper unit is undertaken.

The upper unit as shown in Figs. 3, 6 and 7 consists of four corner posts, two side aprons, two upper end rails, two lower end rails, two drawer runners and a muntin. The other pieces shown in Figs. 6 and 7 not mentioned above are members that are applied after the unit has been assembled. The corner posts if constructed with the finial as an integral part will require four pieces of stock 1¾" square and 7" long. This length allows for 3/8" waste.

When the position of each completed corner post has been decided upon the layout work on it is started. The groove that is to take the side apron, the mortise that is to take the lower end rail, and the dovetail socket that is to take the upper end rail are marked. Refer to Fig. 3. The mortise and the groove can be cut with a hollow mortising chisel set up in the drill press. The dovetail socket is cut by hand. The side aprons will require two

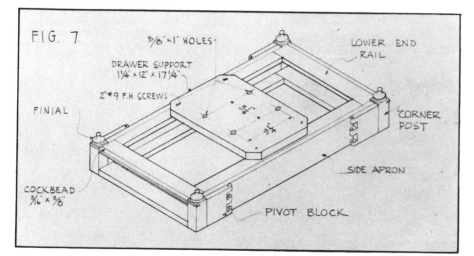

FIG. 7

5/8" × 1" HOLES

DRAWER SUPPORT 1¼" × 12" × 17¼"

2" #9 F.H. SCREWS

FINIAL

COCKBEAD 3/16" × 3/8"

LOWER END RAIL

CORNER POST

SIDE APRON

PIVOT BLOCK

pieces of 7/8" stock, 4½" wide and 33½" long. Bare-faced tenons are to be laid out and cut at each end as shown in Fig. 3 to fit their respective grooves in the corner posts. A 7/8" x ½" rabbet is cut along the lower inside edge of each apron to take the drawer runner. Dovetail sockets are laid out and cut on the upper edge to take the pins on the end of the upper end rails. The corner posts and the aprons can be sandpapered and assembled with glue at this time.

The upper and lower end rails will require four pieces of 7/8" stock, 3" wide and 18½" long. The upper rails have dovetail pins cut on each end to fit the sockets in the corner posts and side aprons as shown in Figs. 3 and 6. Before these pins are cut the layout marked on them should be checked by placing the pins over the post and apron. The lower end rails have bare-faced tenons cut on each end to fit the mortises in the posts. A ¼" x ¾" groove 2" long is cut along the inside edge of each lower end rail to take the tongue on the ends of the drawer runners.

The drawer runners will require two pieces of 7/8" stock, 2" wide and 31½" long. Tongues are cut on each end ¼" thick and ¾" long to fit in the grooves previously cut on the inside edge of the lower end rail. A ¼" x 2" mortise is laid out along the center of the inside edge of each drawer runner. The mortises are cut to a depth of ¾". The muntin requires a piece of 7/8" stock, 2" wide and 16" long. A ¼" x ¾" tongue is cut on each end to fit the mortise in the drawer runners.

Assembly of this portion of the work is done by first gluing the muntin to the drawer runners and then joining the drawer runners to the lower end rails to form a frame. This frame is joined to the corner posts, and the dovetail pin on the upper end rails is set into the sockets in the corner posts and side aprons. The cleats which are used to fasten the table top to the upper unit are installed as shown in Fig. 6. Stop blocks are secured to the drawer runners at the center as shown in Fig. 6.

The brackets that support the drop leaves will require four pieces of 7/8" stock, 4½" wide and 11 7/8" long, while the pivot block will take four pieces 7/8" x 4½" x 5". The hinge for these members is formed by cutting dadoes in the ends of each as shown in Fig. 4. These dadoes are laid out and cut on each member. The ends are rounded at a radius of 7/16" and the members are fitted together. A 3/16" hole is bored through the center of the hinge section to take a 3/16" x 4½" metal pin. The forward end of the bracket is mitered at an angle of 45°. The pivot blocks are secured to the side aprons with 1½" No. 10 flathead screws driven from inside the apron and into the pivot blocks.

The cock bead which is applied to the lower end rails as shown in the photograph and in Fig. 7 can now be set in place. This is made of two pieces of 3/16" x 3/8" stock having one edge rounded at a radius of 3/32". A 3/16" x 9/32" rabbet is cut on the bench saw along the lower edge of the rail and across the corner posts. The cock bead molding is inserted in the rabbet where it is glued in place.

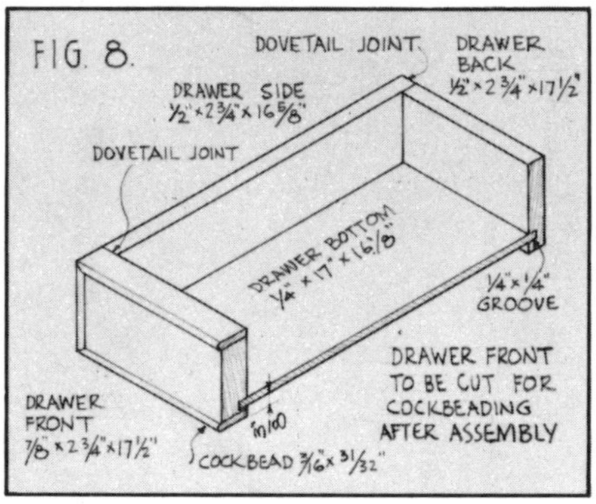
FIG. 8.
DOVETAIL JOINT
DRAWER BACK ½"×2¾"×17½"
DRAWER SIDE ½"×2¾"×16⅝"
DOVETAIL JOINT
DRAWER BOTTOM ¼"×17"×16⅛"
¼"×¼" GROOVE
DRAWER FRONT TO BE CUT FOR COCKBEADING AFTER ASSEMBLY
DRAWER FRONT ⅞"×2¾"×17½"
COCKBEAD 3/16"×31/32"

The drawer support shown in Fig. 7 is made of 1¼" stock, 12" wide and 17¼" long. The corners are cut at an angle of 45° as shown in the plan on the main drawing. Four holes to take the turned pedestals are bored in one of the faces as shown in Fig. 7. These holes must line up with those previously bored in the base block. The drawer support is secured to the drawer runners with wood screws.

The pedestals will require four pieces of 2" square stock 12¾" long including 1" allowance for waste. The overall length of the finished turning is to be 11¾" as shown in Fig. 5. A full-size drawing of the turning should be prepared to insure matching pieces. The pins at each end should be 5/8" in diameter and 1" long so that they will fit in the holes that were bored in the base block and the drawer support. Carving of the pedestals will require the laying out and tracing of the design on each member. The completed pedestals are set in the base block and are then joined to the drawer support.

The two drawers are made as indicated in Fig. 8. The sides are joined to the back and front members by means of dovetail joints. The dimensions given allow for dovetail pins ½" in length. After the drawers have been assembled, the front member is cut for the cock beading.

The main section of the top will require a piece of 13/16" material, 22½" wide and 38" long. The drop leaves will take two pieces the same thickness, 12" wide and 38" long. A rule joint is cut on the butting edges of the drop leaves and center section. The outside corners of the drop leaves are shaped as shown. The hinges which attach the drop leaves to the center section should be located 5" from each end. Since these hinges should be set into gains cut in the underside of the center section and into the drop leaves also, they will not interfere with the pivot blocks. The table top is secured to the upper unit with 1½" No. 8 flathead wood screws.

The finished table deserves the best finish possible. Mahogany stain, filler, shellac and varnish will produce the desired effect.

Chest of Drawers
from the
Richmond Home
of Chief Justice
John Marshall

turned, to obtain the quarter sections without loss of wood on the straight face and edge, it will be necessary to place strips of wrapping paper in the joints between them when gluing. The use of the paper will permit separation of the pieces with a thin-bladed knife, thereby eliminating the need of sawing them apart with a corresponding loss of stock due to a saw kerf.

After the stock has been glued, the work is placed in the lathe between

D ISTINGUISHED in design and perfectly proportioned for use as an heirloom piece in any American home today, this chest of drawers is an example of the fine Colonial-style furniture in the Richmond, Va., residence of John Marshall, chief justice of the United States from 1801 to 1835. It is marked by the typical Colonial details of a quarter-round column at each side and the cutout and shaped feet. Cherry and maple offer the best choice of wood to use in making a reproduction of this chest.

The Marshall house contains many of the original furnishings and portraits in its lovely old paneled rooms. It

is being restored to its former glory and is now a shrine of historic importance in the old section of Richmond.

Construction of the chest should be started with the two corner posts. As shown in Figs. 2 and 3, as well as in the main drawing, each post is made of two pieces ¾″ stock and a quarter-turned and reeded column. The quarter-turned sections will require two pieces of 1⅛″ square stock 33⅞″ long. In order to turn these pieces to shape on the lathe, it will be necessary to glue them together edge to edge, then glue these two pieces to a third piece measuring 1⅛″ x 2¼″ x 33⅞″ as shown in Fig. 1. As these pieces will have to be separated after they are

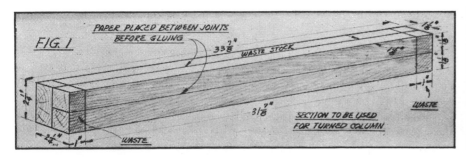

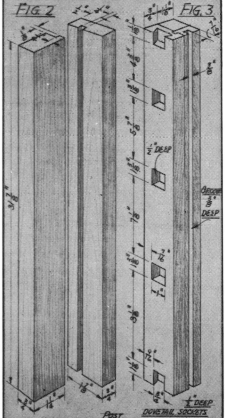

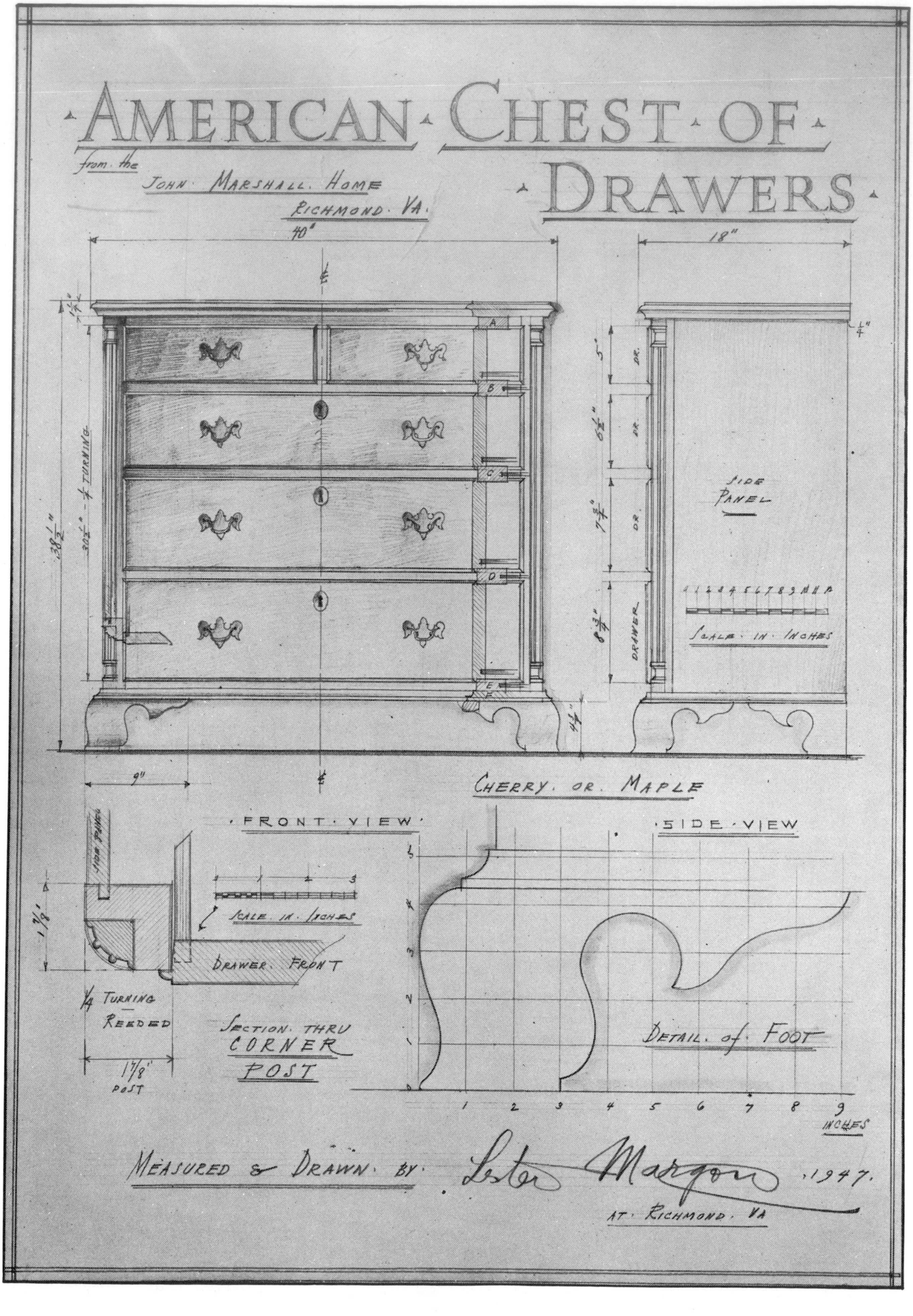

AMERICAN CHEST OF DRAWERS

from the
JOHN · MARSHALL · HOME
RICHMOND · VA.

40"

18"

38½"

20¼" — 4 TURNING

A
B
C
D
E

5"
6¼"
7¾"
8¾"

DR.
DR.
DR.
DRAWER

SIDE PANEL

1 2 3 4 5 6 7 8 9 10 11
SCALE · IN · INCHES

4"

4¼"

CHERRY · OR · MAPLE

9"

1½"

SIDE PANEL

¼ TURNING
REEDED

1½" POST

1 2 3
SCALE · IN · INCHES

DRAWER · FRONT

· FRONT · VIEW ·

· SIDE · VIEW ·

SECTION · THRU
CORNER
POST

DETAIL · OF · FOOT

1 2 3 4 5 6 7 8 9
INCHES

MEASURED & DRAWN · BY · Lester Margon · 1947.

AT · RICHMOND · VA

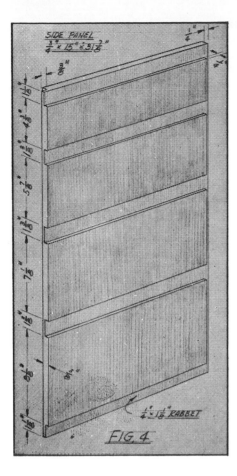

SIDE PANEL
¾" × 15" × 31⅞"

¼" × ⅛" RABBET

FIG. 4

centers, and the section which is to be used for the post should be marked off. The overall length of the required column is 31⅞". This length allows for waste at both ends as shown in Fig. 1. After marking off the limits of the column, the next step is to mark off the section of the column that is to be turned. As shown in the main drawing, the turned section is to be 30½" long, allowing for a ¾" square section at each end. When the turned section has been established, the work of shaping this portion can be undertaken. The 30½" section is to be turned down to a finished outside dimension of 1⅛". The beads near each end of the column are marked off and are then cut to shape with a skew chisel. The reeded section with its two full reeds and two half reeds are left 1⅛" diameter.

The location and width of the reeds should be marked off on the cylinder while the turning is still in the lathe. If the lathe is equipped with an indexing head, there should be no difficulty in dividing each quarter column into three spaces for the reed locations. If the lathe is not equipped with an indexing head, the cylinder should be divided into 12 sections starting at a joint.

Each full reed is to be 3/16" wide and ⅛" high and may be cut on the shaper if a suitable cutter is available. A wood carver's scratch tool with a

cutter ground to the required shape may also be used. With either tool, it will be necessary to prepare a jig for holding the leg while the reeding operation is being done. After the columns have been reeded, the work is separated by forcing a thin-bladed knife through the glue joints. It will be necessary to clean off the paper with a damp cloth or by planing, depending on the type of glue that has been used to join the pieces together. The waste at each end should be cut off square so that the finished column will measure 31⅞" from end to end.

The corner sections of each post as shown in Fig. 2 will require one piece of ¾" × 1⅞" × 31⅞" stock and one piece ¾" × 1¼" × 31⅞". A rabbet is cut along the edge of the 1¼" stock to produce a tongue ⅛" × ¼" as shown in Fig. 2. A ¼" × ⅛" groove is cut along the face of the 1⅞" piece to take the tongue as shown in the same detail. These two pieces are glued together, and the quarter column is glued in the corner as shown in the section through the corner post on the main drawing as well as in Fig. 3.

The assembled corner posts are now prepared to take the drawer rails and side panel. This will require the laying out and cutting of a groove from

end to end for the side panel and the laying out and cutting of mortises and dovetail sockets for the rails as shown in Fig. 3. The groove is cut on the bench saw by means of a dado head set to cut a ⅜" × ⅜" groove. The mortises may be cut by hand or on a drill press with the aid of a hollow mortising attachment. The dovetail sockets can best be cut by hand with a dovetail saw or back saw and a chisel.

Each side panel will require a piece of ¾" stock 15" wide and 31⅞" long. It will be necessary to glue up two or more pieces to obtain a panel of this width. The stock that is being glued together should be large enough to produce an oversize panel. After the glue has set, the panel should be dressed and finished to the required dimensions. The drawer runners are to be set into dadoes and rabbets cut across the inside face as shown in Fig. 4. These dadoes must line up with the mortises and dovetail sockets previously cut in the posts. Cutting of the dadoes and rabbets may be done on the bench saw, or they may be cut by hand with a back saw, chisel and hand router. A ⅜" × ⅜" rabbet is cut along the forward edge of the panel on the outside face to produce a ⅜" × ⅜" tongue which is to join this member to the post. A

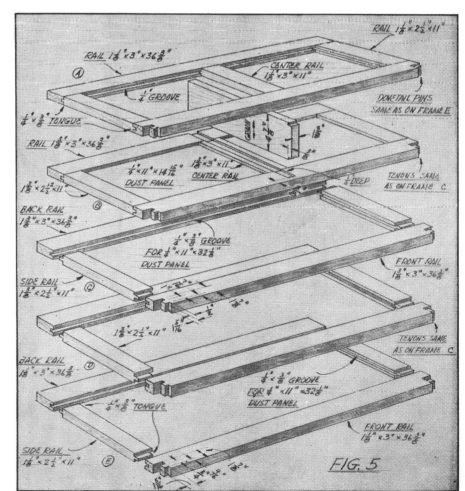

FIG. 5

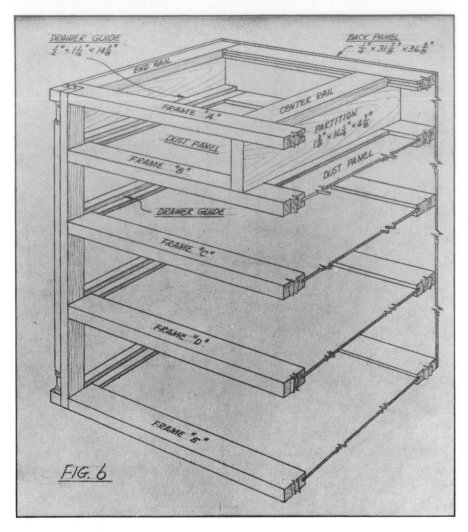

FIG. 6

¼" x ¼" rabbet is cut along the back edge on the inside face to take the back panel. See Fig. 4. The completed side panels can now be glued to their respective corner posts.

The work of preparing the five drawer runners, frames (A), (B), (C), (D) and (E), can now be undertaken. These are shown in Fig. 5. Frame (A), which is the top frame as shown in Fig. 6, has its front and back rails made of 1⅛" x 3" stock 36⅜" long. The outside rails are each made of 1⅛" x 2½" x 11" material while the center rail will require a piece 1⅛" x 3" x 11". Tongues are cut on the end rails to fit into grooves cut

along the inside edge of front and back rails as shown in Fig. 5. Dovetail pins are cut on the ends of the front rail.

Frame (B) has rails made of 1⅜" stock. Front and back rails measure 3" x 36⅜" while the outside rails are 2½" x 11". The center rail is made of 3" x 11" stock. Each member has its inside edge grooved to a depth of ⅜" to take a ¼" panel. Tongues are cut on the end rails to fit into the grooves cut along the edge of front and back rails. Tenons are cut on the ends of the front rail as shown in Fig. 5. Two dust panels made of ¼" stock are cut 11" x 14¹⁵⁄₁₆" to be set inside the frame. Frames (A) and (B) are

glued together. When the glue has set, gains are laid out and cut along the center rail of each frame to take the partition which separates the two upper drawers. The partition is made of 1⅜" stock 16¼" wide and 4⅞" long cut as shown in Fig. 5 to fit the gains.

Frames (C), (D), and (E), as shown in Fig. 5, are prepared in the same manner as frames (A) and (B). The only difference between these is the absence of a center rail and the substitution of a single dust panel.

With the completion of the five frames, these members can be joined to the chest sides. Glue should be applied to all joining surfaces; clamps are used to hold the members in place. Drawer guides, shown in Fig. 6, are made of ½" x 1¹⁄₁₆" x 14⅜" stock glued to each frame as indicated. The back panel is a piece of ¼" material 31⅞" wide and 36⅜" long. It is fastened to the side members as well as to the back rails of each frame with glue and brads.

The bottom frame (F) shown in Fig. 7 is made of 1" x 3" stock. The front rail is to be 39" long, the back rail 35" in length and the two end rails are to measure 17¼" each. The front rail is to be joined to the end rails by means of slip joints. In order to have these slip joints hidden, it will be necessary to miter the corners as shown. The miter and joint should be laid out first, then the miters cut. Following this, cut the tongue and groove of the slip joint. The back rail is joined to the side rails by means of mortise and tenon joints. The frame is glued together; then, after the glue has set, the front and side rails can be molded on the shaper by using a suitable cove cutter. The completed frame is fastened to the carcase with 2" No. 9 flathead screws or with dowels.

The front feet are made of two pieces of 3" stock 4⅜" wide and 9¼" long. As shown in Fig. 8, the butting ends are mitered with grooves cut along the miter to take a spline. Each

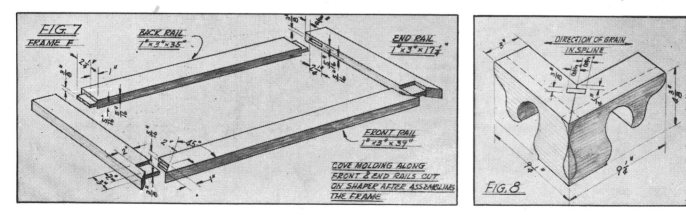

piece is cut to shape on the band saw, then the two are joined with glue. After being glued, the outside faces are molded to the required contour with wood carver's gouges and a plane. The back feet are single pieces the same size and shape as a single corner foot. The completed feet are joined to frame (F) with ½" dowels.

The top is a piece of 1¼" stock 18" wide and 40" long with its forward edge and two ends molded as indicated in the main drawing. It is fastened to the top frame (A) with 2" No. 9 flathead screws driven through the frame rails and into the top.

Each drawer is made according to the detail shown in Fig. 9. Dovetails are used to join the side members to the front and back members, and the drawer bottom is set into a ¼" x ¼"

groove cut along the inside face of the side and front members. The drawer fronts have a 5/16" x ½" rabbet cut along the edges and ends on the inside face. The edges and ends of the drawer fronts are molded with a quarter-round cutter. After the drawers have been glued together and fitted in place, the holes that are to take the hardware should be located and bored.

The work should be stained, then filled with a coat of shellac if a close-grained wood such as maple or cherry has been used. The shellac should be sanded with No. 4/0 sandpaper and the work dusted clean. Three coats of white shellac, each of which should be rubbed down with No. 00 steel wool when dry, will prepare the work for the final operation of waxing and polishing.

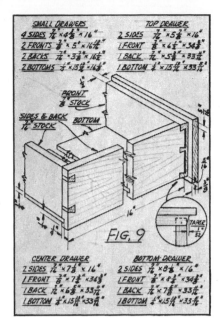

FIG. 9

Duncan Phyfe Lyre-Back Chair

THE CONTINUED popularity of the furniture of Duncan Phyfe is by reason of his excellent craftsmanship, his fine sense of design and proportion and because of his deftness in placing ornament where it would have telling effect. The lyre-back chair was his interpretation of the Directoire mode in the first of the 19th Century when French taste influenced American cabinetmakers.

The delicately carved lyre is a bit of jewelry translated into wood. The brass strings were sturdy as well as ornamental, and the acanthus-leaf carving, so characteristic of the work of Duncan Phyfe, is well employed in this model.

Construction of the chair can be broken down into units: the sides, the back, the rails that join the sides together, and the seat frame. When considered in its essential parts, the project seems less formidable. Wood used throughout is mahogany.

The sides require two pieces 1⅜" x 4" x 17" for the front legs; two pieces 1⅜" x 2⅝" x 13¾" for the side rails and two pieces 1⅛" x 6" x 34" for the back legs, as shown in Fig. 1. A rabbet is cut on the back edge of the front leg to allow for the

sweep of the front leg. This rabbet is ½" deep and extends 2⅝" from the end as shown in Fig. 1. The side rail is joined to the front and back legs by means of mortise-and-tenon joints. In order to locate the position of the mortises in the front and back legs, the three pieces of stock should be arranged on the bench top in their relative positions. The points at which the rail meets back and front legs should be established on both of these members.

Since the upper and lower edges of the rail are to be shaped, this factor must be taken into consideration when the mortise is being laid out. Each mortise should be ⅜" wide and be cut to a depth of 1⅛". After the mortises have been cut, the tenon on each end of the rail should be laid out and finished to fit its respective mortise.

The next step is to lay out full-size patterns of the front leg, back leg and side rail. After these patterns have been traced on each piece of stock, the wood is cut to its rough shape on the band saw or jig saw. The members should now be glued together to produce the side units.

The carving and tapering of the front leg is the next step. The front leg tapers from a thickness of 1⅜" at the top to a thickness of ⅞" at the point where the carved foot starts. This taper should be laid out but should not be cut until after the foot has been shaped with carving tools. After the foot has been completed, the sides of the front leg can be tapered with plane, spokeshave and chisel. The laying out and carving of the single reed on the front of the leg completes this part of the work.

It will be noticed that the side rail which has been made of 1⅜" stock is thicker than the back leg. This difference is necessary because the side rail is to taper from 1⅜" where it meets the front leg to 1⅛" where it joins the back one. Tapering of the side rail should be done with a plane.

The back leg is thickest at the point where the side rail is joined to it. From this point, it tapers to ⅞" at the top, while at the lower end it tapers from 1⅛" to ¹³⁄₁₆". These tapers are cut with a plane. When tapering has been completed, the sawed edges should be dressed smooth with spokeshave and

The Detroit Institute of Arts, shown in above photo, was founded in 1885 and was privately maintained until 1919 when the collections were made a gift to the city of Detroit. This is the home of the fine Duncan Phyfe lyre-back chair. The illustrated piece is one of the finest examples of this type of chair in existence.

A·DUNCAN·PHYFE·LYRE·BACK·CHAIR···
1768-1854

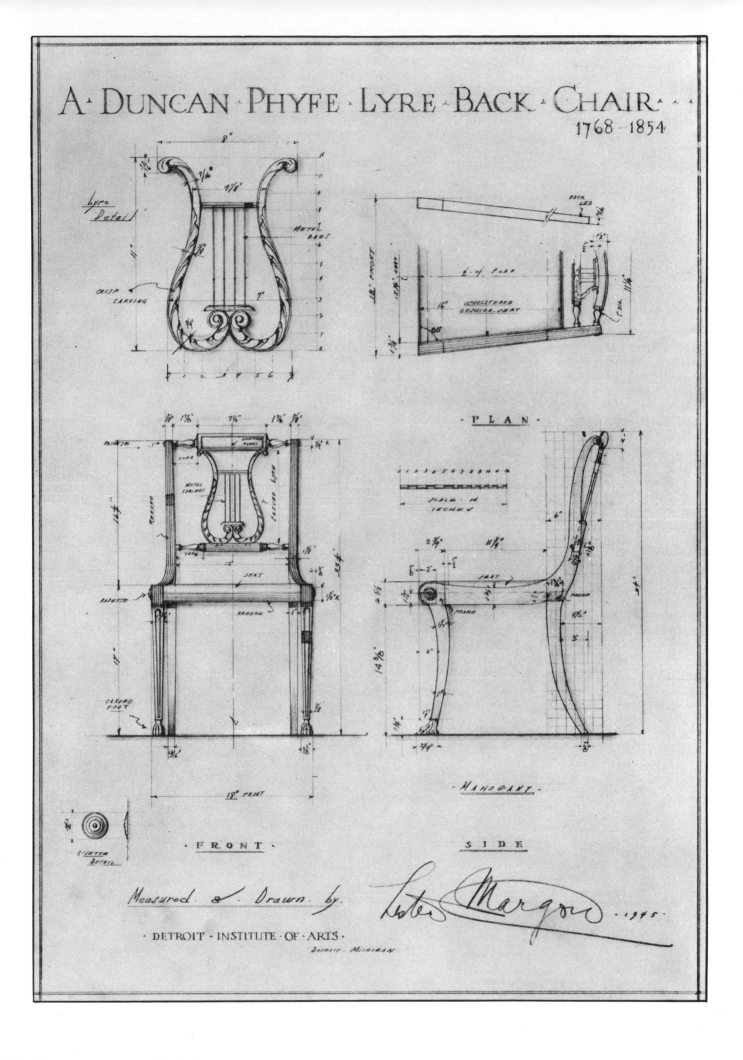

Lyre Detail

CRISP CARVING

METAL RODS

PLAN

UPHOLSTERED CUSHION SEAT

BACK LEG

MAHOGANY

FRONT

SIDE

ROSETTE DETAIL

Measured & Drawn by ~ Lester Margon ~ 1945

DETROIT·INSTITUTE·OF·ARTS
DETROIT·MICHIGAN

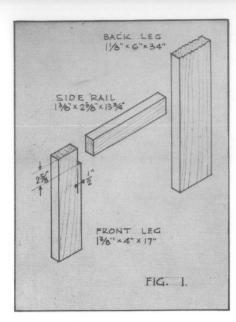

FIG. 1.

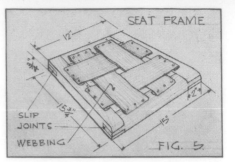

SEAT FRAME

FIG. 5

legs at the same angle. Tenons on the ends of the rails should be cut to fit their respective mortises. The front edge of the forward rail is rounded and reeded. Rounding of the edge should be done with a plane, while the reeding will have to be done the same way in which the side units were reeded. When the work on the front and back rails has been completed, the various members should be assembled temporarily for checking of the distance between the upper part of the back legs. This check-up is necessary in order to determine the length of the upper and lower back stretchers. When the locations of these stretchers have been established on the back legs, the distance between them should be measured. These measurements plus a total of 2″ which is needed for tenons on the ends represent the required lengths of the stock for the stretchers.

chisel. Sandpaper should be used on those surfaces that are not to be reeded.

The laying out of the reeding for carving will require great care. As the drawing shows, the same number of reeds appears at the thickest part of the front leg as appears at the upper end of the back leg. This design requires the diminishing of the width of each reed as it is carried from the front leg to the upper end of the back leg. Reeding is best cut with a wood carver's parting tool and small gouges. Sanding of the reeding can be done after carving has been completed.

The front and back rails that join the side units are made of stock specified in the drawing and in Fig. 3. Mortise-and-tenon joints used to join these members are located by establishing the position of these rails on the side units. The mortises should be ⅜″ wide and be cut to a depth of ⅞″.

Since the front and back rails join the legs at an angle of 85°, it will be necessary to cut these mortises in the

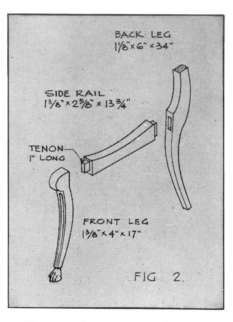

FIG 2.

The stretchers are a combination of turned and square carved sections. The turning is done in the lathe, but the sections between them are carved as shown in the drawing and photograph. Holes are bored in the uprights to take the round tenons on the ends of the stretchers.

The lyre between the stretchers is made of ⅝″ stock as shown in Fig. 4. A full-size pattern of this unit must be made for tracing on the stock. The carved members are cut to shape on the band saw or jig saw and are finished smooth with a spokeshave. Carving tools are used to model the uprights of the lyre. Holes are bored in the upper and lower crosspieces to take the metal rods. The various parts of the lyre are to be joined together by means of dowel joints. In assembly of the lyre,

the metal rods are placed in the crosspieces, then the crosspieces are joined to the upright members. The completed lyre is fastened to the upper and lower back stretchers by means of dowels. After it has been ascertained that all parts fit together, the chair can be assembled permanently.

The rosettes at the outside of the front legs and those at the upper end of the back legs are turned to shape on the lathe. They are glued in place on the chair.

The seat frame as shown in Fig. 5 is made of ¾″ x 2″ stock which is joined at the corners by means of slip joints. The frame should fit loosely in place, as allowance must be made for upholstery. Webbing is stretched over the frame, and the frame is then upholstered with suitable fabric.

The chair should be stained and filled with a paste filler, after which several coats of shellac or clear rubbing varnish should be applied. When the varnish or shellac has set, it should be rubbed down with pumice and rottenstone. An application of wax should be used when polishing the work.

The seat is fastened in place with wood screws driven up through the front and back rails and into the seat frame. Screw holes are counterbored.

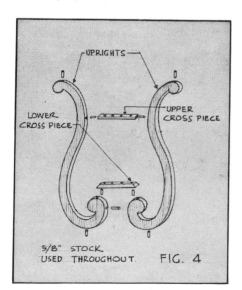

FIG. 4

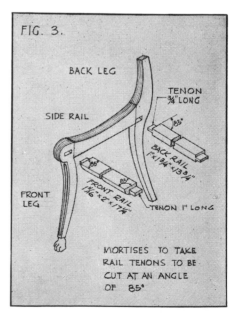

FIG. 3.

Provincial Cradle with Painted Panels

CONSTRUCTION PLANS FOR PILGRIM STYLE OF CRADLE DECORATED BY CANADIAN INDIANS

This unusually fine cradle, constructed by an unknown provincial craftsman, is shown by courtesy of the Antiquarian and Numismatic Society of Montreal

HOW INADEQUATE are the modern contraptions into which babies are placed, compared with the beauty and permanence of the old-fashioned cradle! Not only does the hand that rocks the cradle rule the world, but the hand that makes the cradle plays an essential role in the course of events. Long after a child has grown to manhood the cradle is kept as part of the furnishing of the home as a sort of family shrine. It seems appropriate, therefore, to present construction plans for a cradle that is worthy of making and a pleasure to keep. The cradle selected dates about 1890 and comes from Montreal, Canada. This one is so truly American in its concept and treatment that it is almost entirely free from European influence. Students of early furniture will recognize here a provincial character that is found on furniture of much earlier date, but it must be remembered that provincial craftsmen continued to

follow simple designs even though contemporary styles were changing.

The building in which this cradle is displayed was erected as a residence in 1705 by Claude de Ramezay, governor of Montreal under the French Regime. In 1775 the Chateau was the Headquarters for the Continental Army under Montgomery, and in the spring of 1776 Benjamin Franklin, Charles Carroll of Carollton and Samuel Chase came there as envoys from the Congress to influence the French Canadians to join the colonies in the revolt against British rule. There they met Benedict Arnold, who occupied the Chateau several weeks.

This very fine cradle was undoubtedly made by a white colonist about 1890 and was then given to the Indians of the Iroquois Tribes for decoration. A little later this type of free decoration was no longer used on household articles, religious objects or in costumes. The Indians painted the panels of the cradle all white and with a sharp tool

incised the pattern in line tracery. It then was an easy matter to paint. The design had to be filled in with flat earth colors. The leaves were green; the flowers were pink, yellow and blue; the birds were portrayed with plumage of yellow, blue and green. Everything was idealized as the Indian saw it in his mind's eye.

The design and the construction of this cradle are so simple that reproduction of the original model contains no pitfalls for the home craftsman. The turnings are simple, the panels and rockers are easily cut and materials are readily obtained. For those who do not feel that the Indian decoration would fit into their setting, this is no reason for passing up the entire project. The painting is secondary to the design and simply adds a touch of fantasy to an otherwise practical and important item for the household.

Construction of the cradle is started with the posts. Four pieces of stock $1\frac{5}{8}''$ square and $23''$ long will be required. This length allows for $\frac{1}{4}''$ waste at one end only, the waste being allowed for the upper end. The lower end on which the tenon is to be cut to set the posts in the rockers should be at the dead center of the lathe. After the stock has been cut to size and dressed, the sections which are to be turned are marked off. The relative position of each post must be marked in some manner to designate the faces to be mortised.

The next step is to locate and lay out the various mortises which are cut in these posts to take the side and end members. These mortises as shown in Figs. 1 and 2 are cut to a depth of $\frac{3}{4}''$. Considerable time and energy can be saved when cutting these mortises if equipment is available to convert the drill press into a hollow mortiser or if the work is done on any hollow mortising machine. While the posts, when set in place, are splayed out as shown in the end elevation, nevertheless, the mor-

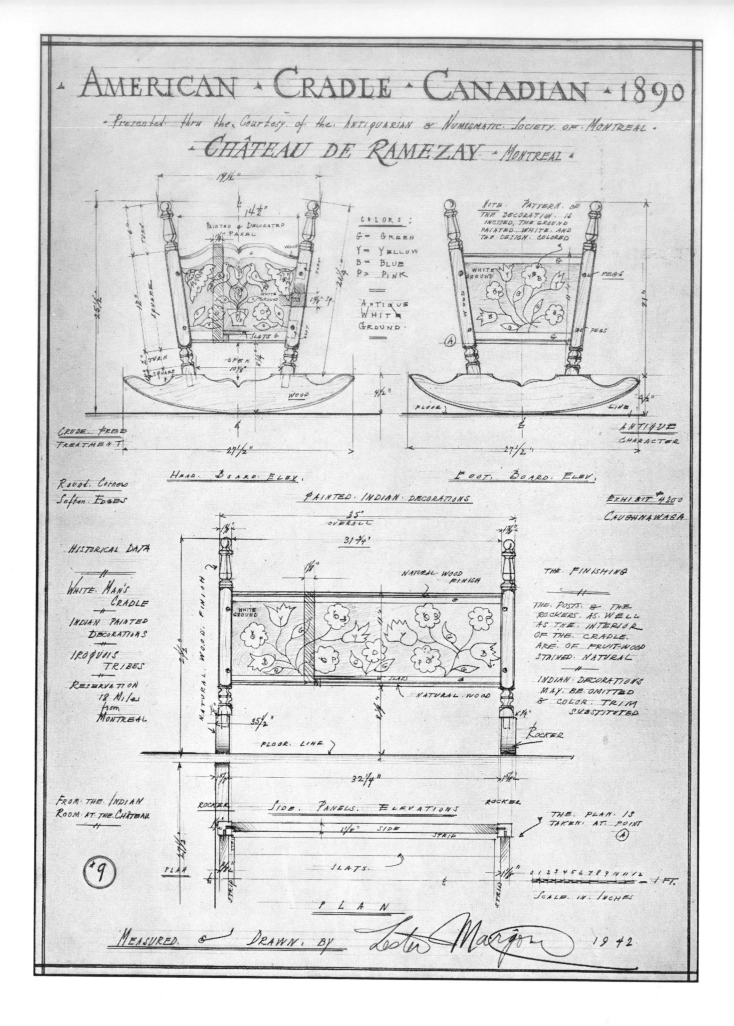

AMERICAN · CRADLE · CANADIAN · 1890

Presented thru the Courtesy of the Antiquarian & Numismatic Society of Montreal

CHÂTEAU DE RAMEZAY · Montreal

COLORS:
G = GREEN
Y = YELLOW
B = BLUE
P = PINK
═ ANTIQUE WHITE GROUND

NOTE: PATTERN OF THE DECORATION IS INCISED, THE GROUND PAINTED WHITE AND THE DESIGN COLORED

CRUDE FREE TREATMENT

HEAD BOARD ELEV.

FOOT BOARD ELEV.

ANTIQUE CHARACTER

ROUND CORNERS
SOFTEN EDGES

PAINTED · INDIAN · DECORATIONS

EXHIBIT # 4200
CAUGHNAWAGA

HISTORICAL DATA

WHITE MAN'S CRADLE
INDIAN PAINTED DECORATIONS
IROQUOIS TRIBES
RESERVATION 18 Miles from MONTREAL

THE FINISHING

THE POSTS & THE ROCKERS AS WELL AS THE INTERIOR OF THE CRADLE ARE OF FRUIT WOOD STAINED NATURAL

INDIAN DECORATIONS MAY BE OMITTED & COLOR TRIM SUBSTITUTED

NATURAL WOOD FINISH

NATURAL WOOD

ROCKER

FROM THE INDIAN ROOM AT THE CHÂTEAU

SIDE · PANELS · ELEVATIONS

THE PLAN IS TAKEN AT POINT Ⓐ

ROCKER

PLAN

SLATS

9

0 1 2 3 4 5 6 7 8 9 10 11 12 = 1 FT.
SCALE IN INCHES

P L A N

MEASURED & DRAWN BY Lester Margon 1942

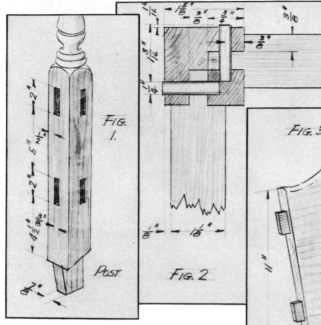

FIG. 1.

POST

FIG. 2

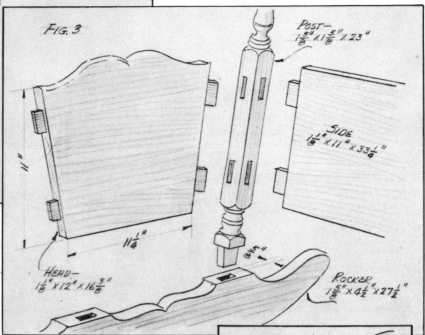

FIG. 3

Fig. 1 shows the post with mortises cut in two adjacent sides for side and end panels. Fig. 2 indicates dowel pins through post and tenon. Figs. 3 and 4 give panel sizes together with locations of tenons on panel

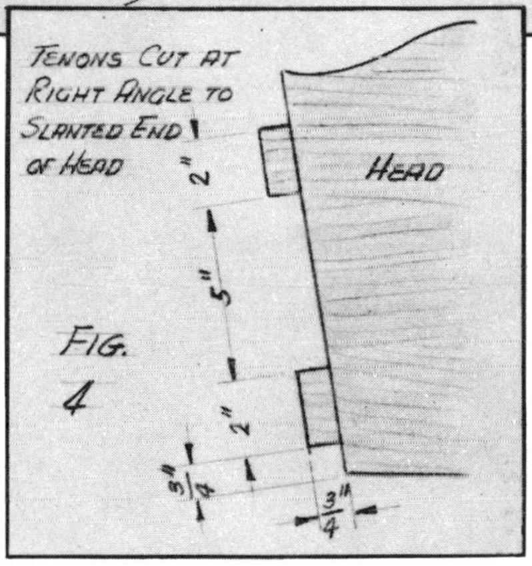

HEAD—
1⅛" x 12" x 16⅜"

POST—
1⅝" x 1⅝" x 23"

SIDE
1⅛" x 11" x 33¼"

ROCKER
1⅝" x 4½" x 27½"

TENONS CUT AT RIGHT ANGLE TO SLANTED END OF HEAD

HEAD

FIG. 4

tises are cut at an angle of 90 degrees to the face of the posts. The tenons on the ends of the headboard and footboard are cut also at an angle of 90 degrees. The splayed effect is achieved by having the ends slanted before the tenons are cut.

After the mortises have been cut each post can be centered for turning in the lathe. The center of each end is located by drawing diagonal lines, then the live and dead centers of the lathe are driven into the stock. As mentioned, the dead center should be placed at the lower end of the post. The first step in turning the posts is to turn down to a rough outside diameter the portions of the post which require shaping on the lathe. The limits of the various cuts are marked off, then with a parting tool and calipers the depths of the various cuts are established. From this point on, the process of shaping entails use of the various turning tools to produce the required shape of the turned sections. The portion that is turned should be sandpapered thoroughly while still in the lathe. The waste wood at the end of each post should be cut free on the lathe with the point of the skew chisel while the lathe is turning over at its slowest speed.

The headboard and footboard are the next members that are to be made up. The headboard is made of a piece of 1⅛" stock, 12" wide and 16⅜" long, while the footboard is made of a piece of stock 1⅛" x 11" x 16". Both members have the ends slanted with the lower portion of each being 12¾" long. After the ends have been cut at the required angle the next step is to cut rabbets on each face along the ends to

produce a tongue ⅜" thick and ¾" long. This can best be done on the bench saw. The next step is to locate the tenons on the tongues according to dimensions given in Fig. 4. The tenons are made by removing that portion of the tongue which is not required. Before this part of the work is done the layout of the tenons should be checked against the mortises which have been cut in the posts. It is important to make certain that the work will line up properly when the time comes for assembly.

After the headboard and footboard have been fitted in place, the two side

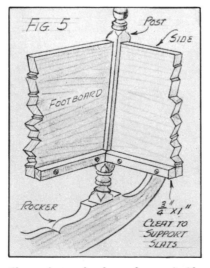

FIG. 5

POST

SIDE

FOOTBOARD

ROCKER

¾" x 1"

CLEAT TO SUPPORT SLATS

Cleats fastened along lower inside edge of panels are to support slats

members can be made up. Two pieces of 1⅛" stock, 11" wide and 33¼" long will be required. These panels are to be joined to the posts by tenons cut on the sides as shown in Fig. 3. The method of laying out and cutting these tenons follows the same procedure as was described for those on the headboard and footboard.

A small bead is cut along the upper and lower edges on the outer face of the sides and footboard members and along the lower edge of the headboard as shown in the various elevations and cross sections of the main drawing. This operation can be done with a hand beader or it can be done on the shaper or drill press equipped with a small cutter of the required shape. The upper portion of the headboard is cut to the required shape on the band saw or jig saw. A half-pattern of this contour will have to be drawn first and then traced on the stock. After the scrolled edge has been cut to shape it is finished with a file and sandpaper.

The two end units consisting of the posts and panels are now assembled temporarily so that the lower square portion of the posts can be cut at the required slant which will permit them to set flush on the rocker. A straightedge placed across the posts will permit a line to be drawn at the required angle on each one. The tenon on the end of each post can now be laid out as shown in Fig. 6. These tenons are to be cut $\frac{7}{8}$" thick and should be located at the center of the post. The cutting of the tenons can be done on the bench saw.

The rockers are made of two pieces of $1\frac{5}{8}$" stock, $4\frac{1}{2}$" wide and $27\frac{1}{2}$" long. Mortises should be located and cut in the upper edge of these members to take the tenons on the end of the posts. These mortises should be spaced $10\frac{1}{8}$" apart and should be equidistant from the center. As shown in Fig. 6 one side of the mortise is cut perpendicular to the edge, while the other side slants at an angle of 99 degrees to conform with the slant of the post. By cutting the mortise in this manner no difficulty will be experienced when the time comes to assemble the head and foot units to the rockers.

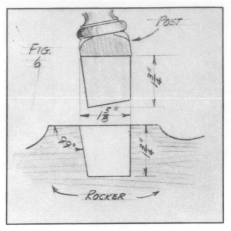

It should be noted that the mortises are located off-center in the main drawing and in Fig. 3. Since the cradle illustrated is an original and the drawing is an authentic copy of the piece, this off-center position of the rockers was carried out in construction sketches. If an authentic reproduction is to be made, the dimensions as given should be followed, but if the craftsman so desires he may make the necessary changes to center the posts over the rockers by placing the mortises in the center of the rockers. After the mortises have been cut in the rockers and the head and foot units are fitted in place temporarily, a half-pattern of the rocker members should be drawn and

traced on the stock. The rockers are taken off and cut to shape either on the band saw or jig saw. Edges are finished by hand with a file and sandpaper.

Assembly of the cradle can now be started. The first step is to assemble the end units permanently. Glue is applied to the tenons and in the mortises. Holes $\frac{1}{4}$" in diameter are bored in the posts through the tenons to take $\frac{1}{4}$" dowels which pin the members together. The side members are now set in place and the tenons are pinned in the same manner. Cleats made of $\frac{3}{4}$" x 1" stock are cut to the required length and fastened to the inside face of the side and end members as shown in Fig. 5 to take the slats which form the bottom. The slats are cut to size and set in place. They may be left loose or may be fastened with $\frac{3}{4}$" No. 5 flathead wood screws. The rockers are now attached to the legs and the tenons are pinned with $\frac{1}{4}$" dowels.

As shown in the drawing the panels are decorated with flowers and birds. These designs are drawn on the panels and then are incised with a wood carver's veiner or parting tool. The main portion of the cradle may be stained a conventional pine or maple shade. The background of each panel is finished with a white ground while the flowers and other decorations are finished as indicated in the drawing.

Desk Used by George Washington

MEASURED DRAWINGS OF A TREASURED ANTIQUE
PRESERVED IN THE NEW YORK CITY HALL

This desk is presented through the courtesy of the Art Commission of the City of New York

IN THE Governor's Room at New York's City Hall a large mahogany desk is carefully guarded because it is the desk of George Washington. On the top is inlaid the following inscription: "WASHINGTON'S WRITING TABLE—1789. This table was used by George Washington from April 1789 to August 1790 during the time that Federal Hall in New York City was the capital of the United States."

This desk is unique in its design because the drawer fronts are carried out on all four sides. In the original model the front and back are identical. The sides and back are false, with fixed panels to carry out the design. The style is an American adaptation of the Louis XVI design.

In reproducing this model for home or office use, the craftsman may consider it necessary to reduce or change the original sizes and proportions. This could readily be done if the length and the depth are kept in the same proportion. The original legs have brass castings at the floor. It would be just as well to make the legs of mahogany with small domes of silence at the floor.

Construction of the desk should be started by making the eight legs. Square stock dressed to $2\frac{1}{4}''$ square will be required. Each leg should be cut to the exact length of $29\frac{1}{4}''$. It will not be necessary to allow any waste at either end for turning, as the square section can be placed at the live center of the lathe while the portion which is to be turned is located at the dead center. Each piece of stock should be centered with great care in order to have the turning line up with the square section when the work has been completed.

The section of the leg which is to be turned should be marked off, then turned down to an outside diameter of $2\frac{1}{4}''$. The various beads, coves and fillets as well as the tapered section which is to be fluted and reeded should be marked off and turned down to the required diameter. Since it will be necessary to turn eight of these legs, it might be advisable to make a full-size pattern to use as a guide in marking off the limits of the various cuts.

When all the legs have been turned, the work of laying out and cutting the flutes and reeds can be undertaken. This can best be done by setting the leg in the lathe. With the aid of the indexing pin in the headstock, locate the ten flutes. These flutes taper, and as they approach the lower end, reeds take the place of the flutes and give the appearance that the reeds are inserted in each flute. The flutes can be cut with a small wood carver's gouge while the reeds can be made with a wood carver's parting tool and a gouge of the correct sweep. The relative position of each leg should be established and marked in some manner for future identification.

Since the desk is made up of two main units joined together with rails to form the knee space, each of these units is identical. The construction notes as given for one are duplicated and applied to the other.

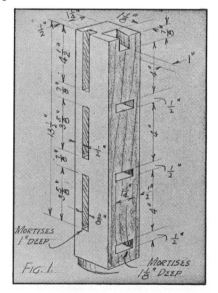

FIG. 1.
MORTISES 1" DEEP
MORTISES $1\frac{1}{8}$" DEEP

· GEORGE · WASHINGTON'S · DESK ·

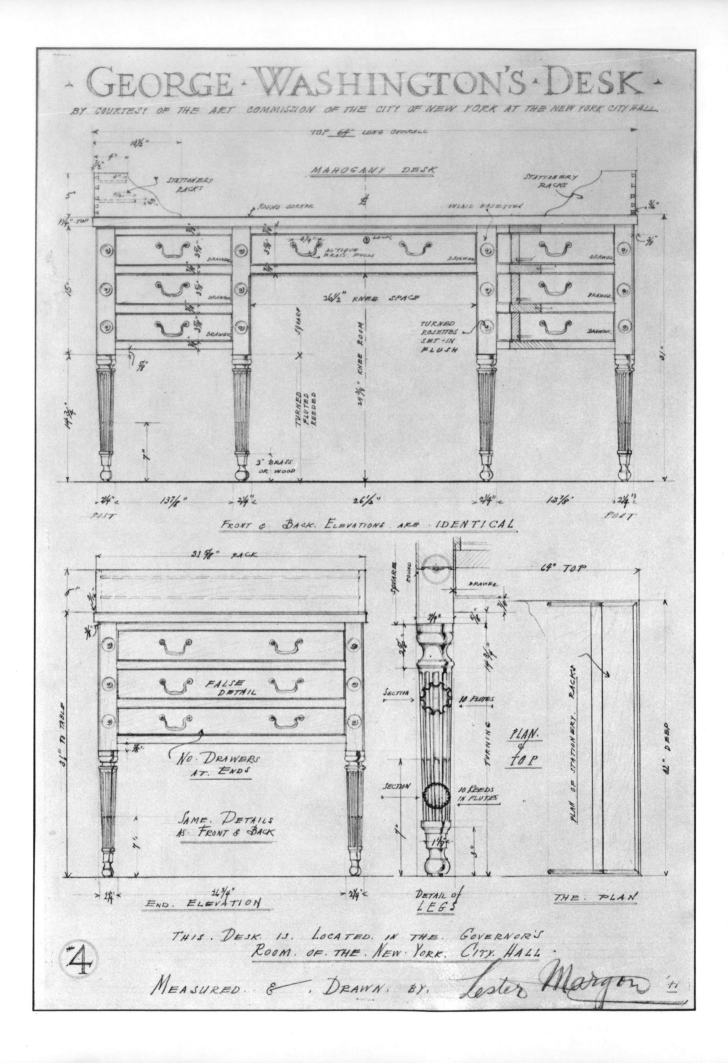

TOP 64" LONG OVERALL

MAHOGANY DESK

STATIONERY RACKS

STATIONERY RACK

ROUND CORNER

INLAID ROSETTES

ANTIQUE BRASS PULLS

LOCK

DRAWER

DRAWER

DRAWER

DRAWER

DRAWER

DRAWER

DRAWER

26½" KNEE SPACE

TURNED ROSETTES SET-IN FLUSH

TURNED FLUTED REEDED

24⅜" KNEE ROOM

3" BRASS OR WOOD

7"

FRONT & BACK ELEVATIONS ARE IDENTICAL

POST   13⅞"   2¼"   26½"   2¼"   13⅞"   POST

31⅝" BACK

FALSE DETAIL

NO DRAWERS AT ENDS

SAME DETAILS AS FRONT & BACK

31" TO TABLE

7"

END ELEVATION

26¾"   2¼"   2¼"

SQUARE   ROUND   DRAWER

SECTION   10 FLUTES

SECTION   10 REEDS IN FLUTES

TURNING

1½"   3"

DETAIL OF LEGS

PLAN OF TOP

64" TOP

PLAN OF STATIONERY RACKS

22" DEEP

THE PLAN

THIS DESK IS LOCATED IN THE GOVERNOR'S ROOM OF THE NEW YORK CITY HALL

#4

MEASURED & DRAWN BY Lester Margon '41

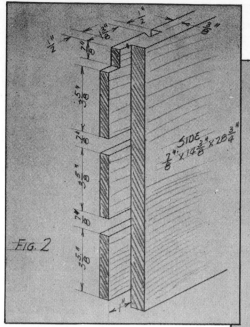

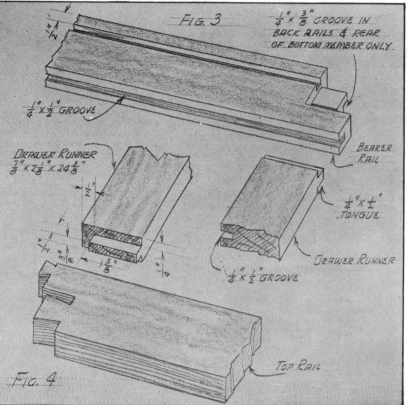

The sides of each unit are made of solid panels $\frac{7}{8}''$ thick. They are to be joined to the legs with mortise and tenon joints. The mortises for the sides are laid out on each leg by following the dimensions given in Fig. 1. These mortises are cut to a depth of $1''$. It should be noted that the top mortise is not $1''$ deep for the full length, but $\frac{7}{8}''$ from the upper end it is cut to a depth of $\frac{1}{2}''$. The drawer bearer rails are also mortised into the legs. The location and size of these mortises also are shown in Fig. 1. The top rails are to be joined to the outside legs with dovetail joints. The rails extend the full width of the desk and are joined to the inside legs as shown in Figs. 7 and 9. The drawer bearer rails above the knee space are joined to the inside legs in the same manner as those in the main unit. The locations of the mortises in the leg to take these rails are shown in Fig. 7.

The original desk was made with false drawer fronts at the back. In order to insert these as shown in Fig. 8, grooves must be cut along the back legs, between the mortises as shown in Fig. 7. The groove shown in Fig. 7 applies specifically to the knee hole section but the grooves in the back of the main units for this same purpose are identical as to size and location.

The location of decorative rosettes should be established on each leg. These rosettes are placed on all outside surfaces of legs. Each rosette is a turning which is inlaid in the square section of the leg. The recess which takes the rosette is $1\frac{1}{4}''$ in diameter and cut to a depth of $\frac{1}{8}''$. This can best be done by starting the circle with a circle cutter or an expansive bit set to the proper size, and then

cleaning out the recess with a hand router. The rosettes are turned on a faceplate in the lathe to the required size and shape. Each piece of stock which is to be used for the rosettes should be glued to a piece of $\frac{3}{4}''$ pine with a piece of paper between the pieces. The $\frac{3}{4}''$ stock is fastened to the faceplate. The inserted paper will make separation easier. The rosettes are glued in place.

The four side panels are now cut to their proper size, $14\frac{3}{8}''$ wide and $28\frac{3}{4}''$ long. The tenons are laid out and cut at each end as shown in Fig. 2 and fitted to their respective mortises. The side panels are grooved as shown in Figs. 2 and 8 to take the drawer runners and the ends of the bearer rails. The two out-

side side members have a $\frac{1}{8}''$ bead cut in them as shown in Fig. 8 to produce false drawer fronts.

The top rails are to be joined to the sides and legs by means of a dovetail joint. The sockets in these members which take the rails are shown in Fig. 2. The dimensions of the socket should be the same as shown for the dovetail in Fig. 5. The two inside panels have a groove cut in them as shown in Fig. 7 to take these top rails. Eight bearer rails in Fig. 8 and the two bearer rails for the center drawer in Fig. 9 are cut to the proper size. The bottom members in Fig. 8 should also be cut to size at this time. The tenons as in Fig. 6 and Fig. 9 should be laid out and cut

This is another view of the top rail with its intricate dovetail. Here the location of a mortise to take the end of the drawer runner is shown

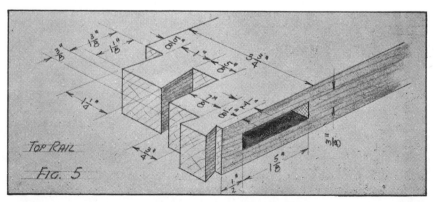

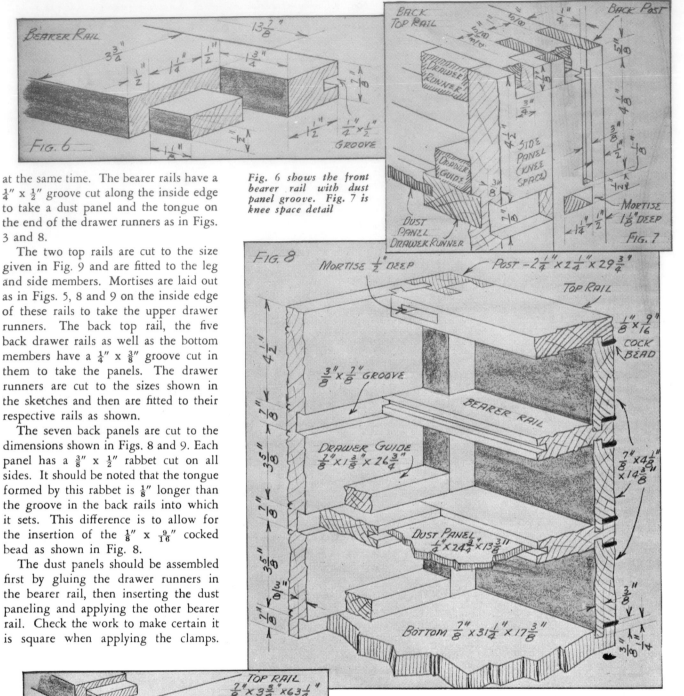

Fig. 6 shows the front bearer rail with dust panel groove. Fig. 7 is knee space detail

at the same time. The bearer rails have a $\frac{1}{4}$" x $\frac{1}{2}$" groove cut along the inside edge to take a dust panel and the tongue on the end of the drawer runners as in Figs. 3 and 8.

The two top rails are cut to the size given in Fig. 9 and are fitted to the leg and side members. Mortises are laid out as in Figs. 5, 8 and 9 on the inside edge of these rails to take the upper drawer runners. The back top rail, the five back drawer rails as well as the bottom members have a $\frac{1}{4}$" x $\frac{3}{8}$" groove cut in them to take the panels. The drawer runners are cut to the sizes shown in the sketches and then are fitted to their respective rails as shown.

The seven back panels are cut to the dimensions shown in Figs. 8 and 9. Each panel has a $\frac{3}{8}$" x $\frac{1}{2}$" rabbet cut on all sides. It should be noted that the tongue formed by this rabbet is $\frac{1}{8}$" longer than the groove in the back rails into which it sets. This difference is to allow for the insertion of the $\frac{1}{8}$" x $\frac{9}{16}$" cocked bead as shown in Fig. 8.

The dust panels should be assembled first by gluing the drawer runners in the bearer rail, then inserting the dust paneling and applying the other bearer rail. Check the work to make certain it is square when applying the clamps.

Fig. 8 shows inside assembly view and explains how the bead is inserted around false fronts. Fig. 9 shows top and bearer rails from the back. Front rails omit false drawer groove

Fig. 10 reveals drawer construction. All four members are joined with dovetails. Cocked bead is applied to front

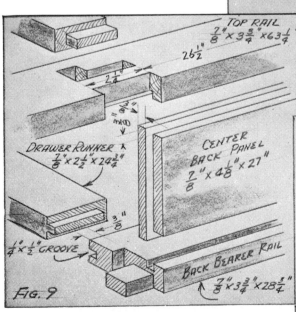

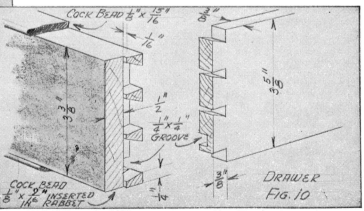

64

The side panels are now assembled with their respective legs and clamped together. When assembling each unit, start by placing the bottom in one of the assembled sides, then insert the various dust panels in their place. The back panels are then slipped in place to tie together the two units. The drawer guides in Fig. 8 are cut to size, then glued and fastened in place with $1\frac{1}{4}''$ No. 7 flat head screws.

The desk top is made up of $1\frac{1}{4}''$ stock, finished to a length of 64″. It will be necessary to glue several pieces together to obtain a panel 32″ wide. The corners of the top are rounded off at a radius of $\frac{3}{16}''$. The top is to be fastened in place with $1\frac{1}{2}''$ No. 10 flat head screws driven through the top rails and drawer runners into the underside of the top. This should not be done until the stationery racks have been made and fastened in place. The sides of the rack are joined to the back with dovetail joints. The two shelves are made of $\frac{5}{16}''$ stock cut to fit in place. The side pieces are cut to shape and dressed with a spokeshave. The rack is fastened to the top with $\frac{1}{4}''$ dowels.

The drawer fronts are made of $\frac{7}{8}''$ stock. The six side drawer fronts should be $13\frac{3}{4}''$ long while the center drawer front measures $26\frac{3}{8}''$ long. This $\frac{1}{8}''$ difference between the drawer front and the opening will be taken up by the cocked bead which is attached to the drawer front as shown in Fig. 10. The drawers are assembled by means of dovetail joints. The drawer pulls are fastened in place as shown in the drawing. It will be necessary to remove these when finishing the desk. The wood should be filled with a mahogany paste filler, then stained a dark-red mahogany color. Four coats of varnish should be applied and rubbed down with pumice stone. Wax is used to polish the desk after the final rubbing.

Butterfly Table *from the* Berkshire Museum

For a superb example of the famous and ever-popular butterfly drop-leaf table Mr. Lester Margon went to Pittsfield, Mass., in the Berkshire Mountains where, displayed in the Berkshire Museum, he found a table truly representative of the type made throughout New England during the Pilgrim Century. With its plain stretchers, double-bottle turnings and graceful leaf support this charming piece is distinctly American and as such is a splendid model for reproduction at the hands of today's craftsman

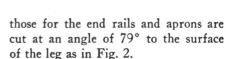

A PIECE of furniture more generally useful than a butterfly table would be hard to find, and certainly there are few pieces that would offer the craftsman more fun and experience in construction.

Work on the butterfly table should be started with the legs. These members are made of four pieces of cherry or maple stock, 1⅝" square and 25½" long. The end of each leg should be cut at an angle of 79° as shown in Fig. 2.

The legs should be arranged in their relative positions and each surface marked. Mortises to take the aprons are laid out ⅜" wide and 3" long and are located ½" from the outside surfaces of the leg. Mortises for the end aprons are located 1 1/16" from the highest point of the upper end, while those for the side aprons are placed 1" from the lowest point of the upper end.

Mortises to take the end rails and side rails, or stretchers, are located 15¾" below the bottom of the mortises for the aprons. For the rails the mortises are to be ⅜" wide and 1¼" long and are located ¼" from the outside surface. The mortises that are to take the side rails and aprons are cut square to the face of the stock, while those for the end rails and aprons are cut at an angle of 79° to the surface of the leg as in Fig. 2.

After the mortises have been completed, the legs can be turned to shape in the lathe. To insure accuracy in producing the four identical legs, a full-size pattern or template should be prepared on paper or cardboard.

The sections that are to be turned should be roughed to an outside diameter of 1 11/16" with the gouge and finished to 1⅝" in diameter with the skew chisel. The beads and coves are marked off and are then cut to their ultimate depth with the parting tool. The skew chisel and roundnose chisel are used to complete the turning. While in the lathe, the leg should be sandpapered with a No. 1 sandpaper and with finer grades down through No. 00.

The aprons are made of ⅞" stock. End aprons call for 4" x 8" stock, while side aprons need 4 1/16" x 20¼" pieces. The end aprons shown in Fig. 1 have each end of the stock cut at an angle of 79 degrees. A barefaced tenon is laid out on each end to fit the leg mortises. After being cut and fitted to their corresponding mortises, the end of each tenon is cut at an angle of 45 degrees.

Present home of the Early American butterfly table illustrated in this article is the Berkshire Museum in Pittsfield, Massachusetts. Pictured above, the museum is outstanding in its permanent collection of furniture and art and enterprising in its special exhibitions. It fosters cultural activities, sponsors art classes, lectures and concerts and inspires the art talents of a community which is the business and cultural center of the Berkshires.

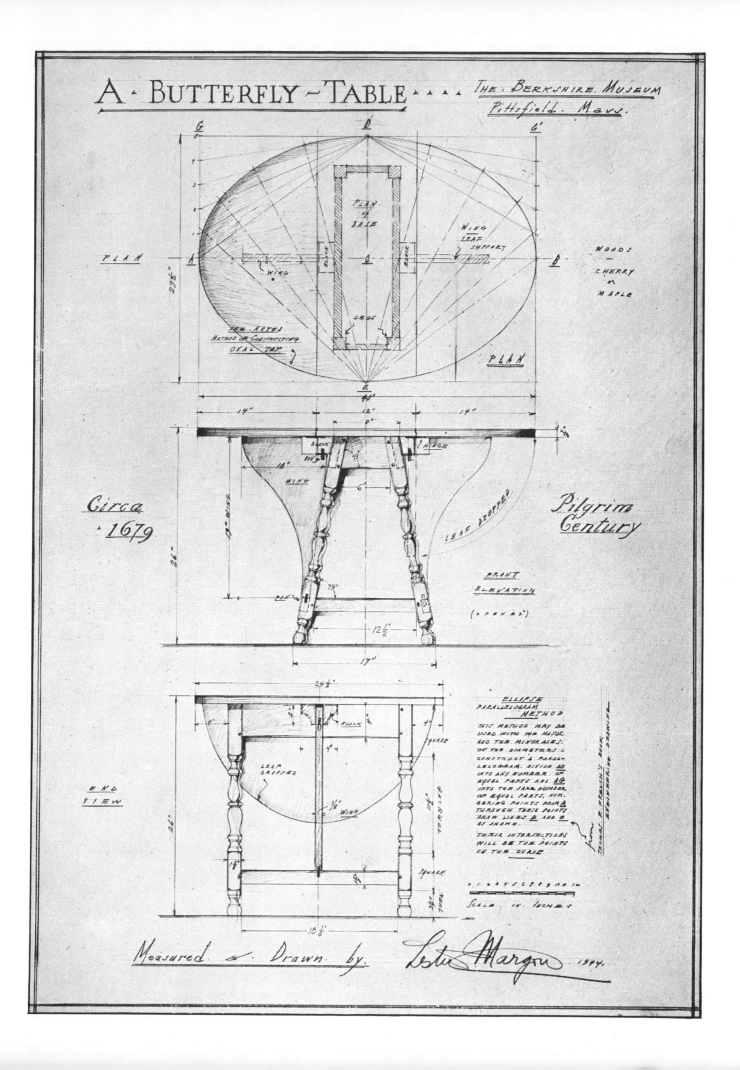

The side aprons have tenons of the same size laid out and cut on each end. These tenons are cut as shown in Fig. 3. The end of each tenon is mitered to butt against the tenons on the end aprons.

The side and end rails are made of 7/8" stock, 1 5/8" wide. The end rails shown in Fig. 1 require two pieces of stock 14 1/2" long. The ends of these members are cut at an angle of 79° in the same manner as was done with the end aprons. The tenon on each end of the rails is 3/8" thick, 1 1/4" wide and 1" long; it is located 1/4" from the

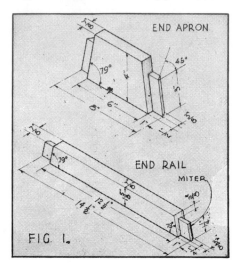

FIG. 1.

outside face of the rail. The fitted tenons are mitered as shown. The side rails require two pieces of stock 20 1/4" long as shown in Fig. 3. The tenons on the ends of side rails are the same size as those on the end rails.

The wings require two pieces of stock 7/8" x 10 1/4" x 19 1/4" as shown in Fig. 4. A full-size pattern of this member should be drawn on heavy wrapping paper for tracing on the stock. The shaping of the wings is done on the band saw or jig saw. Sawed edges are sanded.

The laying out and boring of holes for the pivot dowels must be done accurately. The 3/8" holes for the dowels are located 1/2" from the edge of the wing and are bored parallel to this edge for a depth of 3/4". Dowels 3/8" in diameter and 1 1/2" long are glued in these holes.

The block in which the upper pivot dowel swings is made of 2" stock, 2" wide and 4" long. It is shaped as shown in the end view of the main drawing and in Fig. 4. The 3/8" hole for the pivot dowel is bored at an angle of 83° to the face as shown in Fig. 4. The pivot hole in the lower rail is bored to a depth of 5/8" and at an angle of 86° to the edge.

Assembly of the table can now be undertaken. The side aprons and rails are glued to the legs and set in clamps. After the glue has set, the assembled end units are joined together by placing the side rails and aprons in position. The upper edge of the side aprons should be planed flush with the upper end of the leg. The upper pivot blocks for the wings are fastened to the side aprons with 1 1/2" No. 8 flathead wood screws driven through the apron and into the blocks. The wing should be inserted between the block and rail before the block is fastened in place.

The table top is made of 7/8" stock. The center section is a piece 12" wide and 29 1/2" long, while each drop leaf requires a piece 14" wide and 29 1/2" long. These three pieces should be fastened together temporarily by means of cleats fastened to the underside while the ellipse is laid out and cut as suggested on the main drawing.

Gains are cut as in Fig. 5 to take hinges which attach the leaves to the

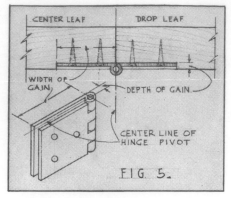

FIG. 5.

center section. Cleats made of 3/4" x 3/4" stock are fastened to the inside face of the aprons with wood screws and the table top is then fastened in place by driving 1 1/4" flathead screws up through the cleats and into the top.

Maple stain and wax comprise one of the best finishes that can be applied to maple. If cherry was used a hand-rubbed oil finish can be undertaken by rubbing in a number of coats of hot linseed oil.

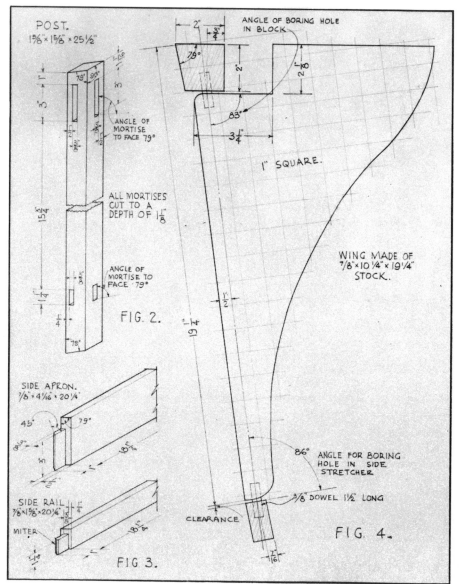

FIG. 2.

FIG. 3.

FIG. 4.

Early American Highboy

In definition a highboy is a chest of drawers supported by a stand, but in terms of the woodworker who makes it, a highboy is his greatest achievement. It is no simple task to reproduce the example shown here. The craftsman who completes it, of course, will have created an heirloom, for this mahogany chest embodies so many of the best features of the Early American cabinetmaker's skill which found its fullest expression during the period between 1690 and 1780 when the highboy was enjoying its greatest popularity. Typical of the highboy is the bonnet top which is a style of broken arch interrupted at the center by a pedestaled finial and set off at the ends by guardian finials of the same design. Shell carving enriches two front panels, and cabriole legs give the appearance of lightness and incomparable grace to the massive ensemble of drawers.

THE highboy is constructed of two separate units, these being the stand and the chest. The chest unit, when completed is simply set on the stand without the use of any type of fastener to hold the upper and lower units together. The purpose of this arrangement is to permit the moving of the highboy should the occasion arise.

The work of construction should be started with the lower section, or stand unit. The framework of this unit consists of four legs, two side panels and the various rails, stiles and dust panels shown in Figs. 9 and 10. The legs, which are the first members to be prepared, are glued-up units built around a post measuring 1⅝" square and 33⅞" long as shown in Fig. 1. To one face of the post, a piece of 1⅛" x 1⅝" x 18⅝" stock is glued and is then dressed flush with the sides of the post. To one of the edges of the glued-up block a piece of 1⅛" x 2¾" x 18⅝" stock is added. At the lower end of the post, to the side opposite the second applied piece, a piece of stock measuring ¾" x 2¾" x 11" is glued. On the fourth side at the lower end a piece of ¾" x 3½" x 11" stock is added. At the upper end

of the first two pieces that were glued to the post, two pieces of 1⅛" x 2" x 4" stock are applied as shown in Fig. 1.

After the stock for the posts has been prepared, the next step is that of laying out a full-size pattern of the cabriole leg. On a piece of cardboard marked off in 1" graph squares the outline of the leg is drawn according to the shape shown in the front elevation on the main drawing. The completed pattern is cut out and is outlined on two adjacent surfaces of the leg stock as shown in

Fig. 1. The leg is cut to its rough shape on the band saw and is then shaped to the required cross sections with chisel, spokeshave and file. The various cross sections are shown in the front elevation of the main drawing. After it has been shaped to the required contour, the leg is sandpapered to remove all tool marks. Initial sanding is done with coarse sandpaper and is followed by the use of finer grades until final sanding is done with a No. 2/0 sandpaper.

The next operation involves the laying out and cutting of mortises and dovetail sockets in the posts to take the various rails and side members. Before any attempt is made to do this layout work, the relative position of each piece should be established on the post. The location and size of the various mortises and dovetail sockets can be found in Fig. 2. The cutting of the mortises can be done with hand tools or on a drill press which is equipped with a ⅜" hollow mortising bit. The depth of all mortises should be ⅞". Cutting of the dovetail sockets at the upper end of the posts requires the use of a back saw or dovetail saw and a chisel.

The next members to be prepared are the end pieces of the lower section. These parts require two pieces of stock ⅞" x 16¾" x 19¾". This size allows for the tenons that are cut on the ends to fit the mortises in the posts. The tenons are laid out on the ends as shown in Fig. 2 and are then cut to fit the mortises in the posts. The lower edge of the side members should be shaped as shown in the side elevation

Present home of the American highboy presented here is the beautiful Cleveland Museum of Art in Cleveland Ohio, which came into possession of the piece through the bequest of the late John Huntington. This is but one of the many pieces of fine furniture displayed at the museum

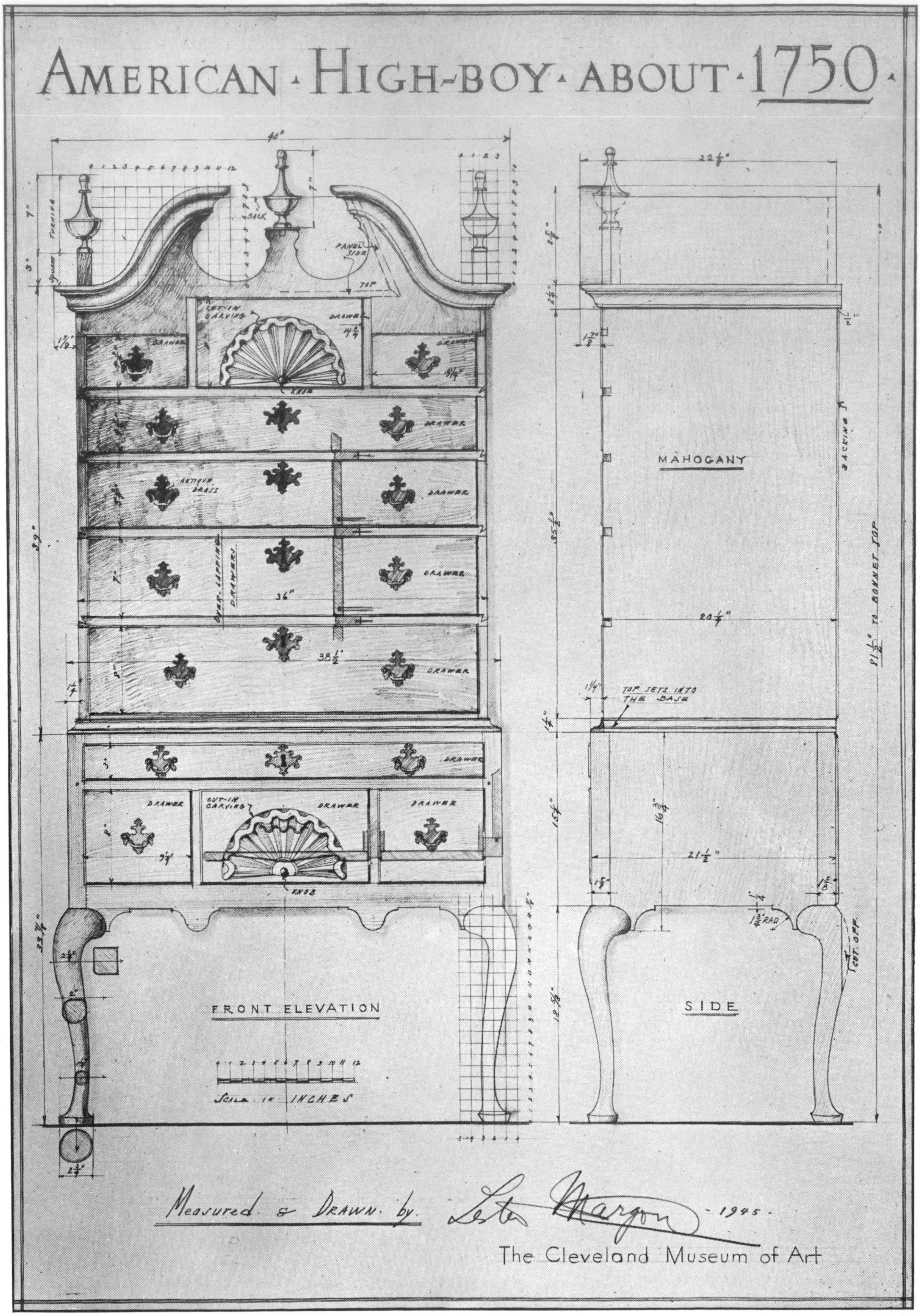

AMERICAN HIGH-BOY ABOUT 1750
FRONT ELEVATION
SIDE
MAHOGANY
SCALE IN INCHES
CUT-IN CARVING
DRAWER
KNOB
ANTIQUE BRASS
OVER-LAPPING DRAWERS
TOP SETS INTO THE BASE
PANEL SIDE
BACK
BACKING
TO BONNET TOP
Measured & Drawn by Lester Margon 1945
The Cleveland Museum of Art

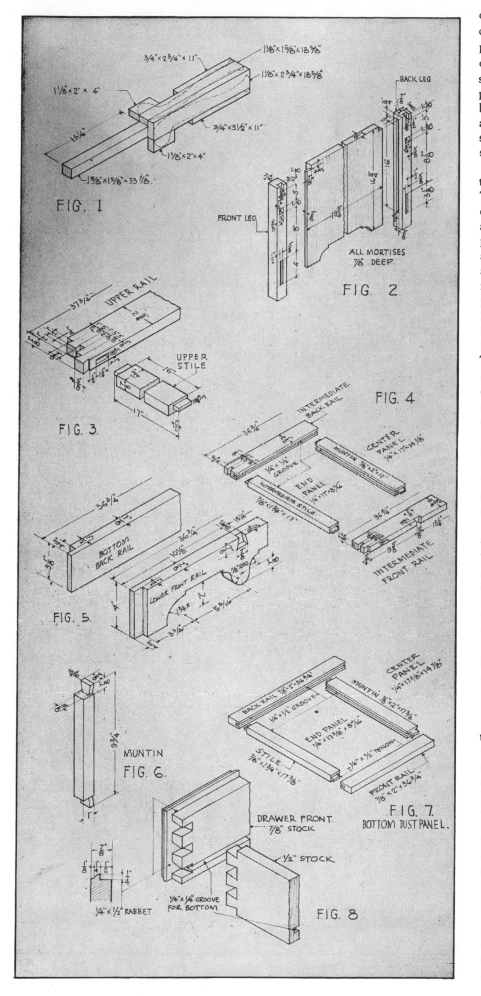

FIG. 1

FIG. 2

FIG. 3

FIG. 4

FIG. 5

FIG. 6

FIG. 7
BOTTOM DUST PANEL.

FIG. 8

of the main drawing. After these curves have been laid out with a compass the stock is cut on the band saw or jig saw. The edge is finished on a sanding drum or with a file and sandpaper. When completed the side members are glued to the legs, and the units are set in clamps. While the glue is setting, work on the upper rails and stiles can be undertaken.

The lower section has three horizontal frames. The upper one is built first. The rails of this upper frame are made of two pieces of ⅞" stock, 2¾" wide and 37¾" long. The stiles require two pieces ⅞" x 1¾" x 17". Dovetail pins are laid out on the ends of each rail as shown in Fig. 3. The outside pin must be cut to fit the socket that was previously cut in the upper end of the leg. The inside pin is to set in a socket that will have to be laid out and cut in the upper edge of the side member. The laying out and cutting of the socket in this member can be done after the clamps have been removed from the end units. Mortises will have to be laid out and cut in the inside of the rails to take the tenons on the ends of the stiles as shown in Fig. 3. Tenons to fit in the mortises are cut on the stiles. The stiles are joined to the rails with glue. The assembled frame should be checked for squareness.

The center frame of the lower unit consists of the intermediate stiles, rails, muntins and dust panels as shown in Fig. 4. The front rail calls for a piece of ⅞" x 2¾" x 36¾" stock, while the back rail requires a piece the same thickness and length but only 2½" wide. Tenons are laid out and cut on the ends of each rail to fit the mortises in the legs shown in Fig. 2. Two stiles are made of ⅞" x 1¾" x 17" stock and two muntins each measuring ⅞" x 2" x 17" are the next members to be prepared. These pieces that make up the intermediate frame are to be grooved to take dust panels. Grooving can be done on the bench saw with the aid of a dado head. After the grooving has been completed, tenons are cut on the ends of each stile and muntin to fit the grooves in the front and back rails. Three dust panels made of ¼" stock are required. All are made of stock measuring 17" wide; two of them are to be 8¹¹⁄₁₆" long, while the third is to be 14⅞" in length.

On the forward edge of the front rail, two dovetail sockets are to be laid out and cut as shown in Fig. 4. They are to take vertical muntins shown in Figs. 6 and 9. These sockets are lo-

71

cated $9\frac{3}{8}''$ from the tenon shoulder at the ends of the rail. When completed, the various members that make up the intermediate frame are assembled.

The bottom section requires lower front and back rails made as shown in Fig. 5. The front rail is made of $\frac{7}{8}''$ stock $4''$ wide and $36\frac{3}{4}''$ long, while the back rail requires a piece $\frac{7}{8}''$ x $3\frac{1}{8}''$ x $36\frac{3}{4}''$. Tenons are cut on the ends of each rail to fit mortises on the legs. As shown in the front elevation of the main drawing the front rail is to be shaped on the lower edge. Dimensions of this cutout are shown in Fig. 5. On the upper edge of the front rail as shown in Fig. 5 the dovetail sockets are to be laid out and cut to take the muntins. These sockets must line up with the ones previously cut in the intermediate front rail.

With the completion of these rails, the lower chest unit, or stand, is now ready for assembly. The intermediate and lower rails are joined to one of the end units; the second end unit is then set in place. The upper rails are next joined to the legs. Clamps hold the carcase together until the glue is dry.

The bottom dust panel as shown in Figs. 7 and 9 is made of two rails $\frac{7}{8}''$ x $2''$ x $36\frac{3}{4}''$, two stiles $\frac{7}{8}''$ x $1\frac{3}{4}''$ x $17\frac{3}{8}''$, two muntins $\frac{7}{8}''$ x $2''$ x $17\frac{3}{8}''$ and three $\frac{1}{4}''$ panels, two of which measure $17\frac{3}{8}''$ x $8\frac{11}{16}''$ while the third measures $17\frac{3}{8}''$ x $14\frac{7}{8}''$. The rails, stiles and muntins are grooved to take the $\frac{1}{4}''$ dust panels. Tenons are cut on the ends of the stiles and muntins to fit into grooved rails. The completed members are joined together with glue. In order to fit the dust panel in the stand each corner will have to be notched to go around the post as shown in Fig. 10. Cleats are attached to the end units and to the lower front rail to support the dust panel. The dust panel is set in place and secured with wood screws.

The two front muntins separating the three lower drawers are made of $\frac{7}{8}''$ x $1''$ x $9\frac{3}{4}''$ stock as shown in Fig. 6. Dovetails are cut at each end to fit the sockets previously cut in the intermediate and lower front rails. Drawer guides are cut and fitted to the work as shown in Fig. 9. The back panel is a piece of $\frac{1}{2}''$ stock, $13\frac{3}{4}''$ x $36\frac{1}{4}''$ with a rabbet cut in the ends and edges as shown in Fig. 10. This panel is fastened in place with brads. To form a rabbet in which the upper chest unit will fit, molding $1\frac{1}{4}''$ x $1\frac{1}{4}''$ is prepared and applied to the upper stiles

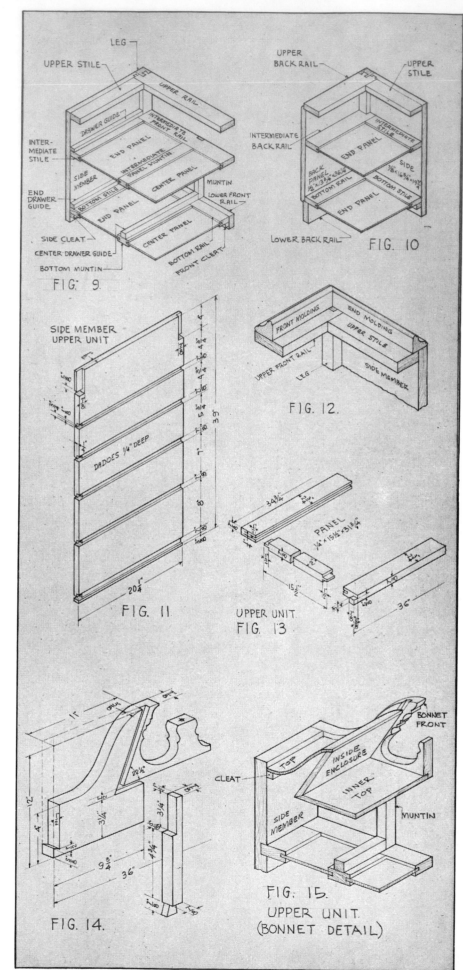

and rail as shown in Fig. 12.

Construction of the upper unit is started with the side members which are made of two pieces of 7/8" stock 20¼" wide and 39" long. Dadoes are to be laid out across the inside face of each piece to take dust panels. The size and locations of these dadoes are shown in Fig. 11. After the dadoes have been cut, the dovetail sockets for the front rails are laid out and cut as shown in the same drawing. A gain and a dovetail socket are laid out and cut at the upper end of the side members, on the edge, to take the front and back members of the bonnet.

The dust panels for the upper unit are shown in Fig. 13. Five of these panels will be needed. Each dust panel consists of a front rail measuring 7/8" x 2¾" x 36", a back rail measuring 7/8" x 2¾" x 34¾", two stiles 7/8" x 2" x 15½" and a ¼" panel 15½" x 31¾". As shown in Fig. 13 the front rail has a dovetail pin laid out and cut in each end to fit sockets cut in the side members. After rails and stiles have been grooved to take the dust panel, tenons are cut on the ends of the stiles to fit the grooved rails. The completed dust panels are assembled to the side members.

The front and back members of the bonnet top shown in Figs. 14 and 15 require two pieces of 7/8" stock 12" wide and 36" long. The ends are cut as shown in Fig. 14 to fit the gains and

dovetails in the end members. At this time it is necessary to lay out a full-size pattern of the bonnet front with the aid of graph squares. After the pattern has been traced on the front member, the grooves and dadoes that take the inside enclosure and inner top members should be laid out. These grooves may be cut with a router. The scrolled edge of the bonnet is cut to shape on the jig saw, and the front member is then joined to the side members. The inner top and inside enclosures are cut to fit in place and are set in the grooves and dadoes when the back bonnet member is being set in place. The top of the bonnet is made of 3/16" stock which is bent as it is being fastened to shaped cleats attached to the bonnet front.

The muntins separating the three upper drawers are made as shown in Fig. 14. Dovetail sockets are cut in the forward edge of the upper dust panel rail to take the pins on the lower end of the muntins. Drawer runners are fitted behind the muntins where they are fastened to the dust panel with glue and brads. The back panel is made of ½" stock rabbeted in the same manner as the back panel for the lower unit.

The molding that is applied to the bonnet front and to side members measures 1⅞" x 2¼" in section. The bonnet front molding will have to be shaped from a solid piece of stock 1⅞" thick

and 5" wide. This is done by cutting the stock to the sweep of the bonnet top and then molding it on the spindle shaper. Three finials are turned to shape, and the two outside ones are set on 1⅛" square posts which are joined to the upper ends of the side members with dowels.

Each of the drawers utilizes 7/8" stock for the front member and ½" stock for the side and back members. These pieces are joined together with dovetail joints as shown in Fig. 8. The drawer fronts should be cut ½" longer and ¼" wider than the width and height of their respective drawer openings. The drawer backs should be the same size as the drawer openings. The drawer sides should be as wide as the drawer back and 19" long. The drawer fronts have a ¼" x ½" rabbet cut on the ends and upper edge; the edge is molded.

It is advisable to install all hardware before any finishing operation is started. After the necessary holes have been bored for the drawer pulls, and the escutcheons have been located the hardware can be removed for finishing the chest. If walnut or mahogany or any other open-grained wood is used, a filler should be applied. Stain and filler should be followed by a number of coats of shellac or varnish, each rubbed down with No. 00 steel wool. Waxing and polishing are the final operations.

Sofa by a Great New York Cabinetmaker

REPRODUCTION OF GENUINE DUNCAN PHYFE SOFA
CHALLENGES SKILL OF TODAY'S BEST CRAFTSMEN

Measured drawings of this Duncan Phyfe masterpiece are presented by courtesy of the Museum of the City of New York

THE MUSEUM of the City of New York bears a fitting inscription in the words of Abraham Lincoln, "I like to see a man proud of the place in which he lives."

In the spirit of these words the museum strives to show the development of The City of New York from earliest times. One of the choicest exhibitions is a New York drawing room of the early 19th Century taken from an old house down on Greenwich Street. The furniture in this room, with the exception of a game table, was made by Duncan Phyfe. One of the finest treasures of the group is the original Duncan Phyfe sofa presented here in measured drawings and photographs so the experienced craftsman of today may reproduce it.

Duncan Phyfe (1768–1854) was one of New York's best and most popular cabinetmakers. This sofa is done in his early and best style when he was under the influence of the great English cabinetmaker Thomas Sheraton.

Despite the historic significance of this sofa it is very much in vogue today and can be reproduced exactly. Of particular interest is the graceful profile of the front posts which are square, turned, carved and reeded as indicated. The enlarged details will afford the necessary assistance to get this just right. The water-leaf carving on the posts is crisp and sharp, but the carving of the panels along the back of the sofa with the ribbons, swags and darts is in bas-relief, very low, not much raised above the background of the panels. The carving here is soft and rounded off like a medal.

The sofa as exhibited is covered in a striped satin. However, any Colonial or Georgian fabric is appropriate. Of course a strictly modern fabric would not do. If you succeed in making a fine reproduc-tion of this sofa, let your local uphol-sterer do the covering unless you are experienced at this work. Sofas like this are not only very costly to purchase in a store but the commercial sofa can never attain the beauty of line or detail of this original Duncan Phyfe model.

Construction of this sofa should be started with the front legs and posts. The two posts are made of 2" square stock finished to an overall length of 25". This piece includes a pin 1" long at the upper end by means of which the leg is to be joined to the arm. The stock which is to be used for these members is set up in the lathe between centers and turned to the shape shown in the draw-ing. With the aid of graph squares a template of the post can be drawn. This will aid greatly in making the posts and legs since all are alike.

After the posts have been turned to the proper shape and size, work on the

DUNCAN·PHYFE·SOFA· 1768 1854

·MUSEM· of·the·CITY·OF·NEW·YORK·

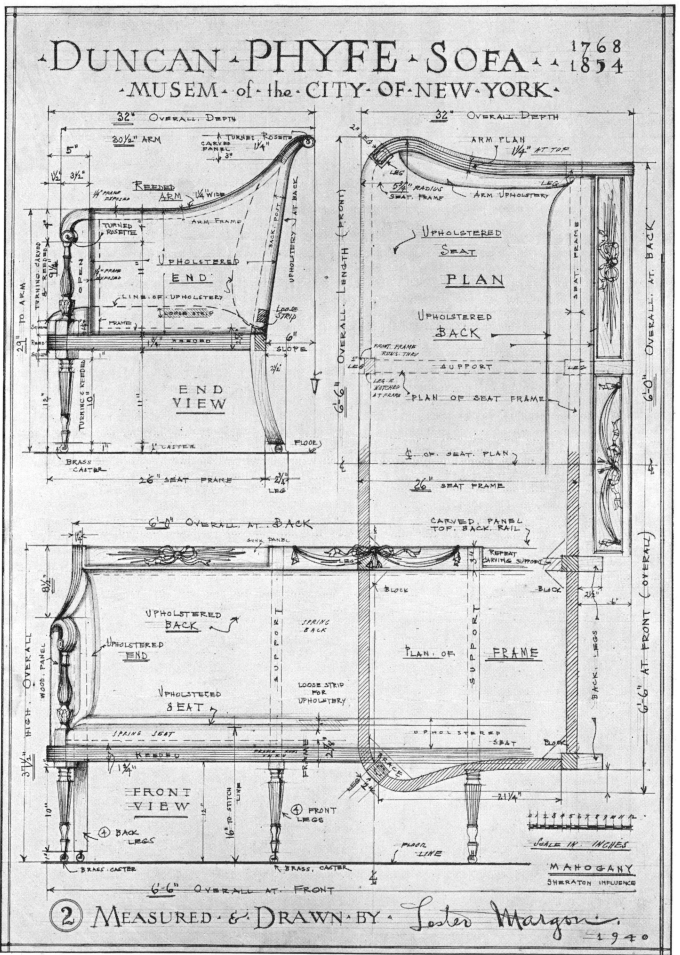

END VIEW

PLAN

UPHOLSTERED SEAT

UPHOLSTERED BACK

PLAN OF SEAT FRAME

℄ OF SEAT PLAN

PLAN OF FRAME

FRONT VIEW

④ BACK LEGS

④ FRONT LEGS

MAHOGANY
SHERATON INFLUENCE

SCALE IN INCHES

② ·MEASURED· & ·DRAWN·BY· Lester Margon

·1940·

two front legs may be started. These are also made of stock 2" square finished to an overall length of 12¾". The lower portion of the template that was used in making the posts should be used when the legs are being turned. The posts and legs should have the turned portions sandpapered while still in the lathe, with the exception of those sections which are to be reeded or carved. If these sections are sandpapered abrasive imbedded in the wood will dull the carving tools. These areas should be laid out with care. The actual cutting should be done with carving tools.

The next step in construction is to make up the back legs of 1¾" stock. The length and width of the stock required for each leg can be determined from the pattern which must also be made. The contour of the leg can be obtained from the drawings. After this pattern has been drawn and cut out it should be traced on the stock. Four of these legs are required. They are cut to shape on the band saw and finished with a spokeshave and smooth plane.

The seat frames, located at the back, are made up of three pieces of 1¼" stock, 2⅝" wide. The lengths of each of these pieces are the same as those shown for carved panels at the top of the back. These dimensions do not allow for the tenons by means of which the frame members are joined to the legs. An additional 1¾" is required for a ⅞" tenon at each end. While these members are being cut to length, it is advisable to cut the stock for the upper back panels at

the same time, as they are all the same length. The location of the seat frame and upper back members should be established on each post. Mortises are located accordingly and cut to a depth of ⅞". The tenons are cut on the ends of each member to fit respective mortises. This completes the basic construction of the back. The fitting of the back unit to the sides will be done later as well as the carving of the upper back panels.

Before the front or side frame members can be made up it will be necessary to lay out full-size patterns of these parts. The complete front frame need not be drawn, as all that will be necessary to obtain its true length as well as the arc at each end is a small section as shown in the plan. These members are made of 1¾" stock. The patterns are placed on the wood and traced. Allowance must be made at each end for tenons 1" long. The stock is cut to shape on the band saw and finished with a spokeshave. The reeding may be done on a shaper.

The location of frame members is established on the front and back posts, then mortises are laid out and cut at these locations. Tenons are cut on the ends of the frame members. The location of the two intermediate front legs is established on the front frame member. As shown in the plan view the frame and legs are notched to fit into one another.

The various completed members should now be temporarily assembled and the overall dimensions checked. The two support members connecting the

intermediate front and back legs are cut to size from 1¾" square stock with allowance for ¾" tenons at each end. Mortises are located and cut in the front and back legs for these members, then the tenons are cut on the ends to fit these mortises.

ARMS REQUIRE GLUED-UP STOCK

The arms are made of stock 4" thick and 6" wide. It will be necessary to draw a full-size pattern of this member, both the side and top views. While these original pieces were made of solid stock it is doubtful if such material can be readily obtained today; therefore, it may be necessary to glue up several pieces of material to obtain a piece of these dimensions. The patterns are traced on the wood then cut to shape on the band saw and finished with a spokeshave.

The upper end of the arm is fitted to the back post and joined to that member with dowels. The vertical frame member connecting the lower side frame member to the arm, directly in the back of the front post, is made of 1" x 1¼" stock cut to the proper length and held in position with dowels. The various loose strips located at the back and sides, to which the upholstery is tacked, are fitted and held in position with dowels. The braces and corner blocks are made up last.

The sofa is assembled permanently with glue, and all dimensions are checked as the work of assembling and clamping is done. Application of the rosettes and the continuation of the reeding around the front legs is done after the work has been glued up. The sofa is sandpapered smooth and then finished in a warm mahogany. Several coats of clear shellac are applied and rubbed down with fine steel wool to produce a smooth surface.

Graph patterns of carved parts shown here should be made and traced to stock for guidance

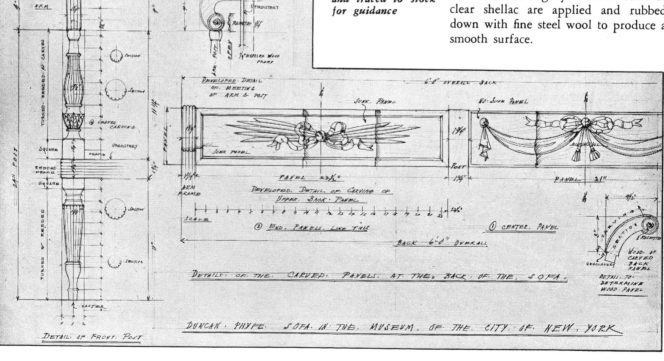

Gate-Leg Dining Table with Oval Top from the Brooklyn Museum

WE HAVE come to accept the gate-leg table as a strictly American Colonial conception. While this may be a bit possessive on our part and not altogether the truth, it is a fact that in no other period do we find the drop-leaf table reaching such charm and distinction as in the Pilgrim Century.

The outstanding model illustrated in the measured drawing, details and photograph herewith is one of the fine treasures found in the Brooklyn Museum's American Wing. When opened, this oval-top table is a full-size dining table; when closed it serves as a very useful side table or console.

Aside from its obvious utility this piece should be recognized for the beauty of its turnings. Just why turnings were so very popular in this period is partly a matter of guesswork, but it is pleasant to believe that cabinetmakers of the period chose this form because they liked to turn. As a result of constant practice they became veritable masters of the art. That the turning process is an art no one can deny. It is a very creative and exacting process to put a square block in the lathe and by the magic of pressing a blade against the revolving wood to fashion these intricate flowing lines interspersed by beads of the most delicate nature.

The maker of this table was not content merely to use a variety of turnings. He probably remembered once seeing a Spanish Renaissance chair with a carved toe. He wanted to show all he knew; so he incorporated this bit of carving into his table. It is just this variation from the routine that gives this table its distinction.

In this presentation the modern craftsman can find not only the opportunity to study and to reproduce a fine table but he also learns by example that it isn't always wise to follow strictly the rules and regulations. By stepping just a bit off the beaten path he may find color, distinction and fantasy.

Construction of the table is divided into four main units which consist of the under portions of the table, the gate legs, the top and drawers. The work is started by building the under portion first. This is made of the four turned and carved pedestal legs, the four turned

·PILGRIM·CENTURY·GATE-LEG·DINING·TABLE·

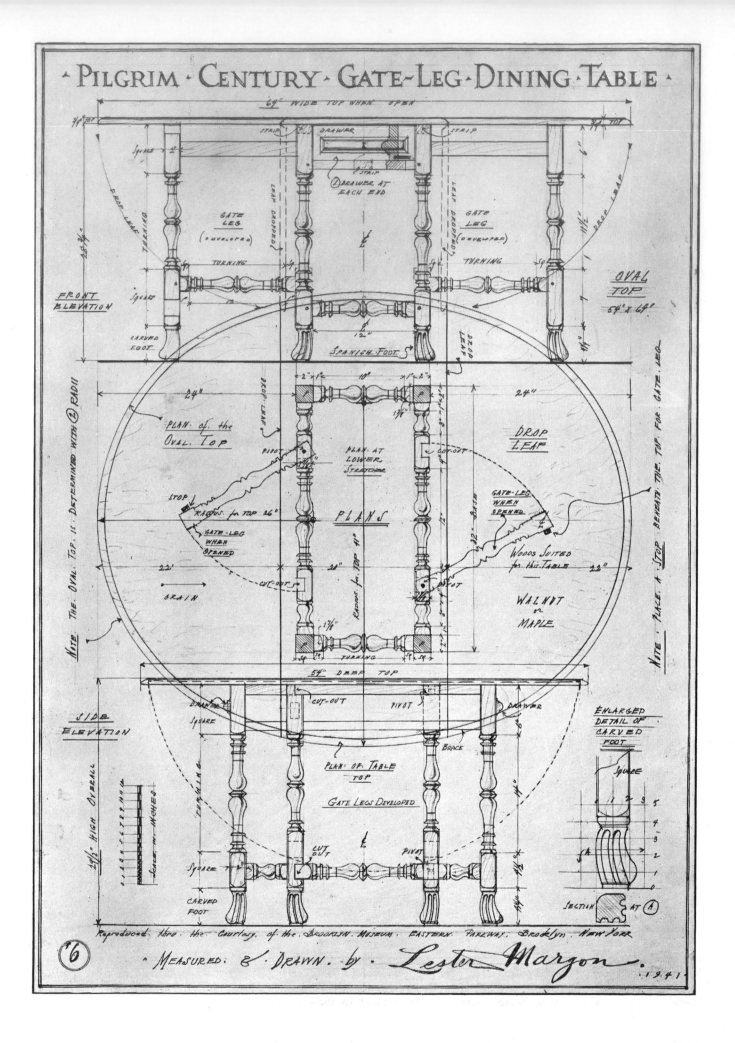

FRONT ELEVATION

OVAL TOP 54" x 64"

PLAN of the OVAL TOP

PLANS

DROP LEAF

Woods Suited for this Table

WALNUT or MAPLE

SIDE ELEVATION

PLAN of TABLE TOP

GATE LEGS DEVELOPED

ENLARGED DETAIL of CARVED FOOT

SECTION AT Ⓐ

NOTE: THE OVAL TOP IS DETERMINED WITH ② RADII

NOTE: PLACE A STOP BENEATH THE TOP FOR GATE LEG

⑥   ·MEASURED·&·DRAWN·by· Lester Margon.   ·1·9·4·1·

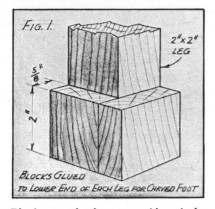

FIG. 1.

2" x 2"
LEG

5/8"

2"

BLOCKS GLUED
TO LOWER END OF EACH LEG FOR CARVED FOOT

Blocks are glued on two sides of the legs so that the feet can be carved

stretchers, the two main upper stretchers, the drawer bearer rails, the brace on which the drawers ride and the cross-piece between the two upper main stretchers. To avoid confusion of the parts it is best to consider, for the moment, that these parts make up the under-structure of the table. Gate legs will be considered later.

The four pedestal legs are made of stock 2" square and 28¾" long. Two ⅝" blocks are glued to two adjacent faces at one end, as shown in Fig. 1, in order that the foot can be carved to the required shape. The various sections of each of these legs which must be turned are marked off as shown in the detail drawing in Fig. 4. For setting up between centers in the lathe the center of each end is now located by drawing diagonal lines. Since four identical turnings are required, accuracy can be greatly increased by cutting out a cardboard templet of the turning. This templet is to be used in checking the work as the shaping progresses.

After setting up the leg in the lathe the portions that are turned should be roughed down to an outside diameter of 2". The limits of the various coves, beads and fillets are marked off on the cylindrical portion of the stock and are then shaped to match the pattern with the aid of the skew, spear-point and round-nose turning chisels. Before the turned leg is removed from the lathe, it should be sandpapered thoroughly with No. ½ and No. 00 sandpaper.

The next step in the construction of this unit is the cutting out and turning of the two main stretchers. These are made of stock 1⅞" square and 30" long. This length allows for a 1" tenon at each end of the stretcher. As with the legs, the portion of each stretcher which must be turned is marked off. The stock is set in the lathe and shaped according to the same procedure as described for making the legs. At each end of the stretcher a tenon measuring 1" long and 1" in

diameter is turned on the stock.

The two short stretchers located below the drawers are the next members to be made up. Two pieces of 1⅞" square stock 14" long are required. They are shaped as shown in Fig. 4, and tenons 1" in diameter and 1" long are turned at each end. The two main upper stretchers are made of 1¼" stock 1¾" wide and 30" long. These members are joined to the legs by means of a dovetail joint. The tail should be 1" long at each end. The drawer bearer rails are made of two pieces of 1" x 2" stock 14" long. This size allows for a 1" tenon on each end. The brace as shown in Fig. 3 is made of 1" x 2" stock 30" long. The cross-piece between the two upper main stretchers is made of ⅞" stock 1¼" wide and 13½" long. This is joined to the stretcher as shown in Fig. 5 by means of a dovetail joint. The tails on the ends of this member are ¾" long. This work completes the various members which go to make up this unit.

Work can now be undertaken to cut the necessary joints by means of which the members are assembled. The tenoned stretchers are joined to the legs by means of the tenon on the ends of the former. The 1" holes in the legs to take these

tenons are located and bored to a depth of 1⅛". The upper stretcher is joined to the legs by means of a dovetail joint. The socket is cut in the end of each leg, then the tail is fitted in place.

The drawer bearer rail is set into a mortise measuring ¾" x 1¼" which is cut to a depth of 1⅛". The top of this rail should be 4¼" below the end of the leg. The mortise must be placed with this location in mind. Mortises are cut in the edge of each bearer rail to take the brace which carries the drawer. These mortises also are cut to a depth of 1⅛". The dovetail sockets which take the crosspiece are cut in the upper stretchers. The short turned stretcher located below the drawer is set into a 1" hole 1⅛" deep which has been bored into the side of each leg. This completes the cutting of the necessary joints to assemble this unit and the various members may be set up at this time to check the work.

Provisions must be made for joining the pivot leg to the table stretchers. As shown in Figs. 2 and 3 a pin is turned on the end of this member. Holes must be located and bored in the upper and lower stretchers to take these pins. Fig. 3 shows the location of these holes. They should be ⅝" in diameter and bored through both members at the points indicated. The foot, which is located below the pivot leg, does not move with the gate but is fastened permanently in place in the lower half of the ⅝" hole that takes the pin on the end of the pivot leg.

As shown in the top view, Fig. 5, and the plan view in the main drawing, a section of both stretchers is cut out to

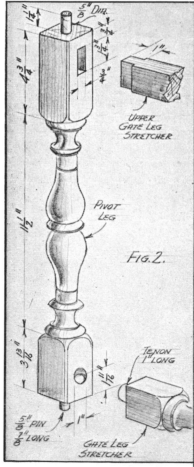

⅝" Dia.

UPPER GATE LEG STRETCHER

1"

PIVOT LEG

FIG. 2.

TENON 1" LONG

⅝" PIN ⅝" LONG

GATE LEG STRETCHER

Fig. 2 shows pivot leg with two gate stretchers. Construction at ends for drawers shown in Fig. 3

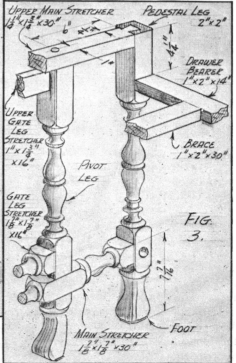

UPPER MAIN STRETCHER
1⅛"x1¾"x30"

PEDESTAL LEG
2"x2"

DRAWER BEARER
1"x2"x14"

UPPER GATE LEG STRETCHER
1"x1¾"x16"

BRACE
1"x2"x30"

PIVOT LEG

GATE LEG STRETCHER
1⅛"x1¾"x16"

FIG. 3.

MAIN STRETCHER
1⅛"x1⅞"x30"

FOOT

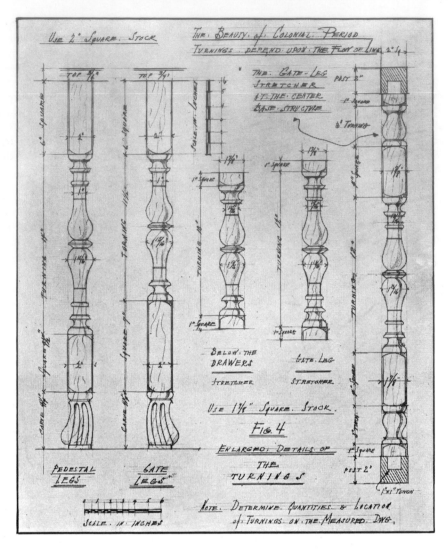

Use 2" Square Stock

THE BEAUTY OF COLONIAL PERIOD
TURNINGS DEPEND UPON THE FLOW OF LINE

THE GATE-LEG
STRETCHER
AT THE CENTER
BASE STRUCTURE

BELOW THE
DRAWERS
STRETCHER

GATE LEG
STRETCHER

Use 1⅞" Square Stock.
FIG. 4
ENLARGED DETAILS OF
THE
TURNINGS

NOTE. DETERMINE QUANTITIES & LOCATION
OF TURNINGS ON THE MEASURED DWG.

PEDESTAL
LEGS

GATE
LEGS

SCALE IN INCHES

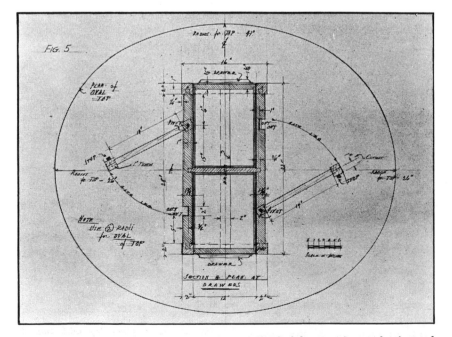

FIG. 5

The oval top fortunately does not require an elliptical layout. It can be drawn by simple method of using a stick with pencil hole and pin as an improvised compass

Successful reproduction of the table will to some extent depend upon crisp, sharp turnings, details of which are shown at left

the corners rounded off as shown in the enlarged detail in the main drawing. The lower gate-leg stretcher is made of 1⅞" square stock 16" long. This allows for a 1" round tenon at each end, 1" long. The upper gate-leg stretcher is made of 1" x 1¾" stock 16" long with a 1" tenon cut on each end. Holes are bored in the lower square sections of the pivot and gate legs to take the 1" tenons on the ends of the lower stretcher, while mortises are cut in the upper square sections of these legs to take the tenons on the ends of the upper stretcher as shown in Fig. 2. The gate leg is notched at the upper and lower square sections to fit in the cuts which were made in the upper and lower main stretchers. The upper recess is shown in Fig. 5 while the lower cut can be seen in the photograph. The latter cut is located 5 9/16" from the bottom of the foot while the former is at the end of the gate leg.

With the completion of these units, the assembly can now be undertaken. The gate-leg members are glued and clamped together. When the clamps are removed the pivot leg is set in the lower main stretcher which in turn is glued to the pedestal legs. Next, the upper main stretcher is set in place after glue has been applied to the dovetail joints. These units are clamped together, then after the clamps are removed the drawer rail, short lower stretcher, brace and crosspiece are set between the two assembled units. The brace should be set in place between the bearer rails first, then this unit along

allow the gate leg to line up with the pedestal legs when in a closed position. This cut measures ¾" deep and 2" long on the upper stretcher and 1" deep and 2" long on the lower turned stretcher.

The gates are the next unit to be made up. Four pieces of stock 2" square and 28¾" long are required for these members. Two blocks of wood ⅝" thick are glued to adjacent faces as shown in Fig. 1 in order to carve the foot. Two of these legs are for the gate while the other two are for the pivot leg and the foot directly below it. They are set up in the lathe and turned in the same manner as described for the turning of the pedestal legs. The two pieces which go to make up pivot legs require additional turning. The upper end of each piece has a ⅝" pin 1¼" long turned on it to act as the pivot. The lower square section is to be left square 1 5/16" above the carved foot and 3 13/16" below the turned section. This will leave a space 1⅞" long in this lower square section which must be turned down to a diameter of ⅝" to produce the pivot pin on the lower end of the pivot leg and the tenon on the end of the foot which joins it to the lower main stretcher.

The feet of all the legs, both pedestal and gate, can now be shaped and carved. The rough shaping can be done on a band saw or jig saw, then with wood carving tools the flutes can be cut and

with the lower stretchers should be set between the legs. The crosspiece is set in place last to complete the assembly.

The table top is made of three pieces of $\frac{3}{4}''$ stock two of which measure 22" x 54" while the third measures $21\frac{1}{4}''$ x 54". These pieces have the joining edges molded with a rule joint cutter as shown in the front elevation. After the joint is cut the three pieces are placed together upside down, then two temporary cleats are fastened on the face to hold the three members in their relative position. The oval top is marked off by first drawing two center lines, then with a compass set for a radius of 26" the end arcs are drawn. The side arcs are made with the compass set for a radius of 41". The top is cut to shape on the band saw or jig saw and is finished smooth with a spokeshave. The edge is molded as shown in the drawing. After this has been done the temporary battens are removed. The top should be sandpapered thoroughly and made ready for assembly.

The hinges can be located and fastened, joining the center section to the drop leaves. Three $1\frac{1}{2}''$ hinges should be used on each leaf. The center section is fastened to the table frame by driving $1\frac{1}{2}''$ flathead screws through the upper main stretchers and into the underside of the top. The stops which are placed on the underside of the drop leaves as shown in Fig. 5 and the plan of the main drawing may be made of $\frac{1}{2}''$ dowels set into the leaf or may be a block of wood glued and nailed to the underside of the drop leaf.

The two drawers are the last units to be constructed. The fronts are made of $1\frac{3}{4}''$ stock $4\frac{1}{4}''$ wide and 12" long. They are shaped as shown in the front elevation of the main drawing. The drawer sides are made of $\frac{1}{2}''$ stock $4\frac{1}{4}''$ wide and 15" long. The drawer backs measure $\frac{1}{2}''$ x $4\frac{1}{4}''$ x 12". These members are joined together by means of dovetail joints, the dovetails in each case being $\frac{1}{2}''$ long. The bottom, which is a piece of $\frac{1}{4}''$ plywood measuring $11\frac{1}{2}''$ x $14\frac{1}{2}''$, is set into a $\frac{1}{4}''$ x $\frac{1}{4}''$ groove cut on the inside face of the drawer members. The drawer locks are set in place to complete the construction of the table.

The finish of the table is optional with the builder. It may be stained or left natural. If open-grained wood has been used, filler should be applied. Several coats of varnish, white shellac or clear lacquer should be applied and each coat should be rubbed down with pumice stone or No. 00 steel wool.

Heirloom Desk of Moderate Dimensions

IDEAL HOME DESK OF KNEE-HOLE BLOCK FRONT VARIETY DATES BACK TO THE 18th CENTURY

One of the finest and simplest remaining examples of the American block front desk, this piece is presented by courtesy of the Metropolitan Museum of Art

get the feeling of something imposing and actually built-out. This type of furniture, known as block front, gives the appearance as though a block of wood had been applied to the front and shaped accordingly. Pieces as elegant as the block front treasure shown here are priceless today.

The desk illustrated in the measured drawing herewith can be used as a knee-hole desk placed against the wall or set in the middle of a room, or it can serve as a chest in almost any room in the house.

The work entailed in its construction demands good wood. Mahogany is the best choice. It should be adequately finished for protection but does not call for a high finish. The size of the piece is particularly good because today all furniture is being scaled down in size due to the cost and scarcity of space, especially in the small house and apartment.

A word might be said for the fine design of the drawer pulls and the "H" hinges on the cupboard door within the knee-hole space. This again has a Dutch character. There are many commercial pulls of this type on the market. The fin-

THIS magnificent example of a knee-hole desk is distinguished for its restraint in design as well as its fine proportions and utility. Every inch of space is used to advantage. There are six small drawers in the pedestals and one long drawer across the top. Above the knee-hole there is a shallow pull-out drawer for small articles. The desk is now on exhibition in the American Wing of the Metropolitan Museum in New York City. It is made of mahogany and dates from the last quarter of the 18th Century.

The serpentine fronts of the French contemporary periods and the preponderant scale of the work of Dutch cabinet makers of the time, all had their influence on furniture that was built in America. While craftsmen in the new land could not and did not wish to copy the European pieces, they did strive to

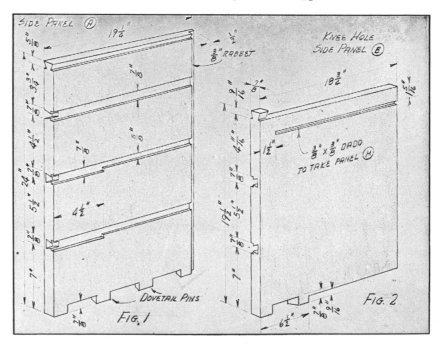

AMERICAN · KNEE-HOLE · CHEST · DESK

Gift of Mrs. Silvester Dering 1930
to the Metropolitan Museum of Art New York

Last Quarter of the 18th Century.

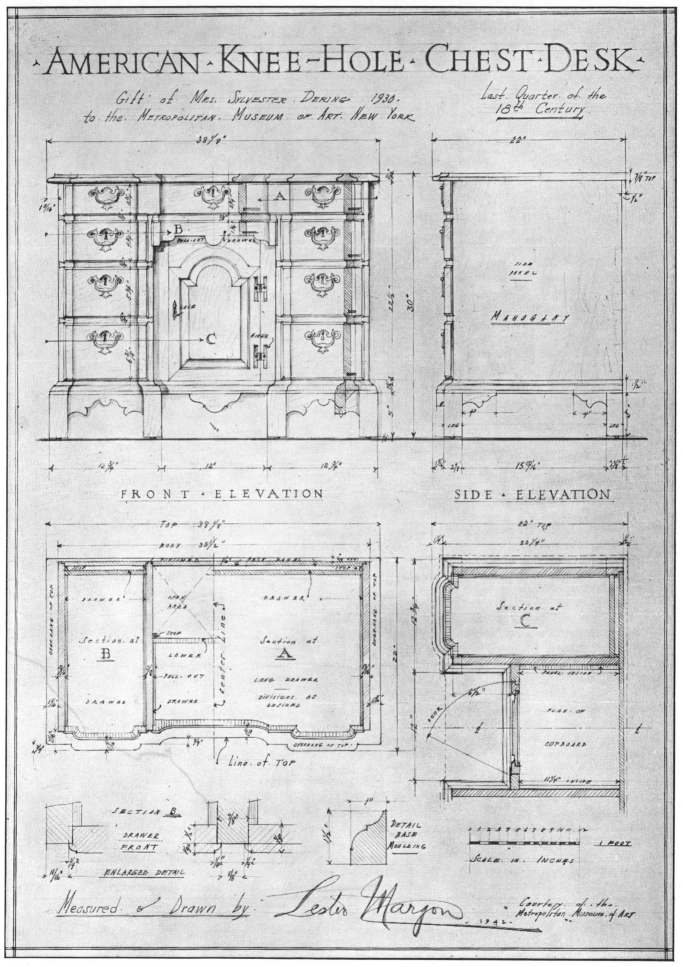

FRONT · ELEVATION

SIDE · ELEVATION

Measured & Drawn by Lester Margon 1942

Courtesy of the Metropolitan Museum of Art

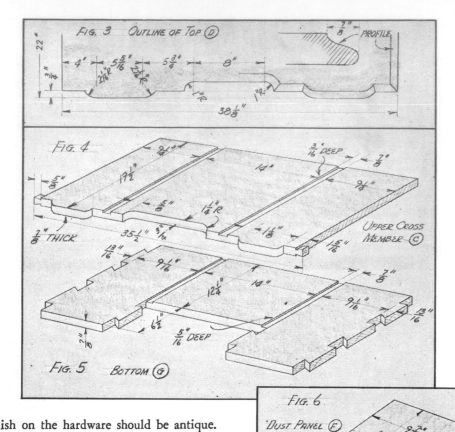

Fig. 3 Outline of Top (D)

Fig. 4

Upper Cross Member (C)

Fig. 5 Bottom (G)

the sockets which have previously been cut in the side members. A $\frac{3}{8}'' \times \frac{3}{8}''$ groove is cut along the back edge to take the dust panel (F). The dust panel is made of $\frac{5}{8}''$ stock $14\frac{5}{8}''$ wide and $9\frac{7}{16}''$ long. A tongue is cut on one edge to fit the groove in the bearer rail as shown in Fig. 6.

The various members (A), (B), (C), (E) and (F) should now be assembled temporarily to check the work for accurate fitting. If everything fits properly the work can be taken apart and the pieces sandpapered thoroughly preparatory to final assembly. Glue should be applied to all joints and where necessary clamps should be used to hold the work together. It is of the utmost importance that all corners be checked with a try square after clamps have been applied in order to make certain that each member is at right angles to the other. Failure to check at this time may bring lasting dis-

ish on the hardware should be antique.

Construction of the desk should be started with the two side panels (A). Two pieces of $1\frac{3}{16}''$ stock $19\frac{1}{4}''$ wide and 24″ long will be required. These panels may be made up by gluing together several pieces of stock to produce a piece the required width. A rabbet $\frac{3}{8}'' \times \frac{1}{2}''$ is cut as in Fig. 1 on the inside face along the back edge to take the back panel.

The work of laying out the various dadoes and dovetails as shown in the drawing should now be done. The utmost care should be exercised when doing this work. All lines should be made with a knife rather than a pencil, while a try square and T-bevel are needed as guides when the lines are scribed. Since the knee-hole side panels (B) must be dadoed like the (A) members to take the bearer rails and the dust panels, these members should also be made up and laid out at this time. The dadoes should be cut on the bench saw with a dado head, while the sockets which take the dovetails on the ends of the drawer bearer rails and the upper cross member (C) should be cut by hand with a fine-tooth dovetail saw and the socket should be cleaned out with a chisel. The dovetail on the upper end of each of these side members may be cut on the bench saw by tilting the table to the required angle and cleaning out the corner by hand with the chisel. The pins on the lower end of the panels can be cut on the bench saw or they may be made by hand with dovetail saw and chisel. The $\frac{3}{8}'' \times \frac{3}{8}''$ dado located on the outside of the knee-

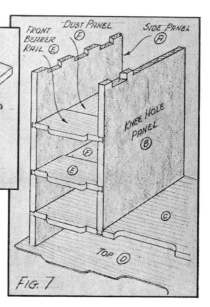

Fig. 6 Dust Panel (E) Front Bearer Rail (E)

hole panel is intended to take the panel on which the small knee-hole drawer rides.

The next member to be made up is the upper cross member (C) shown in Fig. 4. This piece requires $\frac{7}{8}''$ stock $19\frac{1}{2}''$ wide and $35\frac{1}{2}''$ long. The front edge should be laid out and shaped to the contour shown in the drawing. The cutting of the edge to the required shape can be done either on the band saw or jig saw and should be finished by hand with a file and sandpaper. The dovetail on each end which is to fit in the socket cut in the side panels, as well as the dado and dovetail socket across the face for the purpose of taking the knee-hole side panel, should be laid out and cut in the same manner as was those in the side members. When cutting these dovetails and sockets make certain that joining members are fitted to one another.

The front bearer rails (E) are the next members to construct. These require four pieces of $\frac{7}{8}''$ stock $5\frac{1}{4}''$ wide and $10\frac{7}{16}''$ long. The front edge is laid out and cut as shown in Fig. 6; the edge is finished by hand with a file and sandpaper. The dovetails are laid out and cut to fit into

Fig. 7

appointment if any part is not square.

The bottom (G) is made of $\frac{7}{8}''$ stock $18\frac{3}{4}''$ wide and $35\frac{1}{2}''$ long. This piece is laid out and cut to the shape shown in Fig. 5. The dovetails at each end and at the knee-hole space must be laid out and cut to fit those already cut in the ends of the side panels. The dadoes on the face are cut on the bench saw by aid of a dado head. The bottom is now ready to be assembled to the side member. Check the fit before applying glue to join these units.

The top (D) is made of a piece of $\frac{7}{8}''$ stock 22″ wide and $38\frac{1}{8}''$ long. The underside of this member has two dovetail dadoes extending from the back for a length of $19\frac{3}{4}''$ to take the pin on the ends of the side panels. These are laid out and the two parts of the joint are cut and trial-fitted by sliding the back edge of the top into the groove first. After these joints have been fitted properly the next step is to lay out the front edge following the dimensions given in Fig. 3. This edge is cut to shape on the band saw or jig saw and is finished by hand with a file. The molded edge can be cut to a certain point on the spindle shaper if the required shaper cutters are available or if they can be ground, but the inside corners will have to be finished by hand with carving chisels. The entire molding may be cut by hand if no other means is accessible. When completed, the top should be sandpapered and assembled to the case.

The next step is to apply the filler strips (M) to the bottom as shown in Fig. 9. These strips are mitered at each corner and follow the contour of the bottom member (G). They are fastened in place with glue and 1¼″ screws. The base molding is made up as a single length and the members marked (O) are then cut to size and mitered at the corners. This molding is fastened to the bottom with glue and brads. The front molding members (P) are made of 1½″ x 1¾″ stock measuring 12¾″ long. They are shaped as shown in Fig. 8 and fastened in place in the same manner as the other molding strips.

The front leg members (J) are made of two pieces of stock 1½″ thick, 5″ wide and 12¾″ long. The outside face of these members must conform to the shape of the molding member (P) shown in Fig. 8. The cutting of these pieces to the required shape can be done on the band saw, but the face will need finishing with plane, file and sandpaper. A full-size pattern of the scroll work on the face

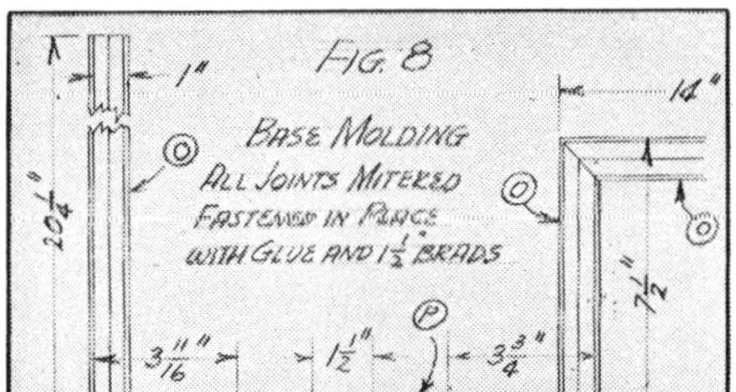

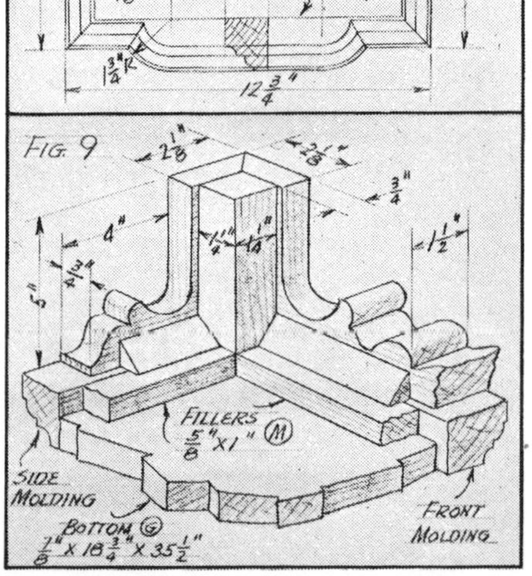

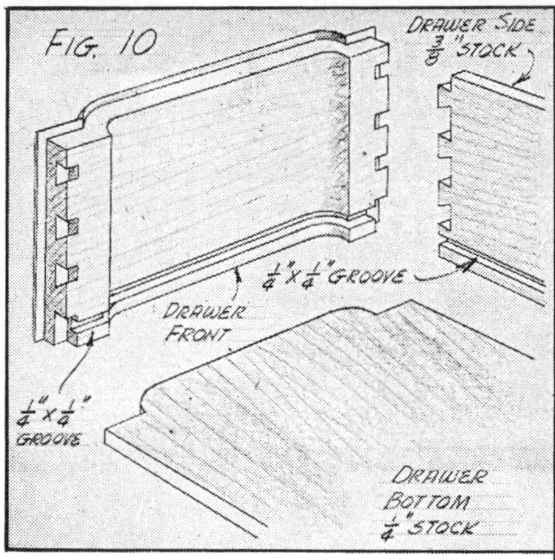

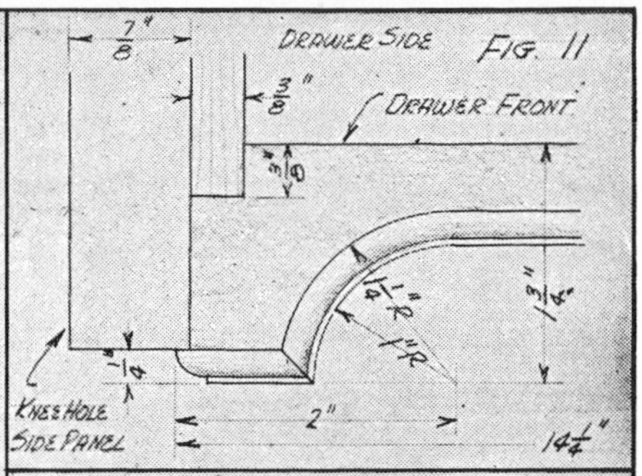

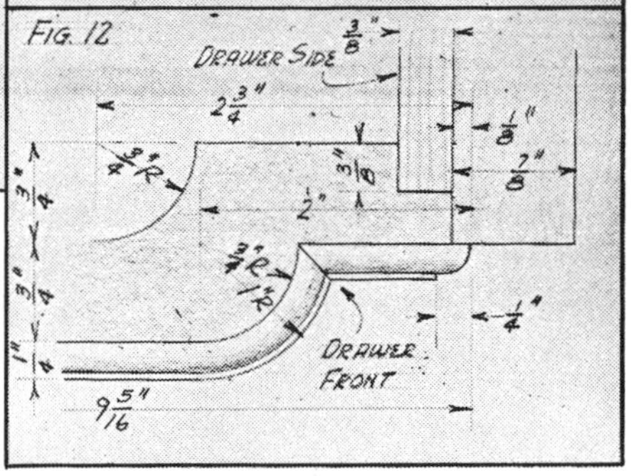

must be drawn and traced on the stock before the piece can be cut to shape on the jig saw. The side leg members (K) are made of ¾″ stock 5″ wide and 6⅛″ long. They are shaped as shown in the drawing. These front and side leg members as well as the side and back leg members are joined together by means of a miter-and-spline joint. The corner blocks are now cut to size and glued in place. After the completed leg units are fastened in place with glue and wood screws, the corner braces are attached with glue to reinforce the assembled units.

The cupboard shown in Fig. 14 is made up as a separate unit and slipped in place from the back. The sides (R) are made of ½″ stock 12″ wide and $16\frac{11}{16}''$ long. The stiles (S) and (T) are made of 1″ stock $16\frac{11}{16}''$ long but are 2¼″ and 1¾″ wide respectively. This difference of ½″ is required on one stile to produce the rabbet which acts as the door stop. The top rail (U) is made of 1″ stock $4\frac{13}{16}''$ wide and 12″ long. The rail is jointed to the stiles by means of mortise and tenon joints. The edges of the stiles are rabbeted to take the side members (R). The top rail is cut to the shape shown in Fig. 14. The various members are now sandpapered and assembled with glue. The cupboard is set in place from the back and is fastened there with screws which pass through the cupboard sides and into the knee-hole side panels. The knee-hole drawer bearer (H) can now be cut to the required size and fitted in place.

The cupboard door shown in Fig. 13 is made up of two stiles (V) plus a bottom rail (W) and a shaped top rail (X). These members are joined together by means of mortise and tenon joints. There is an allowance made in the materials list for tenons 1″ long. The panel sets in a rabbet as shown in the drawing. The rabbet in the top rail may be cut with a router bit or on the spindle shaper equipped with a straight-faced cutter. The molding around the inside edge of the stiles and rails is cut on a spindle shaper. The fielded panel (Y) is made of ⅝″ stock 8¼″ wide and 13¼″ long. It is held in place by means of ¼″ quarter-round molding. A ½″ x ½″ rabbet is cut along the inside edge of one stile as

Bill of Materials

Pcs.	*Th.*	*W.*	*L.*	*Remarks*
2	$\frac{13}{16}''$	19¼″	24″	Side panels (A)
2	⅞″	18¾″	19½″	Knee-hole panels (B)
1	⅞″	19½″	35½″	Upper cross member (C)
1	⅞″	22″	38⅛″	Top (D)
4	⅞″	5¼″	$10\frac{7}{16}''$	Drawer bearer rails (E)
4	⅝″	14⅝″	$9\frac{7}{16}''$	Dust panel (F)
1	⅞″	18¾″	35½″	Bottom (G)
1	⅜″	17¼″	14¾″	Knee-hole bearer (H)
1	½″	$18\frac{15}{16}''$	34⅝″	Back (I)
2	1½″	5″	12¾″	Feet (J)
8	¾″	5″	6⅛″	Feet (K)
6	1¼″	1¼″	5″	Corner blocks (L)
1	⅝″	1″	8′	Filler (M)
1	¾″	¾″	4′	Corner braces (N)
1	1″	1½″	7′	Molding (O)
2	1½″	1¾″	12¾″	Molding (P)
1	1½″	2⅛″	6″	Pendant, knee-hole (Q)
				Cupboard
2	½″	12″	$16\frac{11}{16}''$	Sides (R)
1	1″	2¼″	$16\frac{11}{16}''$	Stile (S)
1	1″	1¾″	$16\frac{11}{16}''$	Stile (T)
1	1″	$4\frac{13}{16}''$	12″	Top rail (U)
2	1″	1½″	11⅞″	Door stiles (V)
1	1″	1½″	10¼″	Door bottom rail (W)
1	1″	4″	10¼″	Door top rail (X)
1	⅝″	8¼″	13¼″	Door panel (Y)
1	¼″	¼″	4′	Quarter-round molding (Z)
				Top Drawer
1	2½″	3¾″	34⅛″	Front
2	⅜″	3¾″	18″	Sides
1	⅜″	3¼″	33⅞″	Back
1	¼″	18⅝″	33⅝″	Bottom
				Upper Side Drawer
2	1¾″	4¾″	$9\frac{5}{16}''$	Fronts
4	⅜″	4¾″	18″	Sides
2	⅜″	4¼″	$9\frac{1}{16}''$	Back
2	¼″	18⅝″	$8\frac{13}{16}''$	Bottom
				Second Side Drawer
2	1¾″	5¾″	$9\frac{5}{16}''$	Fronts
4	⅜″	5¾″	18″	Sides
2	⅜″	5¼″	$9\frac{1}{16}''$	Back
2	¼″	18⅝″	$8\frac{13}{16}''$	Bottom
				Bottom Side Drawer
2	1¾″	6⅜″	$9\frac{5}{16}''$	Fronts
4	⅜″	6⅜″	18″	Sides
2	⅜″	5⅞″	$9\frac{1}{16}''$	Back
2	¼″	18⅝″	$8\frac{13}{16}''$	Bottom
				Center Drawer
1	1¾″	3″	14¼″	Front
2	⅜″	1⅛″	17¼″	Sides
1	⅜″	⅝″	14″	Back
1	¼″	17⅛″	13¾″	Bottom

shown in the drawing. The door is fastened to the cupboard with "H" hinges.

The bill of materials gives a complete cutting list of the various drawer members. The drawer sides are joined to the front members by means of dovetail joints while the drawer backs are joined to the side members in the same manner.

The drawer bottoms are set into grooves $\frac{1}{4}'' \times \frac{1}{4}''$ cut on the inside face of the drawer sides and fronts. See Fig. 10. When cutting the grooves in the drawer fronts a $\frac{1}{4}''$ straight-faced cutter must be used on the shaper in order to follow the contour of the drawer front. The panels in turn must be shaped to fit in these

grooves. The drawer fronts themselves are the only members which present a problem. From the detail sketch of the drawer fronts it is possible to lay out the contour without difficulty. When the shape has been laid out on each drawer front member it is cut on the band saw and finished by hand using a plane, file and sandpaper. The molded front is cut to shape on the shaper set up with a depth collar as a guide. With the exception of the top drawer all the other drawers have a $\frac{1}{4}''$ rabbet cut on the upper edge. This is done with a router bit.

Each drawer as shown in the detail drawings has a $\frac{1}{8}''$ rabbet cut at each end. This is done on the bench saw. The drawers, when assembled, are placed in the desk, and small stop blocks are fastened to the side panels of the case at the back as shown in the main drawing. The back can now be made up and fastened in place with glue and brads. The hardware should be set in place and then removed while the desk is in the process of finishing. The desk is stained and is filled with a paste filler after which several coats of shellac are applied and rubbed down with No. 00 steel wool.

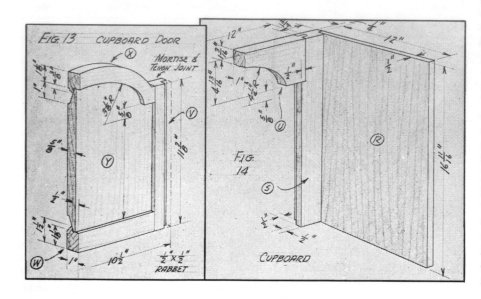

FIG. 13 CUPBOARD DOOR

FIG. 14

CUPBOARD

Upholstered Colonial Wing Chair
from the Brooklyn Museum

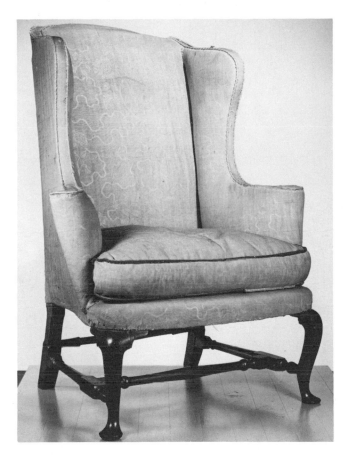

I N ONE of the American rooms of the Brooklyn Museum this exceptionally beautiful chair is a treasured exhibit. It originally came from the living room of the Francis Corbin House at Edenton, North Carolina. Made about 1730, it shows the influence of the Queen Anne style, but it is American made and is covered in the original fabric called "perpetuana," a wool and silk material much favored in the 18th century in America. The fabric is deep red and the piping a darker tone of velvet.

This original chair is made of ma-hogany and finished in walnut. The severe simplicity of the cabriole without any adornment whatsoever and the purity of line of the square and turned stretcher stamps it as American, for the native cabinetmakers of that date were not given to any unnecessary ornamentation. Despite its elegance, its fineness of proportion and beauty of line, this chair is eminently simple and can be reproduced by the home craftsman.

The construction of the wing chair should be started with the cabriole legs. Each leg is made up of three pieces of stock glued together. The main member is a piece of mahogany $2\frac{1}{2}''$ square and $12\frac{1}{2}''$ long. This should have the four sides dressed smooth by hand as it will be necessary to glue two blocks to it. The smaller of these blocks is $2\frac{1}{4}'' \times 2\frac{1}{2}''$ and $3\frac{3}{4}''$ long. The edge of this block which is to butt against the main leg member must be dressed smooth then glued and clamped in place. Allow the stock to remain in the clamp from 12 to 24 hours. After the clamp has been removed the larger block which measures $2\frac{1}{4}'' \times 4\frac{3}{4}'' \times 3\frac{3}{4}''$ is now made ready to be glued in place. On the main leg member, to which the small block has already been glued, the surface that is to take the large block must be dressed true in order to obtain a surface that the larger block can be glued to. After this block has been glued and clamped in place, clamps remain on overnight.

When the clamps have been removed the next step is to lay out and cut the mortises in the legs to take the seat frames. As shown in the detail sketch these mortises are $\frac{3}{8}'' \times 2\frac{1}{2}''$ and $1\frac{1}{2}''$ deep. They are located as shown and may be cut by hand using an auger bit and chisel, or they may be cut on the drill press using a hollow mortise chisel and bit.

Since a cabriole leg requires shaping, a full-size pattern of the outline must be drawn. This can be worked out from the detail shown in the main drawing. Cardboard should be used for the pattern as it will be necessary to trace the outline four times, twice on each leg. The major portion of the shaping should be done on the band saw. The finishing of the legs to conform with the cross sections as shown in the detail must be done by hand with the aid of spokeshave, rasp, and file. The legs should be sandpapered thoroughly, starting with No. $1\frac{1}{2}$ sandpaper and working down through the various grades, finishing with No. 00. These

AMERICAN · WING · CHAIR · c.1730.

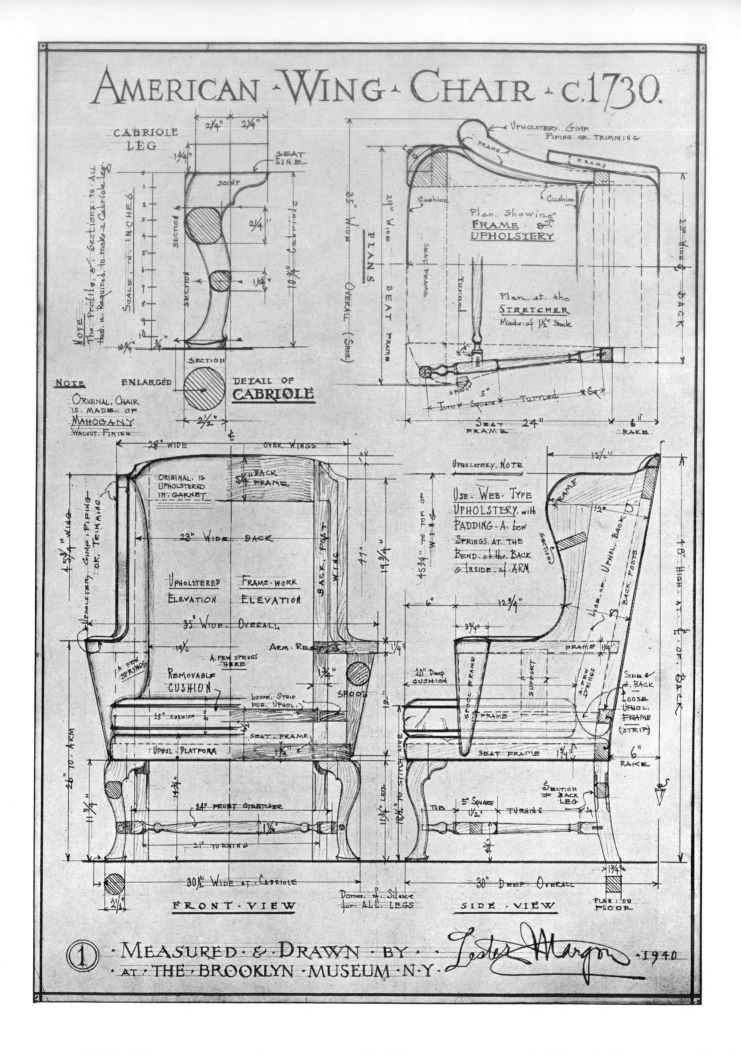

CABRIOLE LEG

SCALE IN INCHES

NOTE. The Profile, & Sections is All that is Required to make a Cabriole Leg.

NOTE. ORIGINAL CHAIR IS MADE OF MAHOGANY Walnut Finish

SECTION ENLARGED DETAIL OF **CABRIOLE**

PLANS

Plan Showing FRAME & UPHOLSTERY

Plan at the STRETCHER Made of 1½" Stock

SEAT FRAME 24" RAKE

ORIGINAL IS UPHOLSTERED IN GARNET

UPHOLSTERED ELEVATION — FRAME·WORK ELEVATION

Removable CUSHION

Domes of Silence for ALL LEGS

FRONT · VIEW

Upholstery. Note

Use Web Type UPHOLSTERY with PADDING - A few SPRINGS at the BEND of the BACK & Inside of ARM

SIDE · VIEW

① · MEASURED · & · DRAWN · BY · *Lester Margon* · 1940 · AT · THE · BROOKLYN · MUSEUM · N·Y·

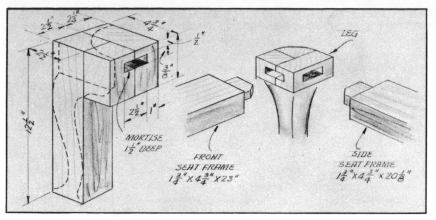

Before the cabriole leg is band sawed to shape from the blocks which have been glued up for the purpose, mortises are cut in the blocks to take the seat frames

are set aside while the work of constructing the back legs and posts is undertaken.

The back legs and posts are made of two pieces of $1\frac{3}{4}$" stock $4\frac{1}{2}$" wide and $48\frac{1}{4}$" long. These members are shaped as shown in the drawing. It is best if a pattern be drawn first, then traced on the two pieces of stock. They are cut to the rough shape on the band saw, then finished by hand with a spokeshave and plane. A small section of the leg is chamfered on the four corners as shown in the cross section on that member.

The locations of the lower rail, seat frame, upholstery frame, arm and wing frames are established on the leg and post. The lower rail and the wing frame are joined to this member by means of dowel joints, while the other three are joined with mortise and tenon joints. The location and size of mortises and the holes for the dowels are given in accompanying layout. When boring the dowel holes and cutting the mortises, keep in mind the angles at which the joining members meet the leg and post. Failure to do this will result in mortises and dowel holes in which the tenons will not line up properly. The rear seat frame, back upholstery strip and back frame member are joined to the posts by means of mortise and tenon joints. The mortises to take these are located and cut on the inside of the posts. The posts should be sandpapered thoroughly.

The next step is to make the seat frames. The front and two side members of these frames are made of $1\frac{3}{4}$" x $4\frac{3}{4}$" stock. The former is 23" long while the latter is $20\frac{1}{8}$" long. This allows for the tenons on each end. The back seat frame is made of a piece of $1\frac{3}{4}$" square stock $21\frac{1}{2}$" long. Tenons are cut on the ends of each of these members to fit their respective mortises. The tenons will have to be mitered as shown in the detail so as not to interfere with one another when they are set in place. The

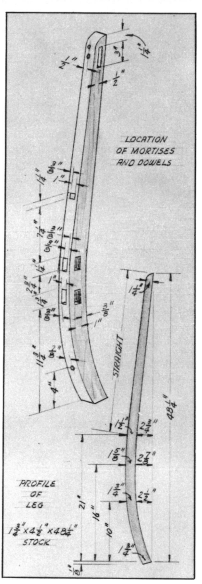

Back legs are cut to shape and the mortises laid out from above sketch

front and side seat frame members are shaped as shown in the drawing. A pattern of the curve should be made and traced on these members while they are set in place. The cutting of the members is done on the band saw, and finishing is done with a spokeshave.

The lower turned rails extending between the cabriole leg and back leg are

the next members to be made. These require two pieces of $1\frac{1}{2}$" square stock 21" long. They are turned in the lathe following the contour shown in the drawing. Care should be taken to have both of them matching. The forward end of each rail has a $\frac{3}{4}$" pin turned on it to fit a hole of the same size bored in the cabriole leg. The square end of the rail must be cut at an angle to butt flush against the back leg. The dowel hole is bored in the end of the rail and a $\frac{3}{8}$" dowel inserted. The hole in the front leg is located and bored to a depth of $\frac{5}{8}$". The front stretcher is made of a piece of $1\frac{1}{2}$" square stock 25" long. The reason for the additional length is to allow for the fitting of the stretcher in place. It is turned to shape in the lathe.

The various finished members of the chair are temporarily assembled at this time in order that the turned stretcher can be fitted in place. It is cut to the proper size, then the $\frac{3}{8}$" holes which are to take the dowels are bored in the ends of the stretcher and the lower rails. With the completion of the lower rails and stretcher the first step in assembly can be undertaken. The side frames and lower rails are glued to the legs.

The back upholstery strip and back frame are the next members to be made. The former is made of a piece of $1\frac{1}{2}$" square stock, while the latter is made of a piece of $1\frac{1}{4}$" x $5\frac{1}{4}$" material. Both of

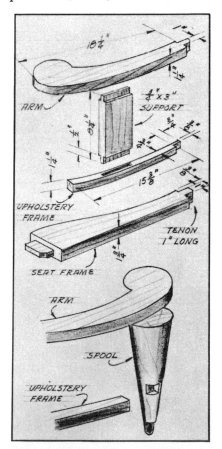

Above details show construction of arms and upholstery frames at sides

these members are 21½" long. Tenons are cut on the ends of both pieces to fit their respective mortises. The back frame has the upper edge shaped as shown in the front and side views. After these members have been fitted the two assembled side units are joined to the various

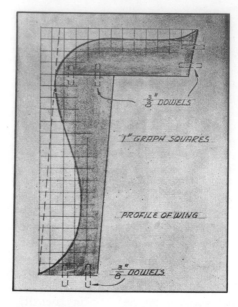

cross members to complete assembly of the main portion of the chair. Care must be taken when applying the clamps so that the chair will not be pulled out of shape. It may be necessary to shape blocks to place between the jaws of the clamp and the wood to prevent this.

The next unit that is constructed is the arms. These consist of four members namely the arm, upholstery frame, support and spool. The arms are made of two pieces of 1¼" x 4¼" stock 19¼" long. As this member is to be shaped, it will be necessary to make a full-size pattern of it. The cutting of the arm is done on the band saw after which a tenon is cut on the end to fit the mortise in the back post. The spool is made of two pieces of 3¾" stock 12½" long. It will be necessary to glue up several pieces of stock to obtain a square this size. The spools are turned in the lathe, then the large end cut to fit against the arm as shown in the drawing. The lower end is notched to fit over the side seat frame.

The upholstery frames are made of two pieces of 1¼" stock 1¾" wide and 16⅜" long cut on an arc to conform with the sweep of arm. The upholstery frame is finished to a width of ¾". A tenon is cut on the back end to fit in the mortise in the post. The support member which is between the arm and the upholstery frame is made of ¾" stock 3" wide and 8¼" long. It is joined to these members by means of mortise and tenon joints as shown in the detail sketch. The mortises are cut in the arm and frame members and the tenons cut on the ends of the support to fit these mortises. The various members are temporarily assembled and placed in position. The gain in the spool which is to take the upholstery frame is cut with a chisel. The support member is glued in place, then the spool attached to arm and frame members with glue and screws. This assembled unit is glued in place using a wood screw to fasten the lower end of the spool to the side seat frame.

The wings are 1" stock. The lengths and widths of the two members that go to make up each wing are shown in the detail drawing. These are joined together as shown, then a pattern of the curve is drawn and traced on the assembled units. They are cut to shape on the band saw. The wings are attached to the arms and back posts by means of ⅜" dowels.

The only portion of the completed chair that must be finished is the lower section as all other woodwork is to be covered by upholstery. As mentioned on the drawing the finish of the chair is walnut. The grain should be filled, then the wood stained with a walnut stain. This is followed by several coats of varnish, each one rubbed down with pumice stone when dry.

The upholstering of the chair is somewhat difficult and should not be undertaken by anyone not familiar with the type of work required for finishing a chair of this kind. If this portion of the work is beyond the ability of the craftsman the chair should be sent to the local upholsterer for finishing.

18th Century Walnut Tip-Top Table

This is another piece reproduced by courtesy of the Metropolitan Museum

ONE of the largest collections of American furniture in existence is owned by the Metropolitan Museum of Art in New York. Ranging from the Pilgrim Century to the Empire interpretations of Duncan Phyfe this collection is outstanding for the quality and authenticity of its pieces. In fact, the resources of the American Wing of the Museum are so extensive that it would be impossible to show its entire collection at one time; therefore, pieces are loaned to other shrines of American history. Such is the case with the tip-top table illustrated in the measured drawing and the accompanying photograph. We

found this table in the beautiful living room of the Dey Mansion at Preakness, New Jersey, a home that served as Washington's headquarters in the Fall of 1780.

While it is true that the American cabinetmakers of Colonial days followed the traditions and fashions of England in the furniture which they made, nevertheless they had neither the time nor inclination to elaborate the forms with intricate carvings and tracery. Instead they took the fundamental form and treated it in the American manner. What they created were works of art.

As you will recognize at once, the excellence of this tip-top table depends

upon the beauty of the silhouette, the fineness of its proportions and the exquisite profiles of the turnings. Here is a task that is not difficult but does require patience and good workmanship. The 34"-diameter top provides a many-purpose table. A simple tilting mechanism in the crow's nest at the top of the pedestal allows the top to be tilted so the table may be placed against the wall where it takes little space.

Construction of the table should be started with the pedestal. A piece of walnut stock 4" square and 24" long will be required. If possible the stock for the pedestal should be one piece but may be glued up. The length of 24" is the rough size allowing $1\frac{3}{8}$" at the ends for waste.

A full-size pattern of the pedestal should be drawn with the aid of graph squares following the outline shown in the drawing. From this pattern the exact location of the various cuts can be determined as well as the diameters at these various points. The stock is turned down to an outside diameter of $3\frac{7}{8}$" with a gouge used for roughing and a skew for finishing the cylinder. When this has been done, the various sections of the turning can be marked off. From a point $\frac{1}{2}$" from the live center end of the stock a 4" section is marked for the bottom of the pedestal. The main portion of the pedestal turning should extend from this mark $13\frac{1}{2}$" toward the other end. From this last established point, the turned pin which passes through the crow's nest is established. The length of the pin should be $4\frac{7}{8}$". Within the $13\frac{1}{2}$" area, the various beads, fillets and coves should be marked off. The diameter at these various points should be established with the use of calipers and a parting tool. From here on the chisels are used.

Before removing the pedestal from the lathe and before cutting off the waste at each end of the stock, the location of each leg should be established. The post is divided into three parts and lines are drawn parallel to the center line of the post at these established points. The

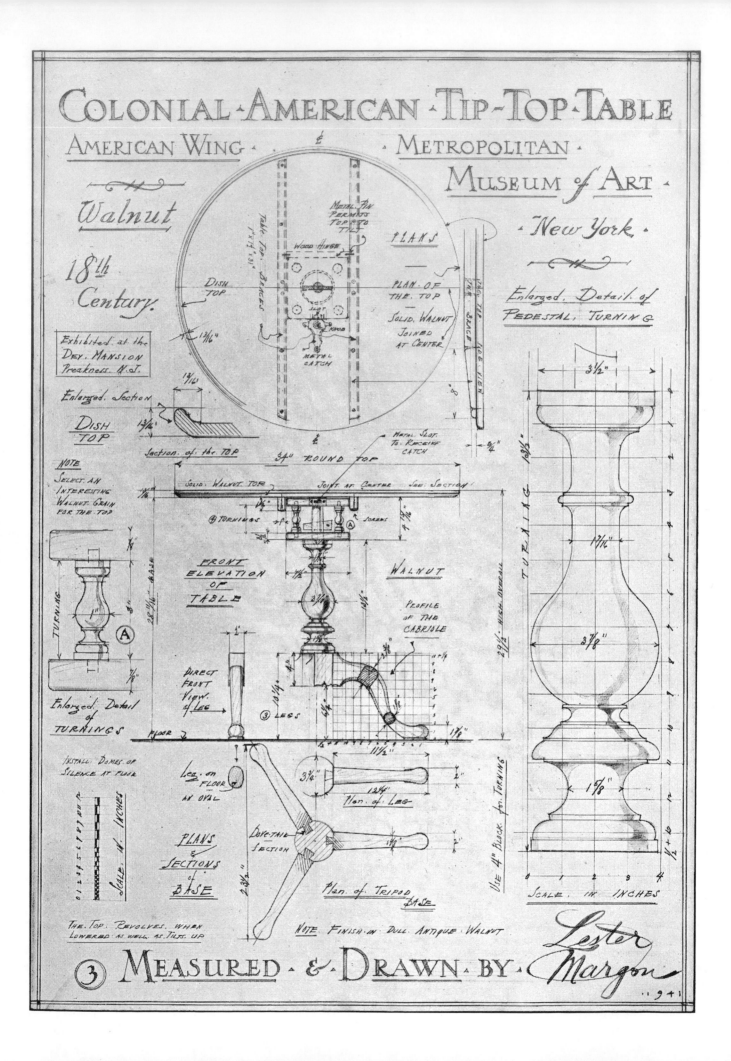

COLONIAL·AMERICAN·TIP-TOP·TABLE

AMERICAN WING · · METROPOLITAN

MUSEUM of ART

Walnut

18th Century.

· New York ·

Exhibited. at. the
Dey. MANSION
Preakness. N. J.

Enlarged. Section
DISH TOP

NOTE
SELECT. AN
INTERESTING
WALNUT. GRAIN
FOR. THE. TOP

Enlarged. Detail.
of TURNINGS

INSTALL. DOMES. OF
SILENCE. AT. FLOOR

SCALE IN INCHES

THE. TOP. REVOLVES. WHEN
LOWERED. AS WELL. AS. TILTS. UP

METAL. PIN.
PERMITS.
TOP. TO
TILT.

WOOD. HINGE

DISH
TOP

PLANS

PLAN. OF.
THE. TOP.

SOLID. WALNUT.
JOINED
AT. CENTER

METAL
CATCH

Section. of. the. TOP

METAL. SLOT.
TO. RECEIVE.
CATCH

34" ROUND TOP

SOLID. WALNUT. TOP

JOINT. AT. CENTER. See. Section.

Enlarged. Detail. of.
PEDESTAL. TURNING

3½"

10⅜"

1⅞/16"

3⅜"

1⅝"

4 TURNINGS

SCREWS

FRONT
ELEVATION
of
TABLE

WALNUT

PROFILE
OF THE
CABRIOLE

DIRECT
FRONT
VIEW.
of. LEG

3 LEGS

FLOOR

LEG. ON
FLOOR
IS. OVAL

PLANS
&
SECTIONS
of
BASE

DOVE-TAIL
SECTION

3¾"

11½"

12¼"

Plan. of. LEG

Plan. of. Tripod
BASE

NOTE. FINISH. IN. DULL. ANTIQUE. WALNUT

SCALE. IN. INCHES

USE 4" BLOCK. FOR. TURNING

29½" HIGH. OVERALL

③ MEASURED · & · DRAWN · BY · Lester Margon

·9·41·

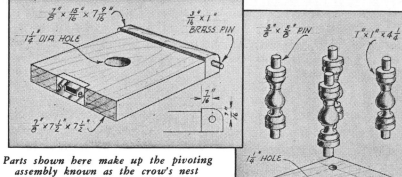

Parts shown here make up the pivoting assembly known as the crow's nest

pedestal is removed from the lathe and the waste stock is cut off with a back saw. The portion of the pedestal against which the legs butt must be made flat. This flat area, 2" wide, should be laid out within two lines 1" each side of the center line. With the stock held securely in the vise a sharp chisel is used to pare down to the lines. The dovetails are laid out on the lower end of the post. The cutting of these dovetails should be done by hand with a sharp chisel.

WOOD KEY LOCKS CROW'S NEST

In the spindle at the upper end of the pedestal a slot must be cut to take the key which locks the crow's nest, with the top attached, to the pedestal. The slot is $\frac{3}{8}$" wide. At its long side it should measure 1" and should taper to $\frac{3}{4}$" at the opposite side. The slot is located so that the bottom is 1" above the pedestal shoulder. It should be cut by hand with auger bit and chisel. The key is made of $\frac{3}{8}$" stock, $1\frac{1}{4}$" wide and $3\frac{1}{4}$" long. It is tapered to fit the slot.

As shown in the front elevation as well as in the detail sketch, the lower end of the post has a broken edge. This ornamentation is typical of early American tripod tables. It is cut into the pedestal with a file.

Three legs are required. Stock 2" thick, 5" wide and 16" long will be needed for each one. A full-size pattern of the leg is drawn on a piece of cardboard with the aid of 1" graph squares. The dovetail tenon should be drawn on this pattern, as the stock for the leg must be cut with this tenon attached. The pattern is traced on the stock, then the leg is cut to shape on a band saw or jig saw. The dovetail tenon is now laid out on each leg and is cut to fit one of the dovetail mortises. Number each leg to correspond to the joint in the pedestal to which it has been fitted.

The legs are now shaped as shown in the plan. The job of tapering them from the top down to the knob foot can be done on the band saw or by hand with a spokeshave. The last step in shaping

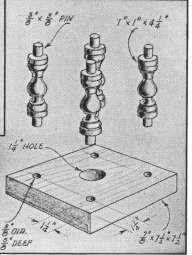

the legs is to round off the corners to conform with the cross sections as shown in the profile and plan views of these members. This work is done with a spokeshave or file. The legs should now be sandpapered.

The crow's nest is the next unit to be made. This unit attaches to the top and revolves on the pedestal. Two pieces of $\frac{7}{8}$" stock $7\frac{1}{2}$" square will be required for the top and bottom. The four turned posts which separate the top and bottom of the crow's nest are turned from stock

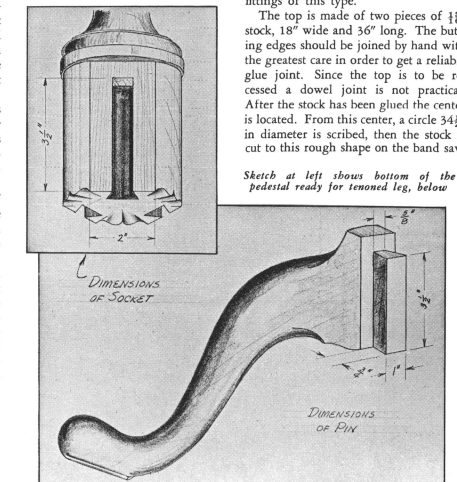

Sketch at left shows bottom of the pedestal ready for tenoned leg, below

$1\frac{1}{4}$" square, $5\frac{1}{2}$" long. The finished spindle will have an overall length of $4\frac{1}{4}$". The top and bottom members have a $1\frac{1}{4}$" hole bored in the center of each. This hole is to take the spindle end of the pedestal and should be a loose fit so that the assembled unit may revolve on the post. The hole should be bored with an expansive bit. The turned posts are to fit in holes bored in the upper and lower members. These holes are placed $1\frac{1}{4}$" in from each side. They are $\frac{3}{8}$" in diameter and $\frac{5}{8}$" deep. The four posts are now turned in the lathe to the shape shown in the detail (A) of the main drawing. After they are removed from the lathe, the waste wood is cut off. They are glued in place to complete the assembly of the crow's nest.

A piece of stock shown in the detail sketch is fastened to one edge of the upper member of the crow's nest with glue and $1\frac{3}{4}$" No. 10 flat head screws. This piece holds the metal pins on which the top tilts. One edge of this strip is rounded off at a radius of $\frac{7}{16}$" as shown in the sketch. The pivot points should be located, then $\frac{3}{16}$" holes are bored to a depth of $\frac{1}{2}$" to take the pins. On the opposite edge of this same member the metal plate which takes the bolt of the catch should be located and set into the wood as shown. Hardware stores have fittings of this type.

The top is made of two pieces of $1\frac{3}{8}$" stock, 18" wide and 36" long. The butting edges should be joined by hand with the greatest care in order to get a reliable glue joint. Since the top is to be recessed a dowel joint is not practical. After the stock has been glued the center is located. From this center, a circle $34\frac{1}{2}$" in diameter is scribed, then the stock is cut to this rough shape on the band saw.

The shaping and recessing of the top to match the enlarged section in the drawing must be done on the lathe. This is possible only by swinging the work outboard, on the opposite end of the headstock. An auxiliary tool rest must be used for this work. When turning stock of this diameter the speed of the lathe should be reduced to a minimum. Sharp turning tools are an absolute necessity if the work is to be done properly. When the turning has been completed, the top should be sandpapered thoroughly before removal from the lathe.

Cleats, or braces, under the table top are made of two pieces of 1″ stock, $1\frac{1}{2}$″ wide and 31″ long. They are shaped as shown in the side view of the top and the front elevation of the table. The taper may be planed, while the rounded edges can be done with a plane and sandpaper. They are fastened to the underside of the table with flat head wood screws. The braces are placed across the grain of the top, located $3\frac{13}{16}$″ each side of the center line. This will place the braces $7\frac{5}{8}$″ apart. Holes are located and bored on the inside faces of these braces to take the metal pins on which the top tilts. These holes are located $\frac{7}{16}$″ from the top edge and $4\frac{3}{16}$″ from the center. They should be $\frac{3}{16}$″ in diameter and $\frac{1}{2}$″ deep. In order to place the top on the crow's nest, one brace will have to be removed to engage the pin. Screws are driven through the brace and into the top.

The finish is started by applying a walnut filler. This is brushed on and rubbed into the grain. When the filler has dried and hardened the surface is given a wash coat of shellac which is rubbed down lightly with fine steel wool or sandpaper. Three coats of shellac are then applied, each rubbed down in the same manner as the wash coat.

Low-Boy from the Pendleton Collection

AMERICAN LOW-BOY OF THE EARLY 18TH CENTURY HAS CARVED CABRIOLE LEGS AND CURVED FRONT

Reproduced by courtesy of the Museum of Art, Rhode Island School of Design

THE PENDLETON Collection of Colonial Furniture was presented by Mr. Charles Pendleton of Providence, Rhode Island, to the Rhode Island School of Design in 1904. His aim in making this collection was to furnish a house as a gentleman of taste and discrimination would have at the end of the 18th Century. The Collection is the result of the work of many years and the repeated elimination of the good for something better.

From its many pieces this walnut low-boy was selected because of its simplicity of design and fineness of proportions but most particularly because of its fitness to take its place in the mod-ern scheme of things for its beauty and utility. In the early days a low-boy functioned as a dressing table but is now commonly used as an occasional table.

The elegance of the shaped front which is followed diligently by the line of the top gives this piece color and class. While the original has a rich, figured veneer on its top, front and sides, many of these American pieces were made in the solid wood. The craftsman can take his choice in this matter.

The front cabriole legs with the in-cised carving at the knee, its typical claw-and-ball foot, stamps it Colonial,

but in spite of this, the piece shows very distinct influence of the Queen Anne period and strong influence of Dutch cabinetmakers. The hardware shown is Louis XV and it was probably put on because it was at hand. It would be more correct to use Old English hardware of this general shape.

Construction of this low-boy is started with the legs. Stock must be glued up for these members. Each front leg is made up of a piece of $3\frac{1}{2}''$ square stock $28\frac{3}{4}''$ long. To one side of these pieces a block $1\frac{1}{2}''$ thick by $3\frac{1}{2}''$ wide and $19''$ long is glued, while against the adjacent side a piece of $1\frac{1}{2}''$ stock, $5''$ wide and $19''$ long is attached. The rear legs are made up of $3\frac{1}{4}''$ square stock $28\frac{3}{4}''$ long to which is glued $1\frac{1}{4}''$ stock, $3\frac{1}{4}''$ wide and $19''$ long and a second piece $4\frac{1}{2}''$ wide of the same length. This is shown in Fig. 1. The narrower pieces are glued and clamped to the square stock first. After the clamps are removed the surface against which the second piece is to be glued should be dressed before glue and clamps are applied.

As shown in Fig. 2 the upper section of each front leg is rounded off at a radius of $2\frac{1}{2}''$ from a center which is located $1''$ from the inside faces. This arc is drawn on the upper ends with a compass or dividers. Since the legs must be mortised and grooved to take the sides and other members, the shaping of the legs should be done last. In leav-ing this part of the work for the final operation the legs are left square so that the laying out of various cuts can be done with ease and the cutting of them either by machine or by hand, with the use of chisels, can be done. The upper portion of the rear legs is left square as shown in Fig. 3 and in the plan.

The next step in making the legs is to locate and cut the grooves that are to take the side members. These grooves measure $\frac{1}{2}''$ wide and are cut to a depth of $\frac{3}{4}''$. As shown in the plan and Fig. 3 the locations of the grooves are different on the front and back

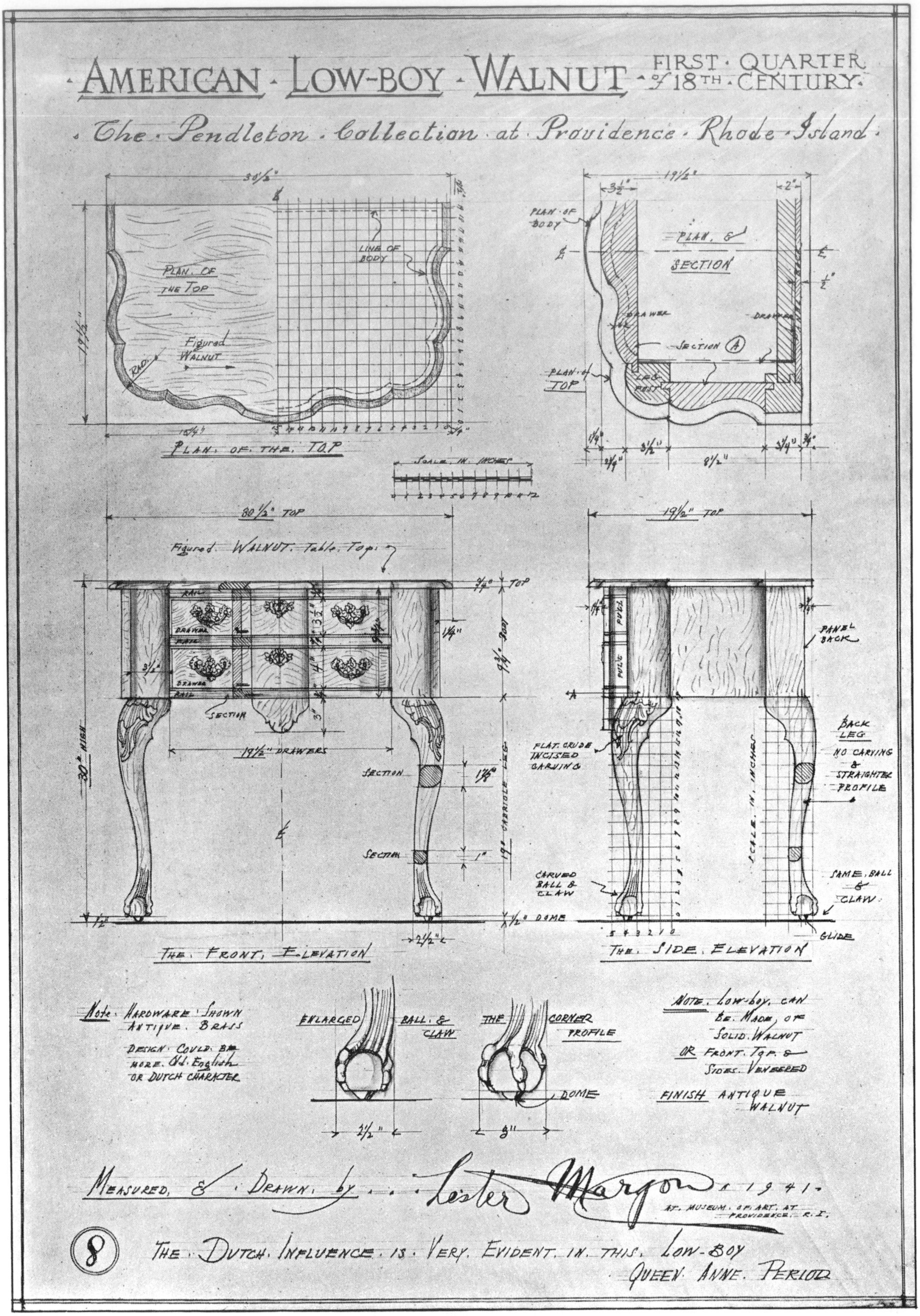

AMERICAN · LOW-BOY · WALNUT FIRST · QUARTER ·of 18TH · CENTURY·

·The·Pendleton·Collection·at·Providence·Rhode·Island·

PLAN· OF
THE·Top

Figured
WALNUT

LINE OF
BODY

PLAN· OF· THE· TOP

PLAN· OF·
BODY

PLAN· &
SECTION

DRAWER   DRAWER

Section A

PLAN·OF·
TOP

SCALE IN INCHES

Figured· WALNUT· Table· Top

DRAWER
RAIL

DRAWER
RAIL

SECTION

19½" DRAWERS

TOP

SECTION

SECTION

½

THE· FRONT· ELEVATION

PANEL
BACK

BACK
LEG
NO CARVING
&
STRAIGHTER
PROFILE

FLAT CRUDE
INCISED
CARVING

SAME BALL
&
CLAW

CARVED
BALL &
CLAW

SCALE IN INCHES

GLIDE

THE· SIDE· ELEVATION

Note· HARDWARE· SHOWN
ANTIQUE· BRASS

DESIGN· COULD· BE
MORE· Old· English·
OR· DUTCH CHARACTER

ENLARGED· BALL· &
CLAW

THE· CORNER
PROFILE

DOME

Note· Low-boy, CAN
BE· MADE· OF·
SOLID· WALNUT·
OR· FRONT· TOP· &
SIDES· VENEERED

FINISH · ANTIQUE ·
WALNUT

MEASURED· &· DRAWN· BY· · · · Lester Margon ·1941·

AT· MUSEUM· OF· ART· AT·
PROVIDENCE· R· I·

(8) THE· DUTCH· INFLUENCE· IS· VERY· EVIDENT· IN· THIS· LOW-BOY
QUEEN· ANNE· PERIOD

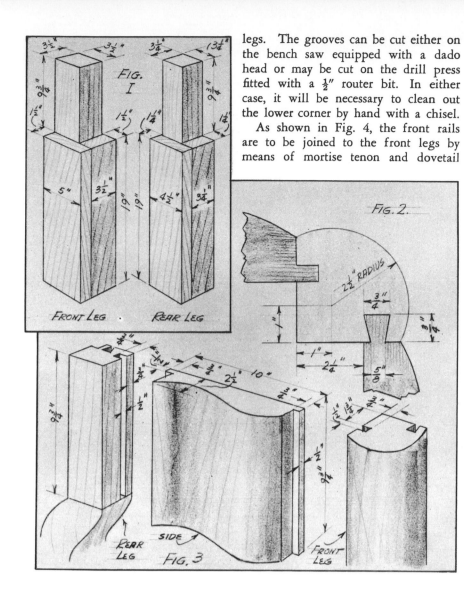

FIG. I

FRONT LEG · REAR LEG

FIG. 2.

REAR LEG   SIDE   FRONT LEG

FIG. 3

legs. The grooves can be cut either on the bench saw equipped with a dado head or may be cut on the drill press fitted with a ½" router bit. In either case, it will be necessary to clean out the lower corner by hand with a chisel.

As shown in Fig. 4, the front rails are to be joined to the front legs by means of mortise tenon and dovetail joints. The location of the mortises and the socket to take the dovetail is laid out as shown in Fig. 4. The cutting of the mortises can be done on the drill press with the machine set up as a hollow mortiser with a ⅜" chisel and bit. The socket for the dovetail can be cut by hand with a back saw or dovetail saw and the wood is removed with a chisel. All these cuts are made to a depth of ¾". The upper and lower back rails are jointed to the back legs in the same manner as the front rails. This is shown in Fig. 5. The mortise for the tenon and the sockets for the dovetail are laid out as shown and cut in the same manner as mentioned before. The rear legs have a ½" x ¾" rabbet cut along the edge, as shown in Fig. 5, to take the back panel. This rabbet starts from the top and extends down along the edge for a distance of 9⅜". As with the grooves, these rabbets may be cut on the bench saw or on the drill press fitted with a router bit. In either case the corner where the rabbet stops must be cut square by hand with a chisel.

SIDES SHAPED FROM SOLID WOOD

The sides are made of two pieces of 2½" stock, 9¾" wide and 10" long. Tongues are cut on each end as shown in Fig. 3. These tongues are ½" thick and ¾" long and should be made to fit

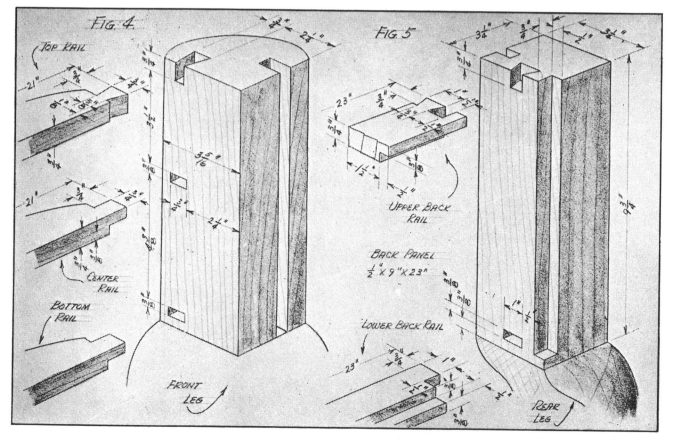

FIG. 4

TOP RAIL

CENTER RAIL

BOTTOM RAIL

FRONT LEG

FIG 5

UPPER BACK RAIL

BACK PANEL
½" X 9" X 23"

LOWER BACK RAIL

REAR LEG

the grooves of the legs. The next step is to lay out the curve of the side pieces as shown in Fig. 3. A pattern of the curve can be developed with the aid of graph squares. The plan drawing of the top shows the outline of the body in dotted line. The important point to keep in mind is that the curve at the ends must coincide with the back leg and the curve of the front leg as shown in the plan and section.

The shaping of these side members is done by first making a series of cuts on the bench saw across the face of the stock. This operation calls for regulating and varying the depth of each cut to conform with the outline of the curve. A wood carver's gouge having a slight sweep is used to rough down the surface after all saw cuts have been made. The surface is then dressed smooth with a spokeshave. The surface should be sandpapered thoroughly to remove all tool marks. No. 1½ sandpaper is used first and successively finer grades are used until finishing is done with No. 00 sandpaper.

The next step is to cut the back rails. These are made of two pieces of ¾″ stock, 2″ wide and 23″ long. These rails are joined to the back legs by means of tenons and dovetails as shown in Fig. 5. Before the tenons and dovetails are laid out and cut, a ⅜″ x ½″ rabbet to take the back panel is cut along the back edge of each member as shown. A tenon ¾″ long is cut on each end of the lower rail to fit the mortise that has been cut in the back leg to take this member. On each end of the upper rail a dovetail is laid out to fit the socket in the leg. This upper rail as shown in Fig. 5 has a projecting end above the rabbet which fills in the rabbet which has been cut in the leg. Before attempting to cut the dovetail make certain that all layout lines are correct. The cutting of the dovetail can be done with a dovetail saw and a chisel.

TOP RAILS DOVETAILED TO LEGS

The three front rails are made of ¾″ stock 3½″ wide, each piece being 21″ long. A dovetail is cut on the ends of the top rail to fit the socket in the leg as shown in Fig. 4. The center and bottom rails have tenons cut on each end to fit the mortises. After these pieces have been fitted in place the next step is to shape the front edge of each rail. A pattern of the contour can be drawn with the aid of graph squares following the outline as shown in the plan of the top. As with the side

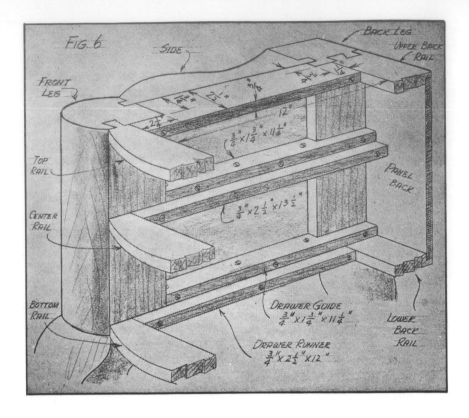

members, care should be taken to make certain that the pattern when traced on the rails meets the leg as shown in the plan and section as well as in Fig. 6. This completes the fitting of the various members that are to be joined to the legs. The work should be assembled temporarily at this time to check the various parts for fit.

The work of shaping and carving the legs can now be undertaken. The upper portion of the front legs are now shaped as shown in the plan and section as well as in Fig. 2, following the arc as previously drawn with the compass. The greater portion of the wood that is to be removed can be cut away with a chisel, then the surface is finished with rasp, file and sandpaper. A full-size pattern of the front and back legs should be drawn with the aid of graph squares shown in the side elevation. The patterns, when completed, are traced on the stock. The legs are cut to shape on the band saw then finished with a spokeshave to the sections shown in the front elevation. The carving of the claw-and-ball foot should be done with carving tools until the shape as shown in the enlarged sketch of this detail is matched. The carving on the leg is of the incised type. A pattern of this carving should be drawn and then traced on each member. The legs should be sandpapered thoroughly.

The pendant which is attached to the lower front rail as shown in the front elevation is made of a piece of 3½″

stock, 5½″ wide and 3″ long. It is shaped to follow the outline of the lower rail, then the lower end of the pendant is cut to the shape shown in the front elevation. It is fastened to the lower rail with glue and 1¾″ No. 10 flathead screws.

With the completion of the work, permanent assembly can now be started. The side members are glued to the legs and clamped together. After the clamps have been removed from these members, the two side units are joined together by inserting the middle and lower front rails and the back rail in the mortises, then the upper front and back rails are set in the dovetail sockets. Clamps are applied to hold the work together. It is of the utmost importance

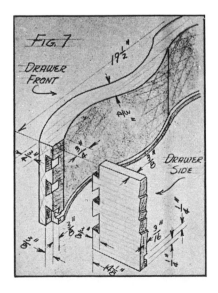

to check the assembled work for squareness before the glue has had time to set. The simplest method of doing this is by checking the diagonal dimensions.

The back panel can now be cut to size and fitted in place. It is fastened with glue and 1″ No. 6 flathead screws. The drawer runners and guides are now cut to the required sizes and fitted in place as shown in Fig. 6.

The top is made of $\frac{3}{4}$″ stock, 19½″ wide and 30½″ long. It may be possible to obtain a single panel this width but if not it can be made up by gluing several pieces together. Dowel joints or good butt joints may be used to assemble the pieces to produce the top panel. A full-size pattern of the top must be drawn as shown in the plan.

The edge of the panel is molded as shown in the front and side elevations.

As noted in the drawing, the top should be of figured walnut. A veneer can be applied or a $\frac{3}{4}$″ veneer walnut panel $\frac{3}{4}$″ thick can be used. The top is fastened to the case by driving 1¼″ No. 10 flathead screws up through the upper front and back rails as well as through the upper cleats attached to the side members.

The drawer fronts are made of 3½″ stock 19½″ long. The upper drawer front is 3½″ wide while the lower drawer front is 4″ wide. The sides are made of $\frac{3}{8}$″ stock 14⅛″ long while the backs are made of the same stock 19½″ long. The drawer members are joined together by means of dovetail joints as shown in Fig. 7. The drawer fronts are shaped as shown in Fig. 7 and the plan and section. These can be cut to shape on the band saw and finished on a sanding drum. The groove which is to take the bottom panel must be cut on the shaper with a straight-face cutter and a depth collar because of the irregular shape. Once the machine is set up to cut the groove in the front member the grooves can also be cut in the side and back members. The bottom panel is cut to fit and the drawers are assembled.

The location of the hardware is established and all necessary holes and gains should be bored and cut to take the drawer pulls and locks. The completed low-boy is stained an antique walnut, then given several coats of white shellac, rubbed down with No. 00 steel wool after it is dry. The hardware should be applied after all work has been completed.

Pennsylvania Pine Table

THERE'S a dash and color to this antique Pennsylvania German table that is altogether exciting. The wood is hard, raspy pine painted a dark reddish color, but worn off in spots to permit the grain to shine through. The corners are rounded, the edges softened, the stretchers worn by the scraping of many feet.

It is great fun to make a piece of this kind because it represents real folk art. You don't have to be too careful. Not one line needs to be straight; the turnings don't have to match exactly; the work is all the better for having a vigorous, freehand look characteristic of the times.

Because of its size, the table is well adapted for use in the living room and elsewhere, or as a breakfast table in a bedroom.

The construction should be started with the legs. Four pieces dressed to 2¼" square and 29¼" long will be required. The first step is to mark their relative positions. On the inside surfaces of each, the mortises that are to take the tenons on the ends of the aprons and stretchers are laid out as shown in Fig. 1. The broken lines drawn at a slant are the angles at which these will eventually be cut, but the actual laying out of the slant should not be done until after the trial assembly of the under structure.

The mortises can best be cut with a hollow mortiser. They must be cut at an angle of 80° to the surface of the leg to allow for the splay. If the drill press is set up as a hollow mortiser, the angle can be obtained by tilting the table. The depth of the mortises at the upper end should be at least 1⅜", while those at the lower end should be 1¼" deep.

After the mortises have been cut, the work of turning the legs can be undertaken. The upper and lower sections of each leg, which are to be square, are marked off. Diagonal lines are drawn on each end to establish centers for mounting in the lathe. With the aid

of a gouge for roughing and a skew chisel for finishing, the section of each leg that is to be worked in the lathe is turned cylindrical in shape to a diameter of 2¼". The various beads, coves and shoulders are marked and the

Its charmingly simple Dutch craftwork makes this piece much easier for the home craftsman to copy than most furniture of museum rank

ultimate depths of the various cuts established with the parting tool and caliper. The heads are shaped with the skew chisel and the coves are worked out with a round-nose chisel or small gouge. All shoulders are finished with the diamond-point or skew chisel.

The aprons will require 1" stock 8¼" wide, the lengths of which are shown in Fig. 2. The ends of each apron are cut at an angle of 80°. Then the tenons are laid out, cut to shape on the bench saw and fitted to their re-

spective mortises. A ⅜" x 5/16" groove is cut along the inside face near the upper edge of each apron member to take the wood buttons, as shown in Fig. 6, by means of which the top is screwed in place.

The end aprons are to have a section removed from the center as shown in Fig. 2 to provide for the drawers. The opening is laid out; then holes are bored at each corner within this area. The actual cutting can be done with a compass or keyhole saw or on the jig saw. The upper edge of the opening will have to be beveled at an angle of 80° to allow for the drawer. The lower edge may be left "as is" as it will not interfere. The drawer runners are supported in gains cut with

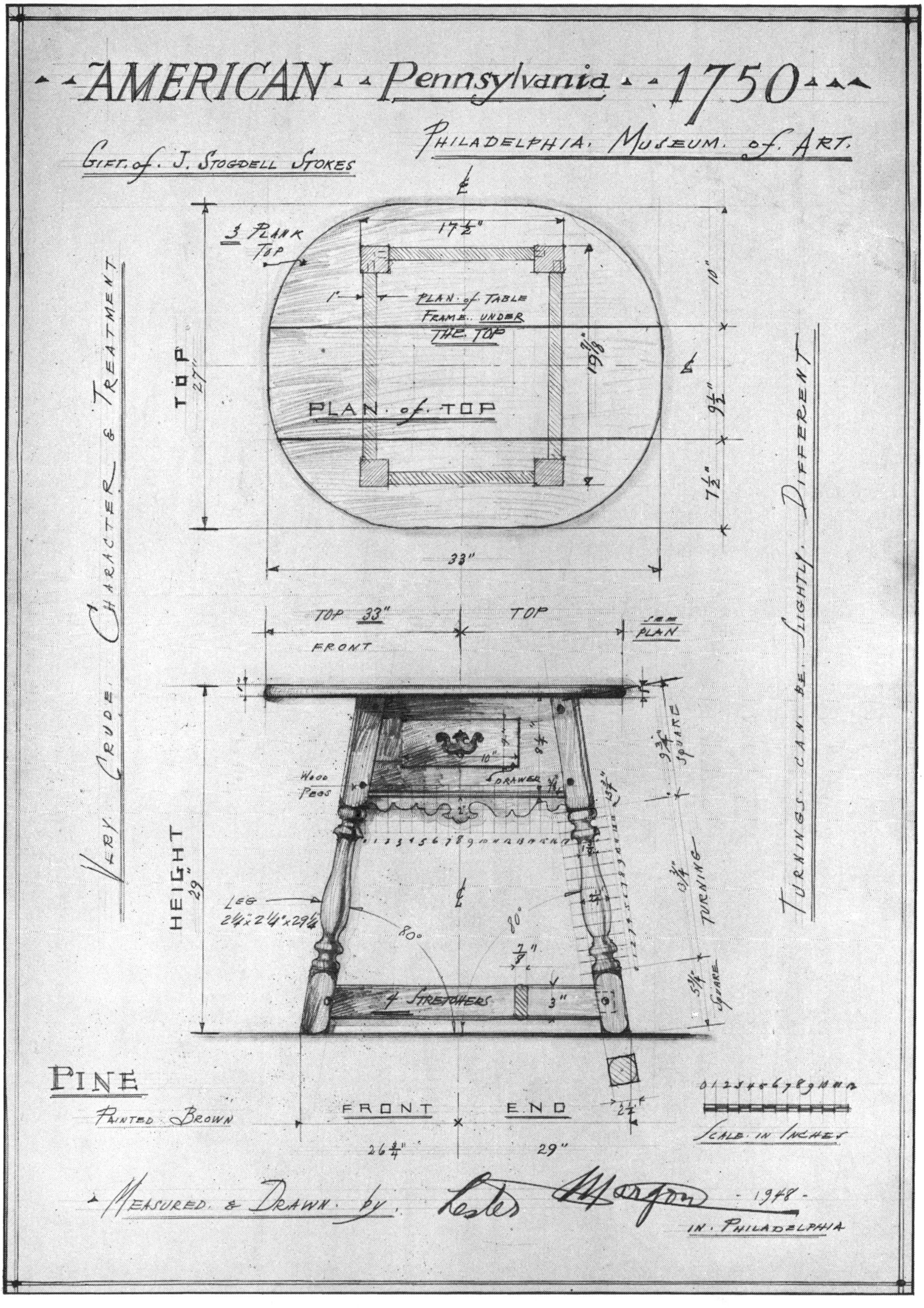

AMERICAN · Pennsylvania · 1750

PHILADELPHIA · MUSEUM · OF · ART.

GIFT · OF · J. STOGDELL STOKES

3 PLANK TOP

TOP 27"

17½"

10"

9½"

PLAN OF TABLE FRAME. UNDER THE TOP

1"

19½"

PLAN of TOP

7½"

33"

VERY · CRUDE · CHARACTER & TREATMENT

TURNINGS · CAN · BE · SLIGHTLY · DIFFERENT

TOP 33"   TOP   SEE PLAN

FRONT

HEIGHT 29

WOOD PEGS

9¾" SQUARE

DRAWER

LEG 2¼" × 2¼" × 29½"

80°

80°

4 STRETCHERS   3"

¾" TURNING

5½" SQUARE

PINE

PAINTED BROWN

FRONT   END

26¼"   29"

0 1 2 3 4 5 6 7 8 9 10 11 12
SCALE · IN · INCHES

· MEASURED · & · DRAWN · BY · Lester Morgan · 1948 ·

IN · PHILADELPHIA

a chisel into the lower edge of the drawer opening in the aprons as shown in Fig. 2.

The stretchers shown in Fig. 3 are cut from 7/8" x 3" stock to the lengths specified. The tenons are laid out, then cut to fit their respective mortises.

The work can now be trial fitted together. At this time, the angles at which the upper and lower ends of the legs must be cut in order that they be parallel to the floor should be laid out. The work is disassembled and the ends of the legs cut. The various pieces should now be sanded, then the work reassembled permanently with glue. Holes 3/8" in diameter are bored through each leg as shown in the main drawing for pegs. These should be square in cross section and tapered so that they may be driven in place. Any projection inside or outside is dressed flush with the leg surface.

The bead molding shown in Fig. 6 is cut from 3/8" x 1 3/16" stock. The scrolls are cut from 1" x 2" stock. Glue and flathead screws should be used to secure the bead and scroll to the lower edge of the aprons.

The drawer runners and guides are made as shown in Fig. 4. The guide is secured to the side of each runner

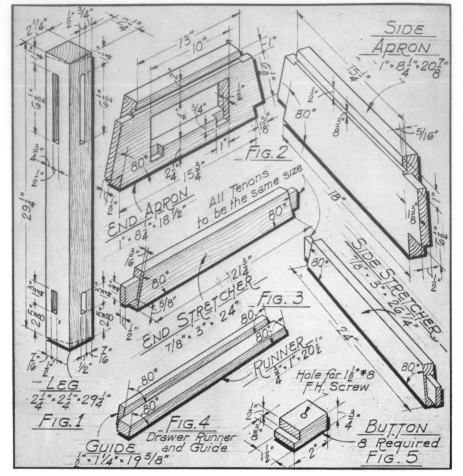

with glue and 1 1/4" No. 7 flathead wood screws. The runner and guide, when assembled, should be set in place in the end aprons as shown in Fig. 6.

Figures 7 and 8 show the drawers. The forward end of each side is cut at 80°. The upper and lower edges of the fronts are beveled at the same angle. The dovetail by means of which the side and front drawer members are joined together is laid out and cut. The drawer bottom is set into a 1/4" x 1/4" groove cut along the inside face of each side and front member. The groove in the front member must be cut at an angle of 80° to the face. Dadoes are cut across the inside face of the side member to take the drawer back. The drawer members are assembled with glue and brads. The drawers are set in place and a stop block is fitted between them and secured to one runner.

The top is made as shown in Fig. 9. Glue the pieces together before laying out and cutting the oval. Buttons, Fig. 5, are cut and fitted to the aprons. A kick rail, Fig. 6, is fitted between the end aprons to prevent the drawers from tipping as they are opened. After the work has been finished, the drawer pulls should be applied.

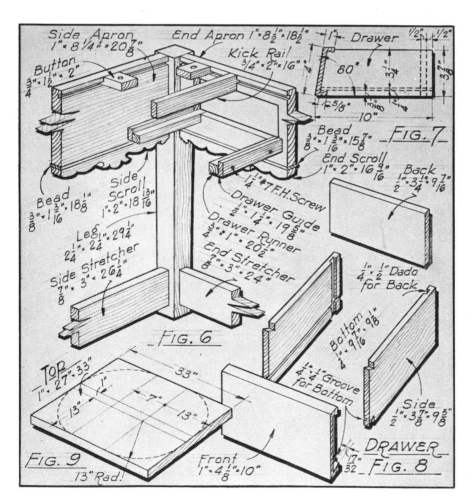

COLONIAL
HIGH-BACK
Chair

Made in Salem, 1782

While legends of witchcraft and the glamor of a Colonial seaport are the remembered features of old Salem, its fame is also perpetuated in the furniture exhibits of various museums. So valuable are its memorabilia that the Salem Maritime National Park Service, in cooperation with the U. S. Department of the Interior, has preserved old buildings and their furnishings, among which is this fine example of a high-back chair made in Salem about 1782. Its tilted back post and split-turning slats mark it as one of the earliest attempts to make Pilgrim-type chairs more comfortable

Among the merchants who gave Salem maritime distinction, few made a greater impression on history than the Derbys. The house at right, now the home of the chair presented here, is the oldest brick dwelling in the town. It was built in 1761 by Capt. Richard Derby for his son, Elias Hasket Derby. Of special interest is the fine paneling in the living room where, at the fireside, stands the fine high-back chair.

CONSTRUCTION of the chair should be started with the back posts. These parts are turnings made of 1¾" x 3¾" stock 48" long. Band saw work is necessary before the stock can be set up in the lathe. The sketch in Fig. 2 shows how the stock must be prepared. One end is laid out to form a 1¾" square. Center lines are drawn on this square and by means of a marking gauge are carried down the opposite faces and along the edge of the stock so that additional center lines can be established on the lower end. The width of the stock required for the leg as well as the curve at the lower end is now laid out. As shown in Fig. 2, the shaded section outside the straight portion of the leg is removed on the band saw. The lathe

centers are driven into the ends of the stock at the intersection of the center lines, and the stock is ready for the lathe.

The turning is to start 1" from the end and extend along the stock for 30" as shown in the sketch. When the stock has been turned down to a rough outside diameter of 1¾" the location of the various coves, beads and square

sections are marked off. A full-size pattern will be helpful.

The turning of the finial should be left until last. After it has been made the stock is removed from the lathe and the section at the lower end that was needed for centering is cut off on the band saw. The remaining curved section of the leg which is still square must be shaped to become round in section. The use of a spokeshave and block plane while the post is held in a vise will produce the round. The planed portion should be sandpapered thoroughly by hand to remove any sharp arris or tool marks. Sanding should be started with No. 1½ sandpaper and finer grades used until No. 00 gives the desired smoothness.

The front legs are made of 1¾" square stock 27" long. This length al-

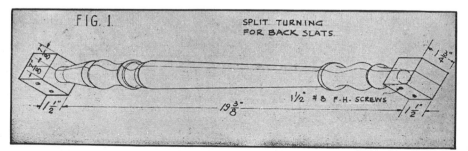

FIG. 1

SPLIT TURNING FOR BACK SLATS.

1½" #8 F.H. SCREWS

19³⁄₈"

· HIGH-BACK · RUSH · SEAT · CHAIR ·

· 1782 ·

Derby · House · Salem · Mass · · · Salem · Maritime · National · Site ·

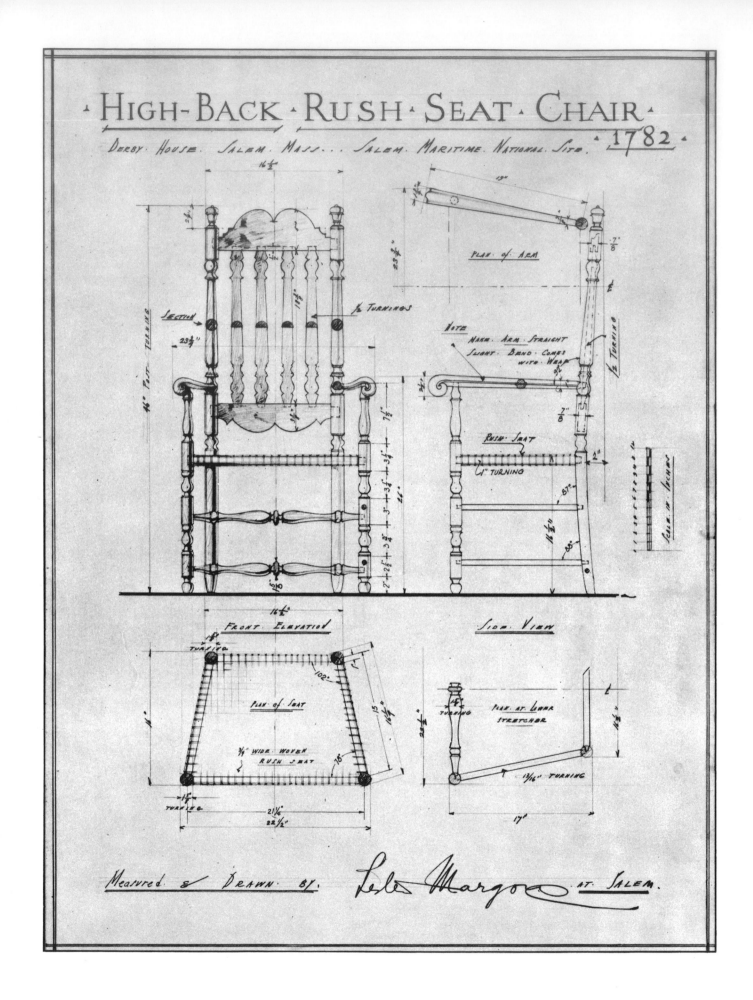

Plan of Arm

Note
Make · Arm · Straight
Slight · Bend · Comes
with · Wear

Section

½ Turnings

Front Elevation

Rush · Seat

1" Turning

Side View

Plan of Seat

¾" Wide · Woven
Rush · Seat

Plan · at · Lower
Stretcher

13/16" Turning

Measured & Drawn by   Lester Margon   at Salem.

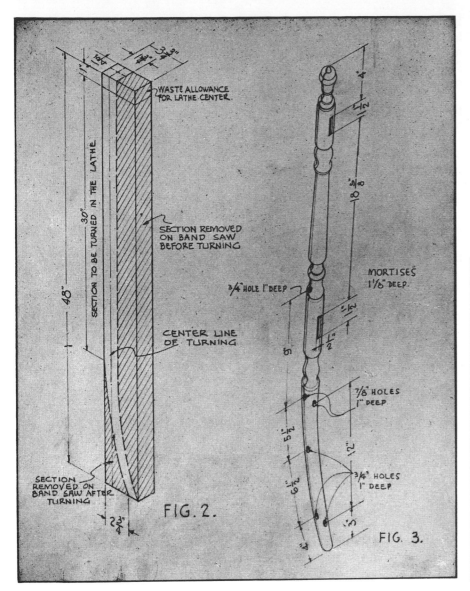

FIG. 2.

WASTE ALLOWANCE FOR LATHE CENTER.

SECTION REMOVED ON BAND SAW BEFORE TURNING

SECTION TO BE TURNED IN THE LATHE

30"

48"

CENTER LINE OF TURNING

SECTION REMOVED ON BAND SAW AFTER TURNING

2¾"

FIG. 3.

MORTISES 1⅛" DEEP.

¾" HOLE 1" DEEP

⅞ HOLES 1" DEEP

¾" HOLES 1" DEEP

end of the leg so that the arm may be joined to it.

The next operation is that of locating and boring holes that are to take the various stretchers and rails. Also, the laying out and cutting of mortises for the upper and lower back rails is done now. Fig. 3 shows the location as well as the diameter and depth of these holes that are to be made in the back posts. The location of the holes in the front legs that are to take the stretchers can be carried over from the back legs. It is important that these holes be located as shown in the plan view.

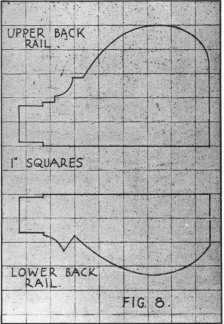

UPPER BACK RAIL.

1" SQUARES

LOWER BACK RAIL.

FIG. 8.

The side stretchers enter the back post so as to form an angle of 102 degrees with the back stretchers, while the holes in the front legs for the side stretchers must be at an angle of 78 degrees to the holes for the front stretchers. Cardboard templets cut at these angles will be useful in checking the boring angle of the bit as it enters the wood. The mortises in the back posts may be hand cut by boring a

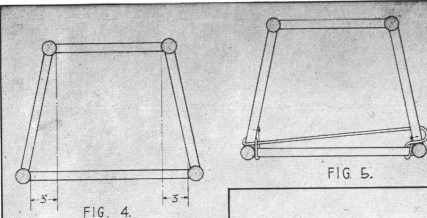

FIG. 4.

3" 3"

FIG. 5.

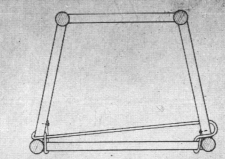

FIG. 6.

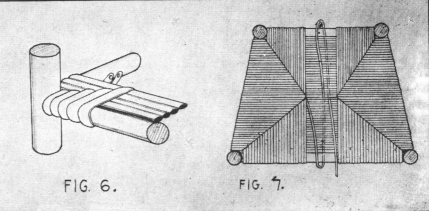

FIG. 7.

lows for waste at the live center of the lathe. The stock is turned down to a rough outside diameter of 1¾" with a gouge and is finished to an outside diameter of 1⅝" with a skew chisel. It is advisable to lay out a full-size drawing of the front legs so as to establish accurate diameter and lengths of the various elements that make up the turnings. A pin ¾" in diameter and ¾" long is turned on the upper series of ½" holes to a depth of 1⅛" and then cleaning out the remaining wood with a chisel, or the work may be done on the drill press.

The lower back stretcher is a turning finished to an outside diameter of 1³⁄₁₆" and an overall length of 15¼". The ends of this turning should have pins ¾" in diameter and 1" long turned on them to fit holes in the back posts. The back seat stretcher is a turning finished to an outside diameter of 1" and to the same overall length as the lower back stretcher. The pins on the ends of this rail are ⅞" in diameter and 1" long.

The upper and lower back rails are bandsawed cutouts made of ⅞" stock having tenons on each end to fit the mortises in the posts and having mortises cut in the straight edge of each member to take the split turnings that form the back. Full-size patterns of these members will have to be laid out to match the outline given in Fig. 8. After the patterns have been traced on the stock, tenons are cut on the ends. The scrolled edge may be cut on band saw or jig saw; edges are finished with file and sandpaper. The mortises that are to take the split turnings should not be laid out until after the turnings have been completed so that they can conform with the end of the turning.

The split turnings require four pieces of ⅞" x 1¾" stock 22⅜" long. Two pieces are fastened together with screws as shown in Fig. 1 to form one turning. There are to be two identical turnings. The contour of each turning should be identical to that of the posts.

From the completed turnings the waste blocks at the end area are cut off with a back saw so as to free each half. Mortises can now be laid out and cut in the upper and lower back rails to take these turnings. With the completion of this part of the work the entire back unit can be assembled.

The front section requires the use of two shaped stretchers made of 1¾" square stock 21¼" long and a seat stretcher finished to an outside diameter of 1". On all three pieces, pins 1" long should be turned at each end to fit the holes in the front legs. The turned members can be assembled with the front legs to form the front unit.

The side stretcher and side seat stretchers are straight turnings having an overall length of 15" with pins 1" long turned on each end to fit holes provided for them in the legs. The two former stretchers are finished to an outside diameter of 1³⁄₁₆" while the seat stretcher should have an outside diameter of 1". These turnings are joined to the previously completed back and front units.

The arms are made of 1¾" stock 2½" wide and 19" long. It is advisable to lay out a pattern of this member and then trace it on the stock. After the stock has been cut to shape on the band saw, the shaping of the arms to conform with the section shown in the main drawing must be done with carving tools. A ¾" hole for a dowel is bored in the end of the arm that is to be joined to the back post. The arm is fitted in place and the hole that is to receive the front leg

is marked. Assembly of the arm completes the woodwork.

Before the seat is woven, the chair should be finished with stain; paste filler is rubbed into the grain and four coats of thin white shellac or three coats of clear varnish should be applied, each being rubbed down with No. 00 steel wool. Wax should be applied last and the surface is then polished with a soft cloth.

The seat is made of rush, either natural or imitation material. The latter is the easier to obtain and to work with but is not as effective looking as the genuine material. The various steps in weaving the seat are shown in Figs. 4 to 7. The length of the back rail must be marked off on the front rail as shown in Fig. 4, this measurement being 3" from each front leg. The triangular sections at each side of the marks must be filled in first. As shown in Fig. 5 the end of the rush is fastened with a tack to the inside of the side rail at the right, then the rush is passed over the front rail, around it and back over the side rail. It is carried under the side rail, across the chair and over the opposite side rail. It is then brought under this rail and over the front rail at the left side, then under the front rail and along the side rail to the left where it is secured with a tack. This operation is repeated until the space remaining along the front rail is equivalent to the length of the back rail. From this point on, the weaving of the seat is one continuous operation. Fig. 7 shows how the center section is filled in.

Early Trumpet-Legged Colonial Highboy

This walnut highboy was photographed and measured at the Brooklyn Museum by courtesy of the Brooklyn Institute of Arts and Sciences

WHEN a chest of drawers is mounted on a stand it is generally known as a highboy. No doubt its origin back at the end of the 17th Century sprang from someone's idea of making an ordinary chest more convenient by eliminating the need for bending over to reach the drawers. The highboy illustrated in photograph and drawings is one of the first pieces made in this country, where its general type was extensively developed by American cabinetmakers of the period. These highboys were often longer, higher and deeper than chests of drawers that were contemporary.

Curiously the date of a highboy may readily be determined by the design and detail of its base. The upper chest of drawers sets into a frame on the top of the base which is often quite heavy and cut deep to receive the drawers. The top chest of drawers and the stand should never be separated because they belong together. The rather simple design of the cornice molding around the top is compensated by the richness of the drawer-front veneers and the fineness of the beading along the stiles.

Wallace Nutting in his book on furniture of the Pilgrim Century suggests that the name highboy was doubtless a sly joke at the often stilted appearance of these chests of drawers on a stand. There are highboys with four, five and six legs but the ones with the six legs are the most rigid and popular.

This example is from the American Rooms of the Brooklyn Museum of the Brooklyn Institute of Arts and Sciences. It was a gift of Frederic B. Pratt and dates from 1690 to 1700.

The original piece was constructed of solid walnut with walnut veneer applied to the drawer fronts and to exposed surfaces of the front, back and sides of the lower unit. Each of the drawer fronts requires matched crotch veneer while the herringbone border around each drawer panel is made by cutting straight-grained walnut veneer at a 45 degree angle. The border inlays are matched as shown in a detail of the main drawing.

The highboy should be made in two separate units and when completed they are placed one on the other but are never fastened together. The upper unit remains in place because of its size and weight. Work should be started with the base unit which, for construction purposes, may likewise be considered as being made up of two parts; namely, the case and the legs. The case requires two side pieces measuring $1'' \times 11\frac{1}{8}'' \times 22''$ and a back and front member each measuring $1'' \times 11\frac{1}{8}'' \times 38''$. When joined together by means or through dovetail joints as shown in Fig. 2, these pieces form a box. The next step is to lay out and cut the front member to allow for the drawer openings as shown in the main drawing and in Fig. 2. The dimensions for these openings are shown in the main drawing.

The next step is to lay out and cut the dovetail sockets in the inner face of the front and back members to take the inside stretchers as shown in Figs. 2 and

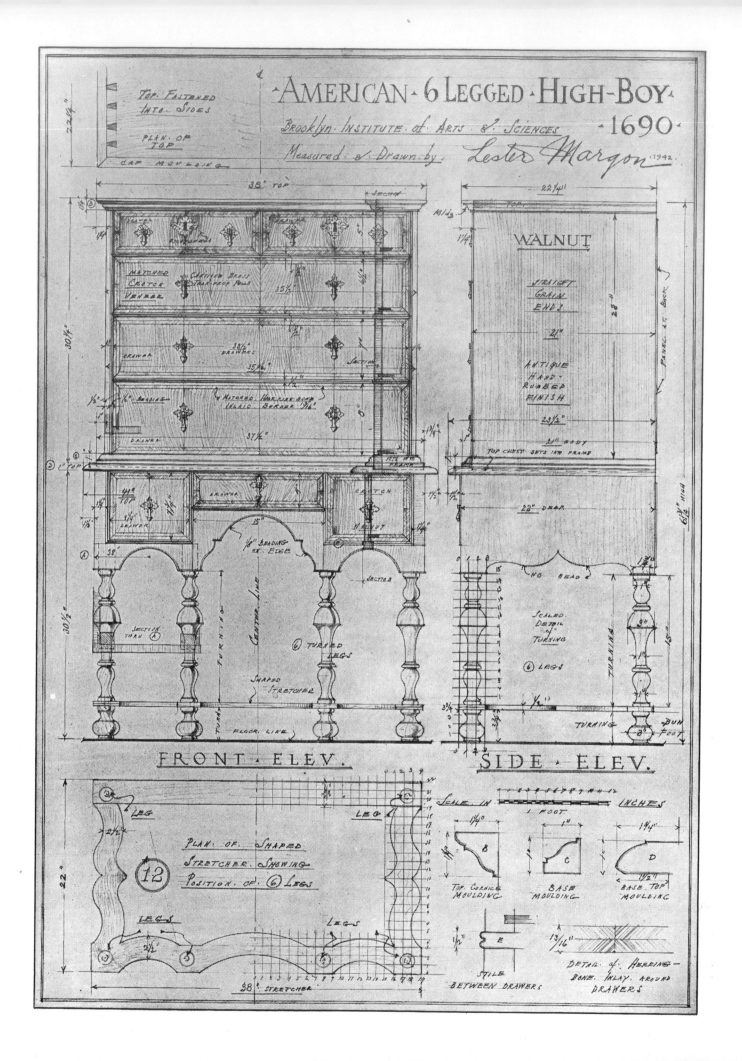

AMERICAN · 6 LEGGED · HIGH · BOY ·
· 1690 ·

Brooklyn · Institute · of · Arts · & · Sciences

Measured · & · Drawn · by · *Lester Margon* · 1942 ·

TOP FASTENED INTO SIDES

PLAN OF TOP

CAP MOULDING

WALNUT

STRAIGHT GRAIN ENDS

ANTIQUE HAND RUBBED FINISH

TOP CHEST SETS INTO FRAME

NO BEAD

SCALED DETAIL OF TURNING

6 LEGS

TURNING

BUN FOOT

MATCHED CROTCH VENEER

CUT OUT BRASS STRAP DROP PULLS

MATCHED HERRING-BONE INLAID BORDER

1/8" BEADING AT EDGE

6 TURNED LEGS

SHAPED STRETCHER

FLOOR LINE

SECTION THRU

CENTER LINE

FRONT · ELEV.

SIDE · ELEV.

LEG

PLAN · OF · SHAPED
STRETCHER · SHOWING
POSITION · OF · 6 · LEGS

(12)

LEGS

38" STRETCHER

SCALE IN   1 FOOT   INCHES

B
TOP CORNICE MOULDING

C
BASE MOULDING

D
BASE TOP MOULDING

E
STILE
BETWEEN DRAWERS

DETAIL OF HERRING-BONE INLAY AROUND DRAWERS

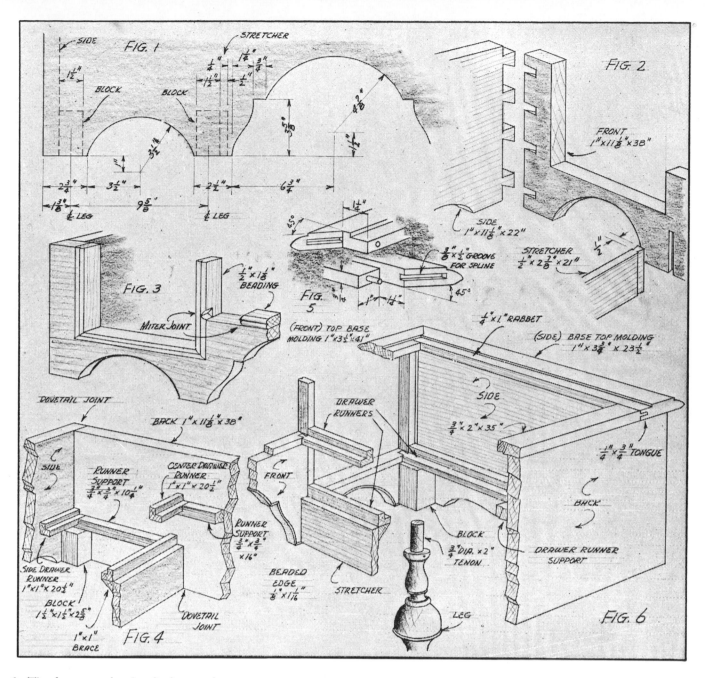

4. The front member has its lower edge shaped as shown in Fig. 1, while the contour of the lower edge of the side members is shown in the main drawing. After these scrolled edges have been laid out they are cut to shape on the band saw or jig saw and finished smooth with a chisel and spokeshave. Sandpaper should not be used on the curves of the front member as a beaded molding is to be glued to these edges. The two inside stretchers are made of $\frac{1}{2}$" stock each being $2\frac{7}{8}$" wide and 21" long. Dovetails as shown in Fig. 2 are cut on the ends of each and the stretchers are then fitted in sockets cut into the face of the front and back member.

The four side members and the two stretchers should be assembled temporarily and if found to fit together properly the work may be reassembled with glue. When clamps are applied it is im-

portant to make certain that the case is kept square. If necessary, two temporary braces of equal length, reaching to diagonal corners of the case, may be set in place and held with brads until the clamps are removed.

The next step is to apply straight-grained walnut veneer to the side members. This veneer should be allowed to lap over the edges a little so that it may be trimmed flush after the glue has set. After the side members have been trimmed veneer is applied to the front and back. The veneers can be held with the aid of a scrap board laid over the surface and held by ordinary hand screws.

The $\frac{1}{8}$" x $1\frac{1}{16}$" beading can now be made up and applied to the scrolled edge of the front piece as well as to the straight edges of the side members. This is a job that will require a consider-

able length of time but not a great deal of work. Since each piece is separate and the ends must be mitered it is necessary to shape the curved pieces first before cutting and mitering the straight pieces. The pieces to be shaped must first be steamed. While this is being done, forms which are the reverse of the curved cuts on the apron must be cut and made ready for use. The steamed stock is placed in position on the edge of the apron and is then forced into shape by use of clamps and the shaped blocks. These parts should remain clamped for at least 24 hours. After the clamps are removed the piece should have the shape of the curve into which it was set and should not lose this shape. They are cut to the required length with the ends mitered to match and fit against the adjoining piece. After the pieces have been fitted as outlined they are glued in place. The corner blocks which receive the tenoned legs are made and glued in place.

The $\frac{1}{2}''$ x $1\frac{1}{8}''$ beading which forms a molded border around the drawers is made up and applied as shown in Fig. 3. It should be noted that the molding at the center drawer space is mitered into the upright molding of the outer drawer spaces. This miter extends halfway through the width of the molding. The drawer runner supports are made up and fastened in place against the back member with $1\frac{1}{2}''$ No. 10 flathead screws. The drawer runners are made as shown in Figs. 4 and 6 and are joined to the front member by means of dovetail joints. The runners are glued in place before the triangular brace between the drawer runner and inside stretcher as shown in Fig. 4 is made up and applied.

The top base molding is made of two pieces of 1" x $3\frac{3}{4}''$ x $23\frac{1}{2}''$ stock for the sides, one piece of 1" x $3\frac{1}{2}''$ x 41" stock for the front and one piece of $\frac{3}{4}''$ x 2" x 35" stock for the back. The two side members and one front member have a $\frac{1}{4}''$ x 1" rabbet cut along the edge as shown in Figs. 5 and 6. The ends of these pieces are joined together as shown in Fig. 5. The back member is joined to the side members by means of a tongue-and-groove joint as shown in Fig. 6. The outer edge of the side and front members is molded as shown in Detail (D) of the main drawing. The four members are assembled with glue to form a frame. Clamps are applied to hold the parts while the glue is given time to set. Be sure that the frame is square and remains so while the clamps are on. After the clamps have been removed, the frame is fastened to the lower case by means of $1\frac{1}{2}''$ No. 10 flathead wood screws driven through the rabbet of the frame and the back mem-

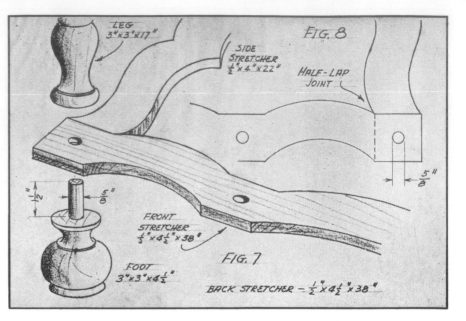

ber and into the edges of the side and back members of the lower case. The upper case is to set in the rabbet of this frame. This work completes the case of the lower unit. Construction of the legs and stretchers can now be undertaken.

Six pieces of stock the rough size of which should be $3\frac{1}{4}''$ square and 17" long are required for the legs, while six pieces $3\frac{1}{4}''$ square and $4\frac{1}{2}''$ long are required for the feet. It should be noticed that no allowance has been made for waste at the ends of the stock. This is because the marks left by the live and dead centers need not be removed as they cannot be seen when the legs and feet are set in place.

Stock for the legs is set up in the lathe and turned down to a rough diameter with a gouge and turned to the finished diameter of 3" with a skew chisel. The limits of the various cuts are marked off on the wood cylinder by taking the necessary measurements from the graph-squared leg drawing in the

side elevation. When the cylinder is being marked the location of the dowel on the upper end of the leg should be placed at the dead center. Parting tool and calipers are used to establish the various depths and from there on the turning is completed in the conventional way. The $\frac{3}{4}''$ x 2" tenon on the upper end, shown in Fig. 6, should be turned last. Each leg should be sandpapered thoroughly before it is removed from the lathe. A $\frac{5}{8}''$ hole bored to a depth of $1\frac{1}{8}''$ is made in the lower end of each leg to take the pin on the foot. Fig. 7 shows the pin. The foot is made up in the same manner as the leg.

The stretchers are made of $\frac{1}{2}''$ stock the lengths and widths of which are given in Fig. 7. A full-size pattern of the front and side stretchers must be enlarged from the main drawing and traced on the stock. Cutting to shape is done on the band saw or jig saw and finishing is accomplished with spokeshave and chisel. The four members

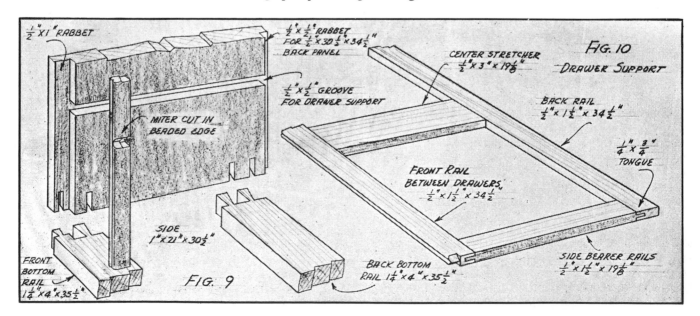

are fitted together by means of half-lap joints. Holes that are to take the pins on the feet should be located as shown in the drawing and bored with a $\frac{5}{8}''$ bit.

The upper case is made of two side members, a top member, two bottom rails, a back panel and three drawer support frames. They are made up in the same order as given. The stock for the sides is cut out to the size given in Fig. 9. A rabbet $\frac{1}{2}'' \times 1''$ is cut along the forward edge for the beaded molding while a $\frac{1}{2}'' \times \frac{1}{2}''$ rabbet is cut along the back edge for the back panel. Dadoes $\frac{1}{2}'' \times \frac{1}{2}''$ are cut across the inside face of the side members to take the drawer support frames. The top is made of a piece of stock $1'' \times 21 \times 35\frac{1}{2}''$. These three members are joined together by means of dovetail joints as shown in a detail of the main drawing. The bottom rails are made up and joined to the sides as shown in Fig. 9. The beaded molding is made and glued in place in the rabbet of the side members.

The three drawer support frames are made up as shown in Fig. 10. They are fitted together by means of tongue-and-groove joints. The partition between the two upper drawers is made up in the form of a frame similar to the one shown in Fig. 10, but having an overall size of $\frac{1}{2}''$ high and $20\frac{5}{8}''$ deep. The drawer support frame for two small drawers has a $\frac{1}{4}'' \times \frac{1}{2}''$ groove cut along the center stretcher up to $\frac{1}{2}''$ of the front. From this point on, a miter cut is made.

A filler made of $\frac{1}{4}'' \times \frac{3}{4}''$ stock is applied to the underside of the top along the front edge as shown in the front elevation of the main drawing. The top and base moldings as shown in Details (B) and (C) of the main drawings are applied with glue and brads.

The drawers are made up to fit the various openings. All joints should be dovetailed and the drawer bottoms which may be made of $\frac{1}{4}''$ plywood are set into grooves cut in the front, side and back members of the drawers. The matched crotch veneer is cut to the required size and is then applied to the drawer fronts. A $1\frac{3}{8}''$ border should be left to take the herringbone inlay. After this inlay is in place the hardware should be applied. In order to finish the cabinet it will be necessary to remove all hardware. The work is stained and then four to six coats of white shellac are applied. Each coat should be rubbed down with fine steel wool. Wax, well rubbed and polished, will complete the work of constructing this magnificent highboy.

Pennsylvania Dutch Wagon-Seat Bench

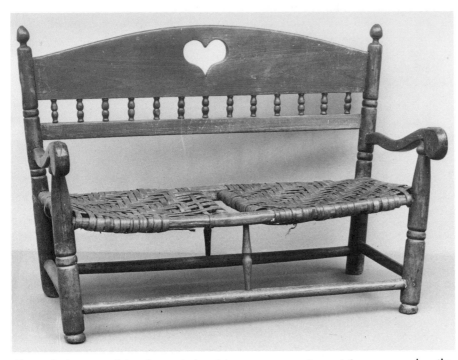

This intriguing type of bench was designed to serve as an extra seat in a wagon when the family went visiting or to market. The original is in the Metropolitan Museum of Art

ONE OF the recent exhibitions at the Metropolitan Museum of Art in New York was a room of Pennsylvania Dutch Arts and Crafts. The display included furniture made by early settlers who endeavored to recreate the comfort and surroundings they had left behind in their former homes. In their new country they incorporated their own native arts and crafts into the brightly painted, and sometimes crudely fashioned, pieces of furniture.

From a vastly intriguing collection of furniture of this period the wagon seat illustrated here has been selected for reproduction. These seats, or benches, were placed inside the wagons for the family to sit on during rides to market or to a neighboring settlement.

It is interesting to see how all four legs incline and to learn how short they are. This was done because the benches were placed on various sorts of blocks inside the wagon, and sometimes on a cleverly devised spring which absorbed the jolts of the wagon. Whatever sort of platform was used, it made up for the short legs. When not in use these wagon seats often became children's benches in the home. For this purpose the benches are well suited today and offer the craftsman an opportunity to reproduce one of the most interesting pieces of this period. Of course, the legs could be made longer than specified if a full-grown bench is considered more practical.

Construction of the bench is started by cutting out the stock for the legs.

The back legs are made of two pieces of 2″ square stock, 30½″ long, including 1″ for waste at the live center, while the front legs are made of two pieces 2″ square and 19″ long. The front legs do not require any waste as the center marks will not show at either end, since one end of the leg rests on the floor and the other end is covered by the arm.

The relative position of each leg should be established, then marked for identification so that the mortises and holes can be laid out in their proper places. The usual procedure is to turn the legs to the required shape first, then lay out and cut the mortises and holes, but since the rails that form the seat frame and the stretchers are at right angles to one another, it will be easier to lay out and cut the mortises and holes first. There will be no difficulty in turning the legs after the holes have been made, provided a fairly high speed is used and the tools are kept sharp.

The locations of the holes for the stretchers and seat frame members are shown in Fig. 1 and in the main drawing. The mortises that are to take the upper and lower back rails, as well as the mortise that is to take the arm, are located in the center of the back leg as shown in Fig. 1. All holes that are to take the stretchers and seat frame members are bored with a 1″ auger bit and are made 1″ deep. The holes in the back legs for the side stretcher and side seat frame members are bored at an angle of 84 degrees, as shown in the side elevation of the main drawing. The holes in the front legs that take the other end of these members are bored at 90 degrees. The holes that are to take the back and front stretcher and the back and front seat frame member are bored at an angle of 86 degrees as shown in the front elevation. The mortise in the back leg, made for the arm, is cut at an angle of 90 degrees.

After the mortises have been cut and

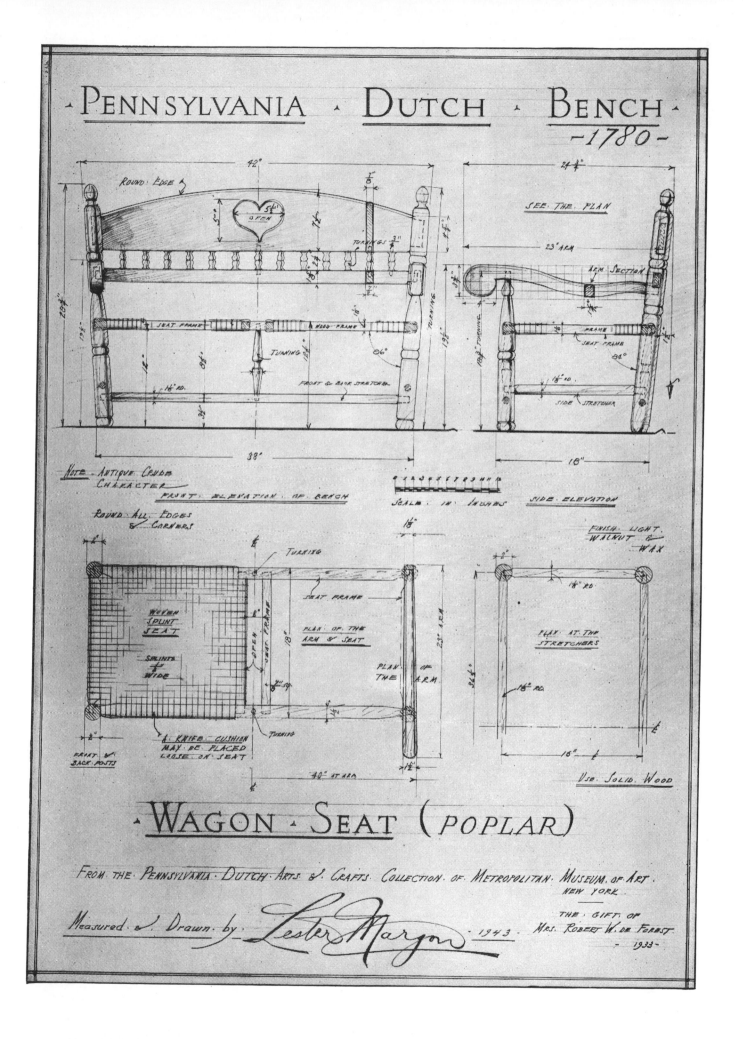

· PENNSYLVANIA · DUTCH · BENCH ·
-1780-

· WAGON · SEAT · (POPLAR)

FROM · THE · PENNSYLVANIA · DUTCH · ARTS · & · CRAFTS · COLLECTION · OF · METROPOLITAN · MUSEUM · OF · ART ·

NEW YORK

Measured & Drawn by Lester Margon · 1943 ·

THE · GIFT · OF
MRS · ROBERT · W · DE FOREST
- 1933 -

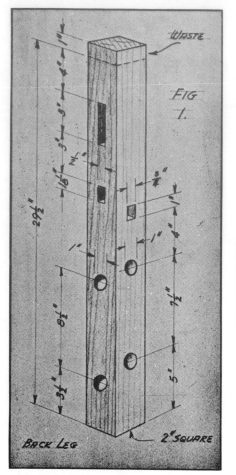

FIG. 1.

BACK LEG 2" SQUARE

WASTE

the holes bored, each member is set up between centers in the lathe and is turned to the required shape. A ¾" tenon, 1" long, is turned on the upper end of the front leg to fit into the arm. When the turnings have been completed, the work should be sandpapered before the waste stock at the upper end of the back legs is cut off.

The side stretchers are made of two pieces of 1⅛" square or round stock, 17" long. If square stock is used, it should be turned down to the required diameter. The finished stretcher should have an overall length of 16" with tenons 1" in diameter and 1" long turned on each end. The front and back stretchers are made of 1⅛" stock 37½" long. They are shaped in the same manner as the side stretchers; they have 1" tenons on each end and have an overall finished length of 36½".

The back and front seat frame members are made of 1⅛" stock, 1½" wide and 39½" long. The tenons on the back member are turned off center as shown in the seat plan and in Fig. 3. The front member has centered tenons. In both cases the finished length of the piece should be 38½". The sides of the seat frame are made of 1⅛" x 1½" stock 17¾" long. The tenons on each end of these members are turned off

center in the same manner as those on the back seat frame member. The finished length of these pieces should be 16¾". Mortises should be located and cut in the edge of the front and back members of the seat frame to take the center pieces as shown in the plan and in Fig. 3. These center frame pieces should be made of ⅞" square stock and should measure 17" long including 1" tenons on each end. All seat frame members should have the upper face as well as the outside edges rounded off as shown so that the splints that are used for the seat can be woven around

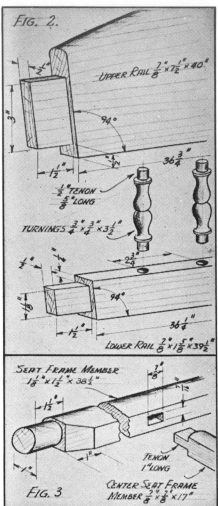

FIG. 2.

UPPER RAIL ⅞" x 7½" x 40"

94°

36¾"

½" TENON ⅝" LONG

TURNINGS ¾" x ¾" x 3½"

94°

36¼"

LOWER RAIL ⅞" x 1⅝" x 39½"

SEAT FRAME MEMBER 1⅛" x 1½" x 38½"

TENON 1" LONG

CENTER SEAT FRAME MEMBER ⅞" x ⅞" x 17"

FIG. 3

the frame without being broken.

The two upright braces between the stretchers and the seat frame are turnings made of 1⅛" stock finished to an overall length of 8½". Tenons, ½" in diameter and ⁹⁄₁₆" long, are turned on each end. Holes are bored in the stretchers and the seat frame to take these turnings.

The arms are made of two pieces of 1⅛" stock 3¾" wide and 23" long. A full-size pattern of these members should be drawn on graph squares and then traced on the stock. A tenon is cut on the end to fit into the mortise in

the back leg. The arm is cut to shape on the band saw or jig saw and is finished with spokeshave and file.

The upper back rail is made of a piece of ⅞" stock 7½" wide and 40" long. Tenons are cut on each and, as shown in Fig. 2, to fit the mortised legs. The upper edge is curved as shown in the front elevation. This is done on band saw or jig saw. The upper edge is then rounded with a spokeshave. The heart-shaped opening is laid out and is cut on the jig saw. The lower rail is made of a piece of ⅞" stock 1⅝" wide and 39½" long. Tenons are cut on each end to fit mortises in the back legs. Holes for the turnings are located and bored in the back rails to a depth of ⅝", using a ½" auger bit.

Assembly of the bench is started by gluing the side stretcher and seat frame to the front leg, then the arm is placed on the end of this member. This assembled unit is joined to the back leg to complete this unit. The two center frame members are joined to the back and front seat frame pieces. The turned braces are set in place and the lower stretchers joined to them. This assembled unit is joined to the completed side unit. The small turnings are set in place between the upper and lower back rails and this unit is assembled to the side unit. The second side unit can now be put together and joined to the rails, front and back seat frame member and the stretchers.

The completed woodwork should be given a coat of light walnut stain and be followed by several coats of wax.

The seats are woven with ½" ash or oak splints. Splints are applied in one direction first, from right to left as shown in Fig. 5. The splints applied from front to back are then woven as shown in the sketch. When it is necessary to join the end of one splint to the next, the pieces are cut with a sharp knife as shown in Fig. 4.

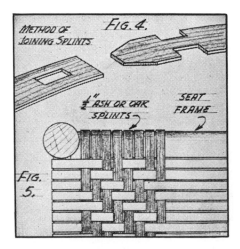

METHOD OF JOINING SPLINTS FIG. 4.

½" ASH OR OAK SPLINTS

SEAT FRAME

FIG. 5.

PENNSYLVANIA ✦ GERMAN ✦ 1765
CUPBOARD

From the fine old kitchen of the Miller of Millbach, which is now exhibited in the Philadelphia Museum of Art, this dresser was chosen because of its unusual and very elaborate scrollwork

POPULARLY, a cupboard like this one from the Philadelphia Museum of Art is known as a Welsh dresser. The upper part is open; the lower portion contains two drawers and is enclosed below them by paneled doors. Of special interest in this particular piece is the way in which the sides have been cut out in exceptionally elaborate scrollwork.

Many of these Pennsylvania cupboards were fancifully painted and even embellished with legends. Reproductions of such pieces usually fit better in a modern home if left unadorned. As they are, basically, peasant pieces, the appearance should have a pleasant, homely quality. Too precise, machine-like accuracy in construction or too fine a finish on this type of furniture would be out of place and would destroy the somewhat primitive, peasant character that is so beguiling.

The construction of the cabinet is divided into two separate units, each being built independently, then assembled. These units are the cupboard or lower unit, shown in the main drawing and in Figs. 1 and 5, and the upper or open shelf unit shown in the main drawing and Fig. 15.

As shown in Fig. 1, the cupboard carcase consists of two end panels, an upper and intermediate frame and bottom. Work should be started with the preparation of the end panels. Two pieces of 1⅛″ stock 15½″ wide and 38¼″ long will be required. As shown in Figs. 1 and 2, the bottom panel is joined to the end panels by means of a dado. The shelf is set into a grain.

The front and back drawer rails as well as the upper front and back rails are to be set into dovetail sockets. The locations and sizes of the dado, gain and dovetail sockets are given in Fig. 2. These are laid out on the in-

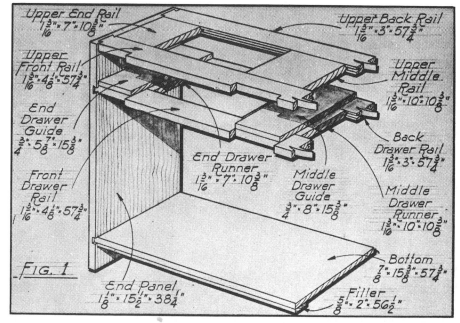

FIG. 1

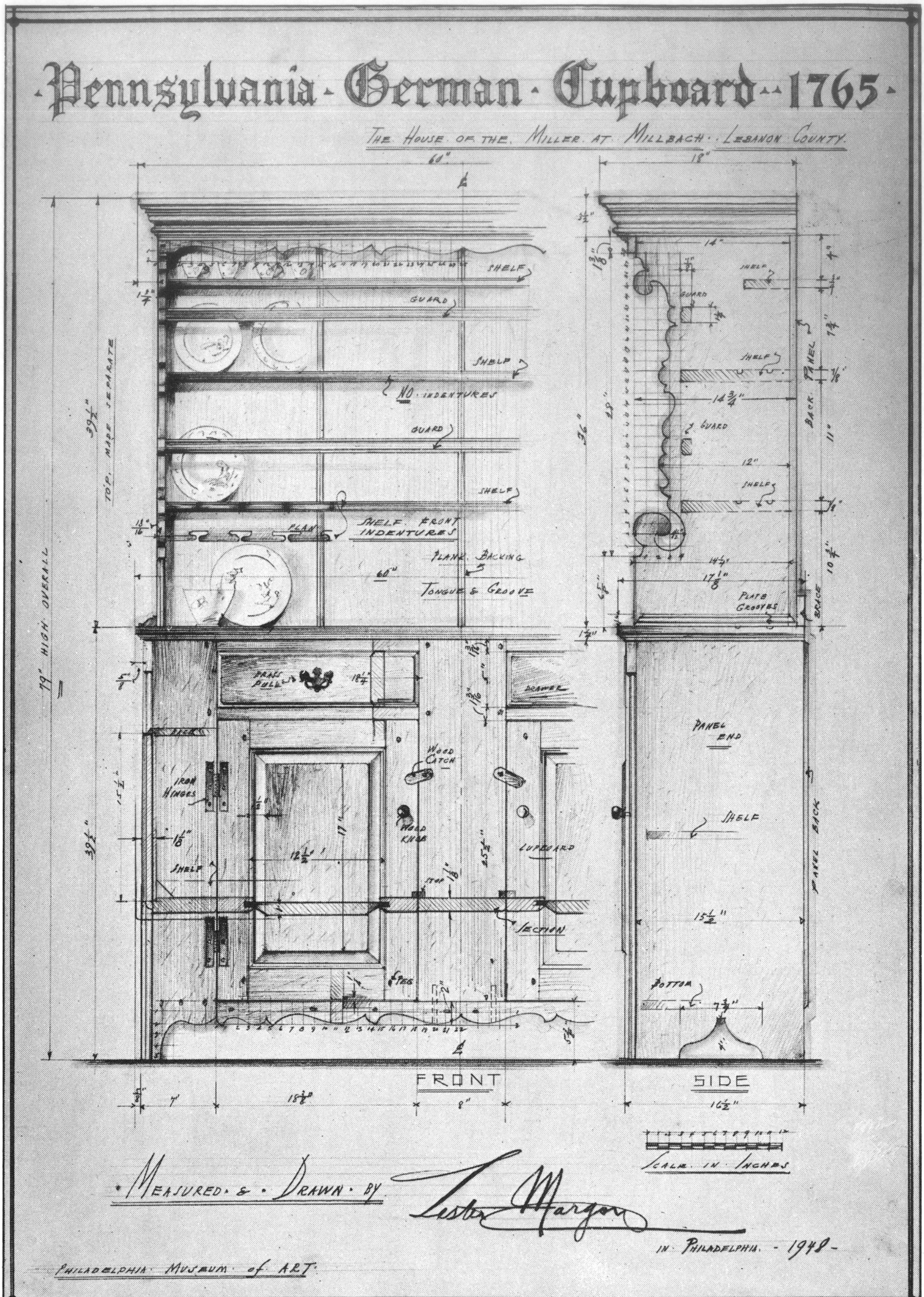

Pennsylvania German Cupboard 1765
THE HOUSE OF THE MILLER AT MILLBACH · LEBANON COUNTY
SHELF
GUARD
NO INDENTURES
SHELF FRONT INDENTURES
PLAN
PLANK BACKING
TONGUE & GROOVE
TOP, MADE SEPARATE
79" HIGH OVERALL
BRASS PULLS
DRAWER
IRON HINGES
WOOD CATCH
WOOD KNOB
CUPBOARD
SECTION
PANEL END
BACK PANEL
PLATE GROOVES
BRACE
PANEL BACK
BOTTOM
FRONT
SIDE
SCALE IN INCHES
MEASURED & DRAWN BY
Lester Margon
IN PHILADELPHIA - 1948 -
PHILADELPHIA MUSEUM of ART

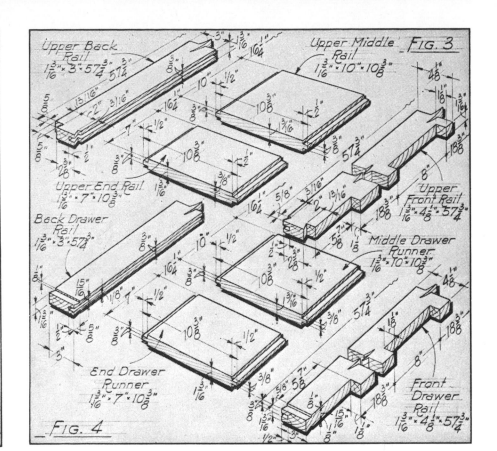

FIG. 2

End Panel $1\frac{1}{8}'' \times 15\frac{1}{2}'' \times 38\frac{1}{4}''$

FIG. 3

Upper Back Rail $1\frac{3}{16}'' \times 3'' \times 57\frac{3}{4}''$

Upper Middle Rail $1\frac{3}{16}'' \times 10'' \times 10\frac{3}{8}''$

Upper End Rail $1\frac{3}{16}'' \times 7'' \times 10\frac{3}{8}''$

Upper Front Rail $1\frac{3}{16}'' \times 4\frac{1}{8}'' \times 57\frac{3}{4}''$

FIG. 4

Back Drawer Rail $1\frac{3}{16}'' \times 3'' \times 57\frac{3}{4}''$

Middle Drawer Runner $1\frac{3}{16}'' \times 10'' \times 10\frac{3}{8}''$

End Drawer Runner $1\frac{3}{16}'' \times 7'' \times 10\frac{3}{8}''$

Front Drawer Rail $1\frac{3}{16}'' \times 4\frac{1}{8}'' \times 57\frac{3}{4}''$

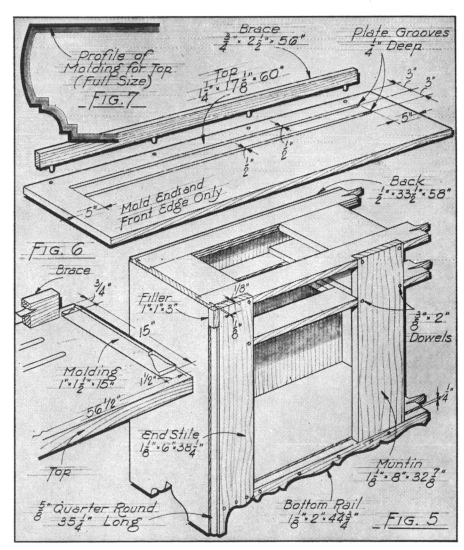

Profile of Molding for Top (Full Size) **FIG. 7**

Brace $\frac{3}{4}'' \times 2\frac{1}{2}'' \times 56''$

Plate Grooves $\frac{1}{4}''$ Deep

Top $1\frac{1}{4}'' \times 17\frac{7}{8}'' \times 60''$

FIG. 6

Mold Ends and Front Edge Only

Back $\frac{1}{2}'' \times 33\frac{1}{2}'' \times 58''$

Brace

Filler $1'' \times 1'' \times 3''$

Dowels $\frac{3}{8}'' \times 2''$

Molding $1'' \times 1\frac{1}{2}'' \times 15''$

Top

$\frac{5}{8}''$ Quarter Round $35\frac{1}{4}''$ Long

End Stile $1\frac{1}{8}'' \times 6'' \times 38\frac{1}{4}''$

Muntin $1\frac{1}{8}'' \times 8'' \times 32\frac{7}{8}''$

Bottom Rail $1\frac{1}{8}'' \times 2'' \times 44\frac{3}{4}''$

FIG. 5

side face of each end panel. The cutting of the dado and gain may be done on the bench saw with the aid of a dado saw. The cleaning out of the forward end of the gain will have to be done by hand with a chisel. The cutting of the dovetail sockets must of necessity be hand work, requiring the use of a back saw or dovetail saw, a chisel and a router if one is available.

The cut-out at the lower end of the end panels will require the preparation of a pattern; then the outline traced on the stock at its proper location. The cutting out of this section can be done on the band or jig saw. The surfaces are dressed with a file and sandpaper. With the completion of the end panels, work on the upper and middle frames can be undertaken.

As shown in Figs. 3 and 4, the various members in both frames are identical, therefore the cutting and dressing of the pieces for each frame should be done at the same time. The upper back rail in Fig. 3 and the back drawer rail in Fig. 4 will require the preparation of two pieces of $1\frac{3}{16}'' \times 3''$ x $57\frac{3}{4}''$. The front rails will require two pieces $1\frac{3}{16}'' \times 4\frac{1}{8}'' \times 57\frac{3}{4}''$. The end rails and drawer runners will take four pieces $1\frac{3}{16}'' \times 7'' \times 10\frac{3}{8}''$ while the middle rail and drawer runner will take two pieces $1\frac{3}{16}'' \times 10'' \times 10\frac{3}{8}''$.

A $\frac{3}{8}'' \times \frac{1}{2}''$ groove is cut along the inside edge of the front and back rails

$\frac{3}{8}''$ from the upper face as shown in Figs. 3 and 4. These grooves are to take the tongues cut on the ends of the short rails and drawer runners. The tongues on the ends of these latter members should be $\frac{3}{8}''$ thick and $\frac{1}{2}''$ long, being located $\frac{3}{8}''$ from the upper face. The tongues are produced by cutting rabbets on both faces of the drawer runners and short rails.

As shown in Fig. 3, dovetails are cut on the ends of the front and back rails to fit the sockets previously made in the end panels. These dovetails are laid out following the dimension given in the sketch; then the layout is checked against the socket before the dovetail is cut. A dovetail saw or back saw can be used for the cutting of the dovetail. Fitting of the dovetail to the socket should be done with a chisel.

Figure 4 shows the dovetail that is to be laid out and cut on the ends of the drawer rails. After these are laid out, the shoulders of the dovetails are cut with a saw, but the shaping of the cheeks should be done with the chisel. These dovetails are fitted to the sockets in the end panels. They slide in from the outer edges.

The final step in the preparation of these units is the cutting of the recesses in the front rails as shown in Figs. 3 and 4 to take the end stiles and muntin as shown in Fig. 5.

With the completion of this por-

tion of the work, the upper frame, consisting of the upper front and back rails, the upper end rails and the upper middle rail, can be glued up. After the clamps have been applied to the assembled frame, it is important that the frame be checked for squareness. If the frame should be out of square, a slight shifting of the clamps will bring it back into line.

While the frame is in the clamps, the work of preparing the bottom panel and filler as shown in Fig. 1 can be undertaken. After these pieces have been cut to size, the bottom panel is fitted to the dadoes previously cut for this purpose in the end panels.

Assembling of the carcase will require the joining of the end panels to the bottom, then applying clamps to hold them in position. The assembled upper frame can be set in place and glue applied to all butting surfaces of the joints. The middle frame will have to be assembled within the carcase. To do this, the back drawer rail is slid into the dovetail sockets from the back; then the various drawer runners are set into the groove in the forward edge of this member. The front drawer rail is finally joined to the runners and end panels by sliding the dovetails into the sockets from the forward edge of the cabinet. Clamps should be applied wherever necessary to pull up the pieces and hold them

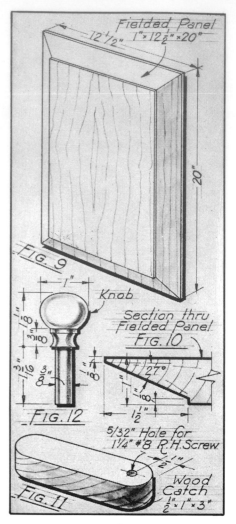

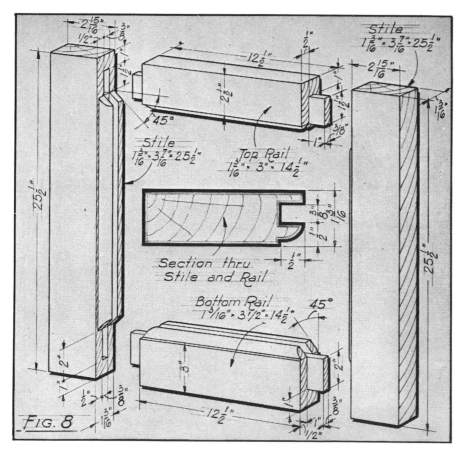

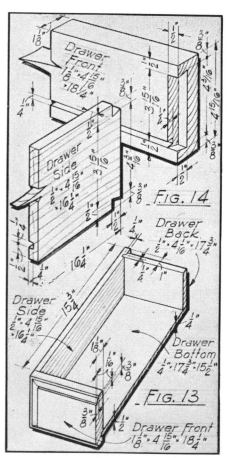

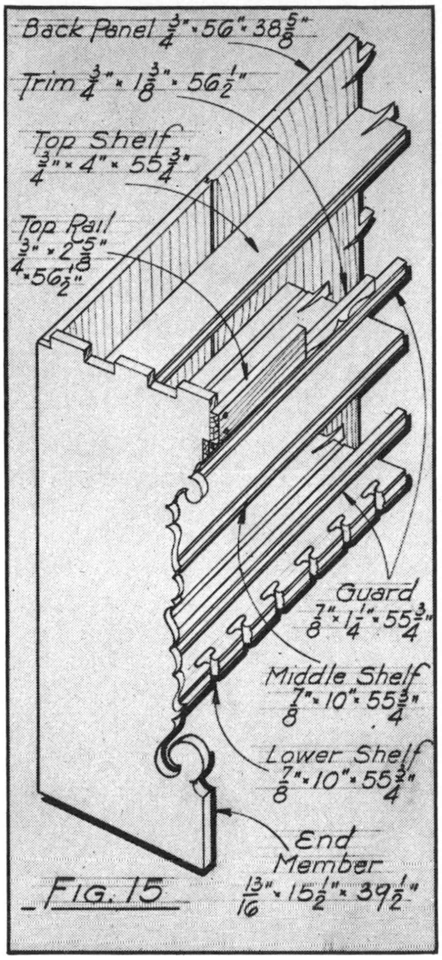
Back Panel 3/4"×56"×38 5/8"
Trim 3/4"×1 3/4"×56 1/2"
Top Shelf 3/4"×4"×55 3/4"
Top Rail 3/4"×2 5/8"×56 1/2"
Guard 7/8"×1 1/4"×55 3/4"
Middle Shelf 7/8"×10"×55 3/4"
Lower Shelf 7/8"×10"×55 3/4"
End Member 13/16"×15 1/2"×39 1/2"
FIG. 15

securely in position while the glue is given time to set.

As shown in Fig. 1, the drawer guides are cut to the sizes specified, then glued to the middle frame as indicated. The filler strip attached to the under face at the forward edge of the bottom is glued in place and held by clamps.

The shelf will require a piece of 3/4″ stock 14½″ wide and 57¾″ long. The ends of this member are fitted to the gains cut into the end panels, then slid in from the back.

The end stiles as shown in Fig. 5 require two pieces of 1⅛″ stock 6″ wide and 38¼″ long. A full-size pattern of the contour at the lower end of these members will have to be prepared and traced on the stock. The band or jig saw can be used to cut these members to shape.

A ⅛″ x ⅛″ rabbet is cut along the inside face at the outer edge of each stile as shown in Fig. 5. The stiles are glued to the various butting members, then ⅜″ holes 2″ deep are bored as indicated to take tapered pins made of hardwood. These pins should be slightly less than ⅜″ square at the small end and 7/16″ square at the large end and should be 2½″ long. Glue is applied to the hole and the sides of the pins; then the pins are driven into the holes. The excess of the pin remaining outside the hole can be dressed flush with the surface after the glue has set.

The muntin shown in Fig. 5 is cut to the required size and secured in the same manner as the stiles. The bottom rail will require a piece of 1⅛″ x 2″ x 44¾″ stock with the lower edge shaped to the contour shown in the front view of the main drawing. This member is secured to the carcase bottom in the same manner as stiles and muntin. As shown in the front view, two wood pins are inserted from the underside of the bottom rail to secure the lower end of the muntin.

The back panel, shown in Fig. 5, can now be prepared, cut to size and glued in place. Filler blocks made of 1″ square stock 3″ long are cut and glued in the rabbet at the outer corners of the carcase. A ⅝″ quarter-round 35¼″ long completes the filling in of this rabbet as shown in Fig. 5.

As shown in Fig. 6, the top is cut to size and the two ends and forward edge are molded as shown in Fig. 7. The plate grooves are located and cut with a router bit set up in the drill press or in a power-driven portable router. They may be cut by hand with the aid of a gouge. The brace to which

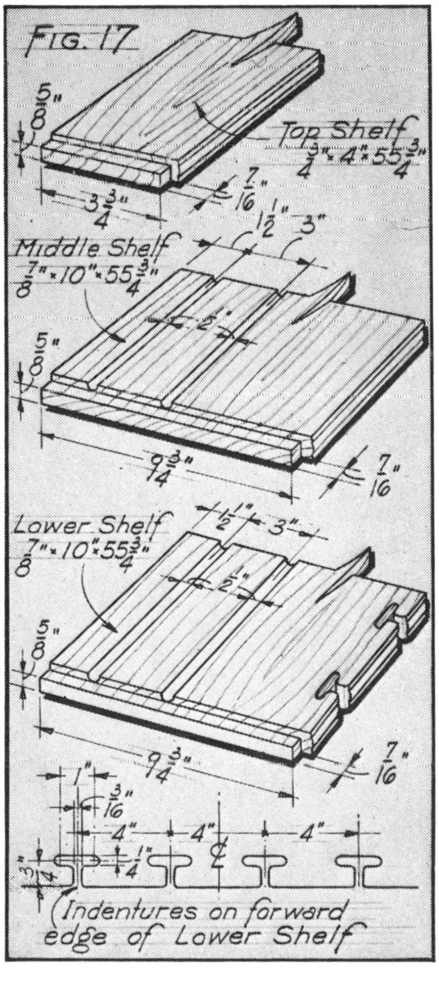
FIG. 17
Top Shelf 3/4"×4"×55 3/4"
Middle Shelf 7/8"×10"×55 3/4"
Lower Shelf 7/8"×10"×55 3/4"
Indentures on forward edge of Lower Shelf

the upper unit is secured is cut to size and joined to the top by means of dowels. Two strips made of 1″ x 1½″ x 15″ stock molded on both ends and one edge are glued to the upper face of the top at the location shown in Fig. 6. The top is fastened in place by driving 1¾″ No. 8 flathead screws through the members of the top frame and into the undersurface.

Each door frame as shown in Fig. 8 will require two stiles and two rails cut to the sizes given. The inside edge of each member is grooved and molded as shown in section. Mortises are laid out and cut on the inside edge of the stiles; then tenons are cut on the ends of the rails to fit these mortises. The molding on all members

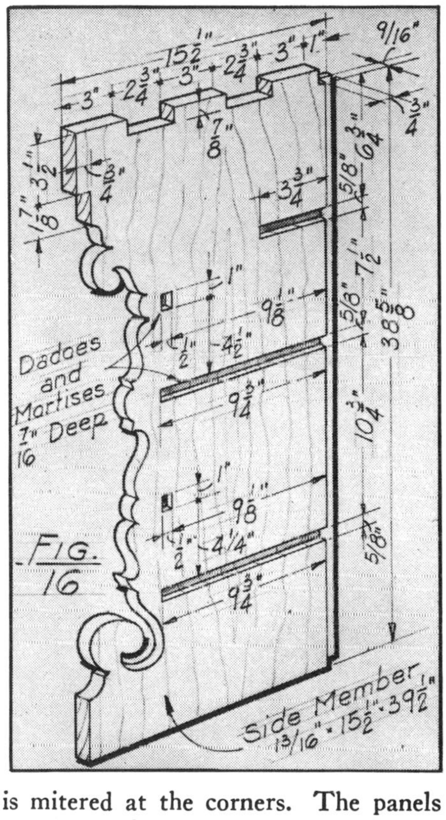
FIG. 16
Dadoes and Mortises 7/16" Deep
Side Member 13/16"×15 1/2"×39 1/2"

is mitered at the corners. The panels are cut to the size and shape shown in Fig. 9. The cutting of the bevel to produce the fielded panel can be done on the bench saw, using a hollow-ground planer saw. The dimensions for the fielding are shown in Fig. 10. The panels should be sandpapered thoroughly before they are assembled.

When the doors have been completed, they should be fitted to the cabinet and hung with wrought iron H-hinges. The wood catches are made up as shown in Fig. 11 and secured to the cabinet with 1¼″ No. 8 roundhead wood screws. The door pull or knob is a turning shaped as shown in Fig. 12. It is secured to the door stile by boring a ⅜″ hole in this member and gluing it in place.

The drawers will require stock as specified in Fig. 13. A ¼" x ¼" groove is cut on the inside face of the front and side members ½" from the lower edge to take the bottom panel. The side members are joined to the front member by means of a dovetail, the details of which are shown in

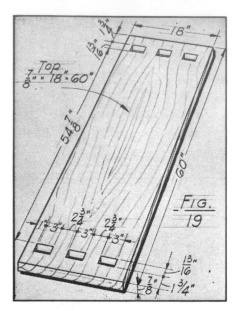

Fig. 14. The drawer back has a ¼" x ¼" rabbet cut along each end which fits a dado cut across the inside face of the drawer sides as shown in Fig. 13. The outer face of the drawer front has a molding cut on the edges and ends. The drawers are assembled by gluing the side members to the front members, then inserting the back. The drawer bottom is slid into the grooves from the back. The drawer pulls should be similar in design to those shown in the photograph and on the main drawing. They should be installed at this time.

Strips of wood ½" x 1" x 25½" should be glued to the inside face of the muntin as shown in the front view on the main drawing to act as door stops.

The upper unit shown in Fig. 15 should be started by preparing the side members. Two pieces of stock 13/16" x 15½" x 39½" will be needed. The gains and mortises that are to take the shelves and guards should be laid out

as shown in Fig. 16. Cutting of the gains may be done on the bench saw. The forward portion of the gain will have to be cleaned out by hand. The mortises can best be cut by hand. A ¾" x 9/16" rabbet is cut along the inside face at the rear edge to take the back panel. Pins are laid out at the upper end as shown in Fig. 16 to take the top member. Cutting of these pins

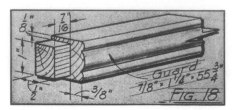

can best be done on the bench saw.

The scrolled forward edge will require the laying out of a full-size pattern, then the tracing of this pattern on the stock. The cutting out of the contour can be done on the band or jig saw. The finishing of the sawn edge is done with a file and sandpaper.

The shelves are cut to the sizes given in Fig. 17. Tenons are laid out and cut at each end to fit the gains in the side members. Plate grooves are cut in the middle and lower shelves in the same manner as were those cut in the cupboard top. The forward edge of the lower shelf has indentures laid out and cut as shown in the detail. This forms a spoon rack. The forward edges of all three shelves are molded.

The plate guards shown in Fig. 18 are cut to the required size. Tenons are laid out at each end, then they are cut to fit their respective mortises in the side members. The forward surface of the guards is molded. The upper unit is assembled by joining the shelves and guards to the end members.

The top rail shown in Figs. 15 and 20 is joined to the end members with wood pins. The trim shown in the same figures is cut to size; then the lower edge is scrolled as shown in the front view of the main drawing. The trim is also secured in place with wood pins. The top shown in Fig. 19 has three mortises laid out and cut as in-

dicated to take the pins on the upper end of the side members. The top is joined to the side members with glue.

Figure 20 shows the various components that make up the crown molding. The moldings are cut to the shapes indicated and secured with glue. The back panel shown in Fig. 15 is the final member to be set in place. This panel requires four pieces of ¾" stock joined together edge to edge by means of a tongue-and-groove or splined joint. The forward surface at the joint should be beveled to produce a V-joint. The back panel is secured to the shelf members with wood pins.

Finishing of the cupboard will require the removal of all hardware. The work may be stained or left natural, depending on individual choice and the kind of wood that has been used for construction. The protective finish

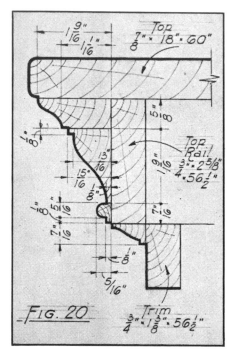

may be produced by wax, linseed oil, varnish, or lacquer. If either varnish or lacquer is used, it should be of the type that produces a flat finish rather than one that dries with a gloss.

The upper unit need not be fastened to the cupboard as the weight of this section will be sufficient to keep it in place and it will be easier to move.

Colonial
SEWING
TABLE

By courtesy of the Metropolitan Museum of Art · · · drawings of an exceptionally beautiful piece on display in the American Wing. It was a gift of Mrs. Russell Sage

*S*O IMPORTANT was the sewing table regarded in colonial days that cabinetmakers spared no pains to make it as attractive as possible. Today it is still an essential piece of furniture in every home and equally deserving of the finest possible styling and the most careful construction.

The model illustrated combines the best characteristics of the Sheraton period as it was interpreted in America. It is, indeed, the last word in refinement in Colonial sewing tables. Crotch satinwood used with mahogany always gives an elegant effect, and the application of rosettes to the top as if continuing the leg turnings is a detail *par excellence*. The use of the silk bag gives the piece a feminine touch and adds to its dainty appearance.

As shown in Fig. 1, the main section of the sewing table is built of a framework which, when completed, has the veneers applied before the legs are joined to the corner blocks. The construction of this main section should be started with the preparation of the stock that is required for the sides, back and corner blocks. These members are made of 7/8″ stock 3¾″ wide. The sides require two pieces 10 9/16″ long; the front corner blocks require two pieces 3 3/16″ long; the rear corner blocks require two pieces 3″ long, and the back requires one piece 16⅛″.

In order to join these members together to produce the octagonal shape of the unit, both ends of the side, rear corner block and back members are cut at an angle of 67½°, as shown in Figs. 3 and 4. The ends of the front corner blocks that are to be joined to the side member must also be cut at this angle as shown in Fig. 3. The beveling of these ends can be done by tilting the bench saw table at the required angle, then cutting the bevel. The forward end of the front corner blocks are cut at the angles shown in

the same figure. Two angles are cut.

To join these mitered pieces together, a spline is used. This requires the cutting of a ⅛″ groove, ⅜″ deep in the butting ends of each member as shown in Fig. 4. This is done on the bench saw by tilting the table to the required angle of 67½° and setting the blade to cut to a depth of ⅜″. Six splines are required. These splines should be ⅛″ thick, ¾″ long and 3¾″ wide. Keep in mind that the splines must be cut with the grain running the short way for maximum

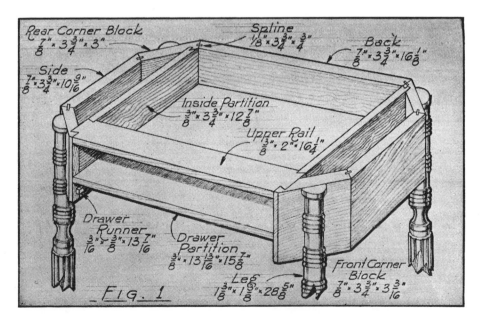

FIG. 1

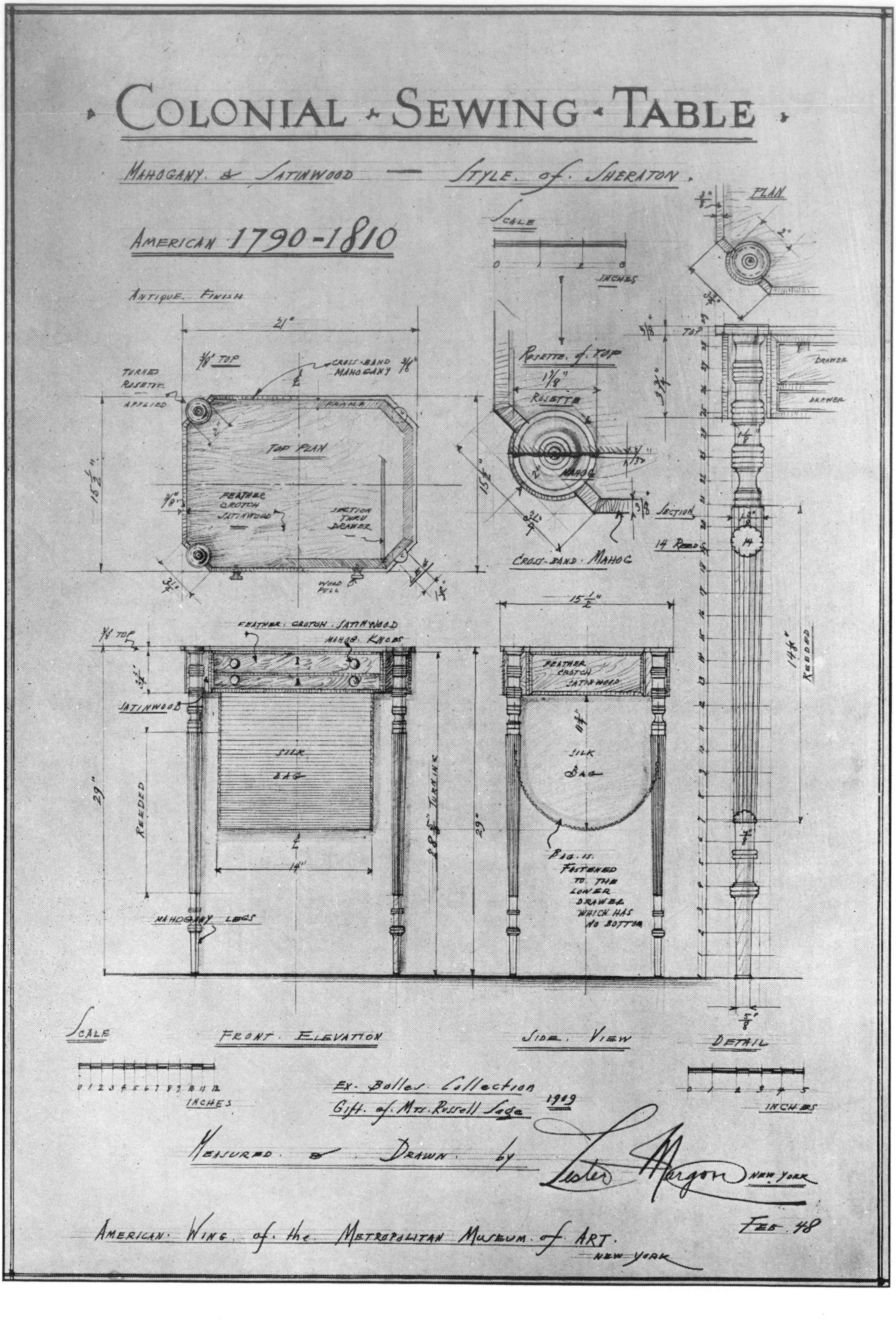

COLONIAL · SEWING · TABLE ·

MAHOGANY & SATINWOOD — STYLE OF SHERATON.

AMERICAN 1790-1810

ANTIQUE FINISH

PLAN

SCALE
0   6
INCHES

TOP PLAN

CROSS-BAND MAHOGANY 3/8"

TURNED ROSETTE APPLIED

FEATHER CROTCH SATINWOOD

SECTION THRU DRAWER

WOOD PULL

ROSETTE OF TOP
1 1/8"
ROSETTE

MAHOG.

CROSS-BAND MAHOG.

DRAWER

DRAWER

14

14 REEDS

REEDED

KEEDED

SECTION

FEATHER CROTCH SATINWOOD
MAHOG. KNOBS

SATINWOOD

REEDED

MAHOGANY LEGS

FRONT ELEVATION

29"

28 3/4" TURNING

14"

15 1/2"

FEATHER CROTCH SATINWOOD

SILK BAG

BAG IS FASTENED TO THE LOWER DRAWER WHICH HAS NO BOTTOM

SIDE VIEW

29"

DETAIL

5/8"

SCALE
0 1 2 3 4 5 6 7 8 9 10 11 12
INCHES

INCHES
0   3   5

Ex. Bolles Collection
Gift of Mrs. Russell Sage   1909

MEASURED & DRAWN by   Lester G. Margon   NEW YORK

AMERICAN WING of the METROPOLITAN MUSEUM of ART.
NEW YORK

FIG. 48

strength in the finished splined joint.

The inside partition is to be joined to the front and rear corner blocks by means of a dado and rabbet joint as shown in Fig. 3. The dado is to be $\frac{3}{16}$″ wide and cut at an angle of 45°. The inside partitions are to be made of $\frac{3}{8}$″ stock $3\frac{3}{4}$″ wide. Each one is to be $12\frac{7}{8}$″ long. The ends are cut as shown in Fig. 2.

With the completion of these various members, assembling of the end units as shown in Fig. 3 can be undertaken. The front and rear corner blocks are joined to the side member by gluing the splines in the grooves. The inside partition is slipped into the dadoes. After the glue has been given time to set, the $\frac{3}{8}$″ x $\frac{3}{16}$″ groove that is to take the drawer partition is laid out and cut. The cutting of the groove can be done on the bench saw or on the drill press, using a $\frac{3}{8}$″ router bit. In either case, the forward and rear corners of the groove will have to be completed by hand with a chisel. The drawer runners, which are pieces of $\frac{3}{16}$″ x $\frac{3}{8}$″ stock $13\frac{7}{16}$″ long, are secured to the inside partitions as shown

in Fig. 3, using glue and $\frac{3}{4}$″ No. 5 flathead wood screws. Make certain that the drawer runner is parallel to the drawer partition groove.

The drawer partition is a piece of $\frac{3}{8}$″ stock $13\frac{13}{16}$″ wide and $15\frac{7}{8}$″ long. The rear corners are mitered at an angle of 45°, while the forward corners have a rabbet cut in them as shown in Fig. 4. The upper rail, as shown in the same figure, is a piece of $\frac{3}{8}$″ stock 2″ wide and $16\frac{1}{4}$″ long. This member is joined to the end units by means of a dovetail joint laid out and cut as shown. The drawer partition, upper rail and back members are trial fitted to the end units; then if the work has been found to fit, the pieces are disassembled and reassembled with glue spread on all butting surfaces. Assembling should be done by joining the back member to one end unit, then placing the drawer partition in this unit. The other end unit is then joined to the back and drawer partition. The upper rail is placed between the end units last.

With the complete assembly of the carcase, the outer surfaces should be

dressed flush with one another preparatory to applying the veneer. The outer faces of the corner blocks, side and back members are to have a satinwood veneer applied to them, allowing for the application of a $\frac{3}{8}$″ border on each panel of cross-band mahogany. The mahogany cross-band is applied to the panels, as well as to the front of the drawer partition, upper rail and the forward end of the front corner blocks as shown.

The legs are made of $1\frac{1}{2}$″ square stock 30″ long. The finished leg has an overall length of $28\frac{5}{8}$″ and a maximum outside diameter of $1\frac{3}{8}$″. The stock is set up in the lathe between centers and turned down to a finished outside diameter of $1\frac{3}{8}$″. The various beads, coves and tapers are marked off on the cylinder; then the stock is turned to shape. Before cutting off the waste at each end, the reeding as shown in the leg detail of the main drawing is cut on the spindle shaper. The upper end of each leg is cut as shown in Fig. 5. The completed legs are joined to the carcase with glue and $1\frac{1}{2}$″ No. 8 flathead screws. The

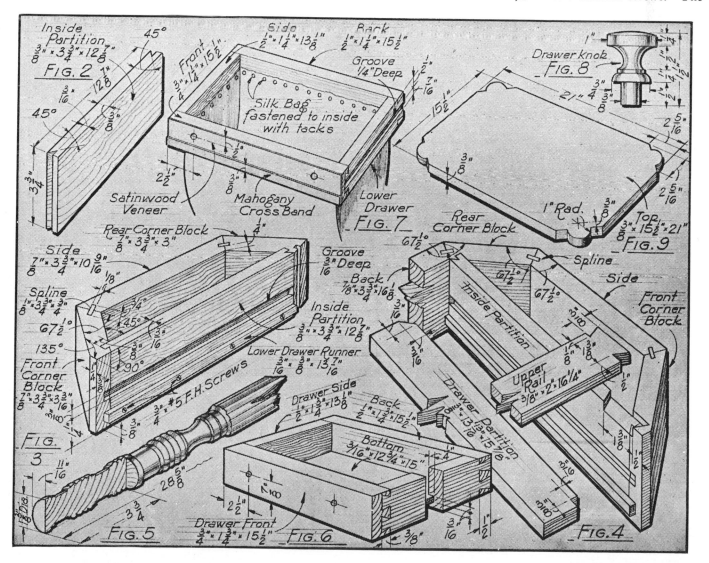

screws are driven through the corner blocks and into the legs.

The upper and lower drawers are constructed of $\frac{3}{4}''$ and $\frac{1}{2}''$ stock as shown in Figs. 6 and 7. A $\frac{3}{16}''$ x $\frac{1}{4}''$ groove is cut on the inside faces of the side, back and front members of the upper drawer to take the $\frac{3}{16}''$ plywood bottom. The side members are joined to the front and back members by means of dovetail joints. As shown in Fig. 7, a $\frac{7}{16}''$ x $\frac{1}{4}''$ groove is cut along the outer face on the side members of the lower drawer to fit the drawer runners previously secured to the inner partition of the carcase. After the drawers have been assembled, the veneer is applied.

The drawer knobs are turnings as shown in Fig. 8. These are secured to the drawer fronts with glue at the locations indicated in Figs. 6 and 7.

The top is made of $\frac{3}{8}''$ stock $15\frac{1}{2}''$ wide and $21''$ long. The stock is laid out as shown in Fig. 9, then cut to shape on the band saw. A satinwood veneer is applied to top allowing for a $\frac{3}{8}''$ border of cross-band mahogany. As shown in the detail of the corner on the main drawing, the cross-band is carried out under the turned mahogany rosette. The edges of the table top should also have mahogany cross-band applied to them. The ornamental rosettes applied at the corners of the top are turned from mahogany and glued in place. The completed top is glued to the carcase.

The silk bag attached to the inside of the lower drawer frame as shown in Fig. 7 is made to conform to the size shown in the front elevation and side view of the main drawing.

The finish should be natural, being built up by applying a number of coats of white shellac and rubbing each one down with No. 00 or No. 000 steel wool, or with very fine sandpaper.

MAHOGANY
BREAK FRONT

MAGNIFICENT is an over-used word, but it may truthfully be applied to this Eighteenth Century break-front cabinet. Taken from a manor house near Surrey, England, it is on exhibition in the Museum of Art of the Rhode Island School of Design, Providence, R. I. Its owner, Miss Lucy T. Aldrich, and the Museum granted special permission for making the accompanying measured drawings.

Of special interest is the dignity of the pediment and entablature. Even the selection of the wood is noteworthy for restraint in graining and figure. The interior of the upper cabinet is covered with pongee in the original, but a conventional wood finish might be preferable in a reproduction, or the interior could be painted, if desired.

Although this is an English model, numerous American pieces found their inspiration in similar cabinets brought over from the Mother Country. Many of those break fronts, however, are so large that they will not fit into a room of moderate proportions.

Break-front cabinets of the size shown in the photograph and main drawing are constructed as two units independent of one another. This is necessary for purposes of moving. A cabinet of this overall size would be extremely difficult to handle and in many instances could not be moved from the shop to the room in which it is to be placed.

The units consist of the lower cupboard shown in Fig. 1 and the upper cabinet shown in Fig. 6. The original was made of solid mahogany throughout, but mahogany veneer panels may be substituted for the wider members. Door rails, stiles, muntins and moldings should be made of solid stock.

Construction should be started with the lower unit as shown in Fig. 1. The end members as shown in Fig. 2 will require two pieces of ¾" stock 10½" wide and 36" long. A ⅜" x ⅜" rabbet is cut along the rear edge to take the back panel. A ⅜" x ¾" rabbet is cut along the inner face of the upper end to take the top member. A ⅜" x ¾" dado is cut across the inside face to take the bottom member.

The end cupboard partitions require two pieces of ⅝" stock 10½" wide and 35⅜" long. A ⅜" x ⅜" rabbet is cut along the back edge to take the back panel and a ⅜" x ¾" dado is

Fine Arts Museum, Rhode Island School of Design

cut across the inside face to take the bottom. To provide for the adjustable shelves, a series of holes will have to be bored in the inside faces of the cupboard partitions and the end members as shown in Fig. 2 to take the shelf supports. These holes are bored to a depth of ⅜".

The center cupboard partitions require two pieces of ¾" stock 13¼" wide and 36" long. A ⅜" x ⅜" rabbet is cut along the rear edge to take the back panel. A ⅜" x ¾" dado is cut across the inside face to take the bottom member. In order to fit this member around the projection of the center cupboard, a tongue will have to be cut in the upper end at the front as shown in Fig. 2. This tongue is ⅜" thick, ⅜" high and 2¾" wide, being flush on the outer face. Holes for the shelf supports are located and bored in the inner faces of these members as shown in Fig. 2.

The cupboard bottoms will require two pieces of ¾" stock 10½" x 17⅜" and one piece ¾" x 13¼" x 35¼". Each of these members has a ⅜" x ⅜" rabbet cut along the upper face at the rear edge as shown in Fig. 1 to take the back panel.

The cupboard top and the top and bottom of the upper cabinet are identical in size and shape. It is of the utmost importance that these three members be identical, therefore it is advisable to make them at the same time. These members require three

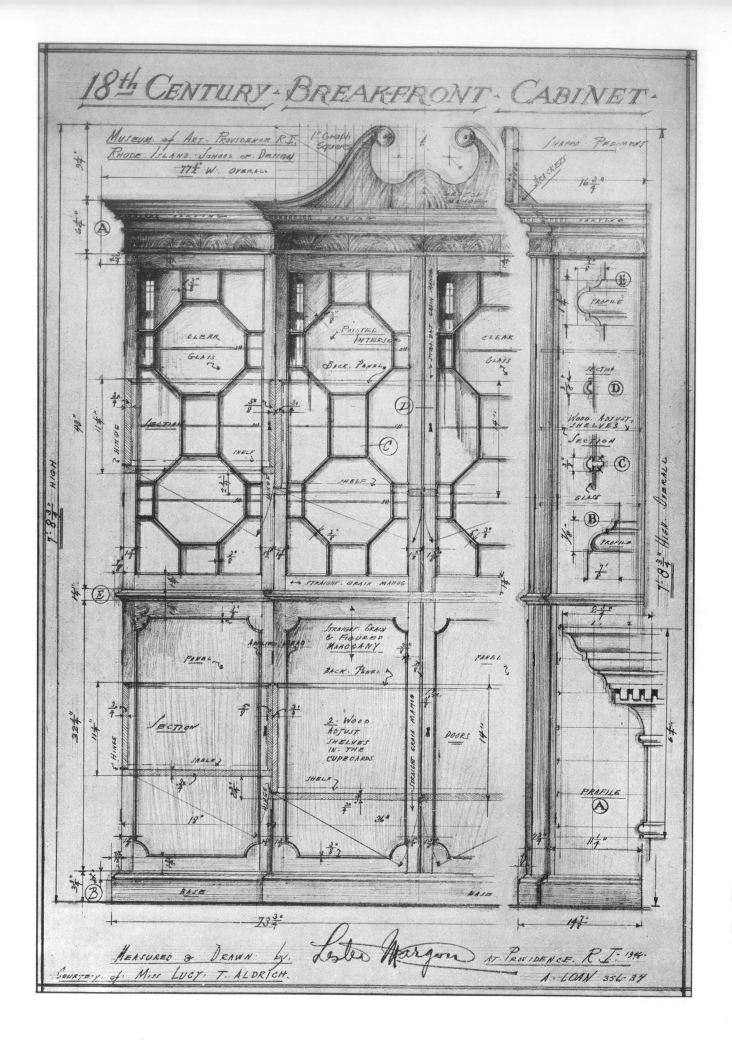

18ᵗʰ CENTURY · BREAKFRONT · CABINET ·

MUSEUM. of ART. PROVIDENCE R.I.
RHODE. ISLAND. SCHOOL of DESIGN
77½" W. OVERALL

SHAPED PEDIMENT

CLEAR GLASS

PAINTED INTERIOR

BACK. PANEL

CLEAR GLASS

SHELF

STRAIGHT. GRAIN. MAHOG

PROFILE

WOOD. ADJUST. SHELVES

SECTION

GLASS

PROFILE

STRAIGHT. GRAIN & FIGURED MAHOGANY

BACK. PANEL

2- WOOD ADJUST SHELVES IN THE CUPBOARDS

PANEL

DOORS

PROFILE

BASE

BASE

MEASURED & DRAWN by Lester Margon AT PROVIDENCE. R.I. 1948.
COURTESY of MISS LUCY T. ALDRICH.

A· LOAN 356·34

pieces of ¾″ stock 13¼″ wide and 71¼″ long as shown in Fig. 3. Dadoes 1⅜″ wide are cut to a depth of ⅜″ across one face of each member to take the partition members. These dadoes have their outer edge located 17″ from the end as shown in Fig. 3. A ⅜″ x ⅜″ rabbet is cut along the rear edge to take the back panels. The projection of the center section is produced by removing stock from the forward edge at both sides of the center section. When laying out the stock for the projection, the center section must

be 35¼″ long with the cuts being made ⅜″ beyond the inside shoulder of the dado as shown in Fig. 3.

The back panels are made of ⅜″ plywood having a mahogany facing on at least one side. The end cupboard backs will require two pieces of stock 17⅜″ x 32″ while the center cupboard back will require one piece 35¼″ x 32″. It is important that these panels be square as they will be needed to help square the cabinet during assembly.

Assembling the cupboard unit will require the gluing together of the cen-

ter cupboard partition and the end cupboard partition as shown in Fig. 2. The center cupboard bottom is glued in the dadoes of the center cupboard partitions. Clamps should be used to hold the work together. The cupboard top is joined to the center partitions, glue being applied to all butting surfaces. This assembled section is checked for squareness; then the center cupboard back placed in the rabbets and fastened to the partitions, top and bottom with glue and 1½″ brads.

Once the back panel is secured, the rear clamp can be removed. The end cupboard bottom is joined to the end partition; then the end member is joined to the bottom and top. All butting surfaces of the various joints should be covered with glue before the parts are assembled. The work is checked for squareness and the back panels are applied. Long bar clamps should be used to hold the cabinet together while the glue is given time to set.

As shown in Fig. 2, front aprons made of ¾″ x 3¾″ solid mahogany are applied to the front of the cupboard. Two of these are to be 18″ long and the third should be 36″ in length. These are glued in place. Brads may be used to secure them to the partitions and end members as these aprons will have their faces covered with the base molding as shown in Fig. 4. Triangular strips cut from ¾″ square stock are glued between the underface of the bottom and the inner face of the apron as shown in Figs. 1 and 4.

The base is made from ⅞″ x 2⅞″ stock as shown in Fig. 4. This base stock extends along the front and the sides, being mitered at each corner. The base member is applied with glue, hand-screws being used to hold it to the apron while the glue is given time to set. The base molding shown in detail at B in the main drawing is made from ¾″ x ⅞″ stock. The edge of the stock is molded on the shaper, then cut to lengths and fitted to the base as shown in Fig. 4. All butting corners are mitered. Glue and 1″ brads are used to fasten the moldings in place. The brads should be set and the holes filled during the finishing process.

The molding between the upper cabinet and the lower cupboard requires 1¼″ x 3″ stock. The detail at E in the main drawing shows the contour of the molded edge. After the stock is molded on the shaper, it is cut and fitted to the top of the cupboard unit as shown in Fig. 5. The butting corners are mitered; then the pieces are secured to the top with glue and 1¾″ No. 8

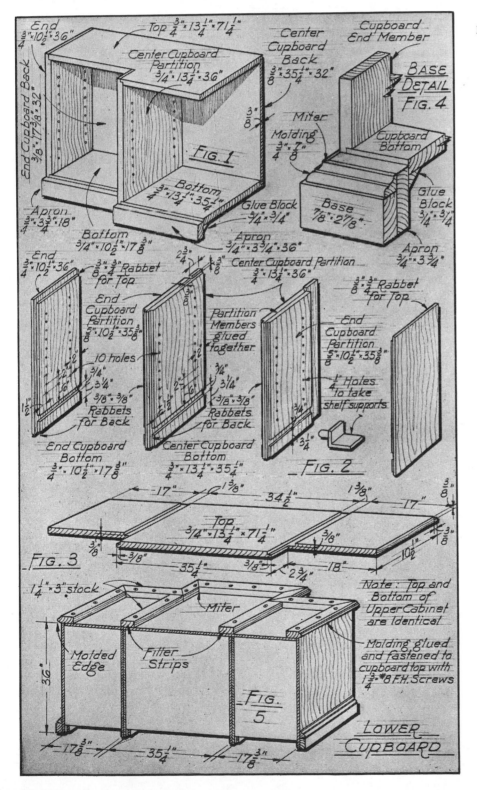

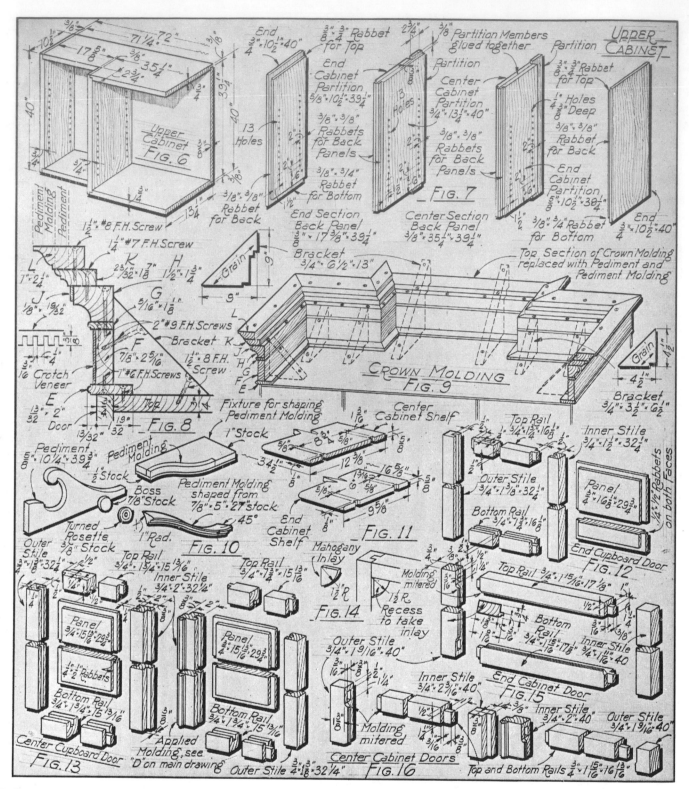

flathead screws. Filler strips made of the same size stock are secured to the top as shown in Fig. 5.

The upper cabinet unit shown in Fig. 6 requires two end members 3/4″ x 10½″ x 40″, two end cabinet partitions 5/8″ x 10½″ x 39¼″ and two center cabinet partitions 3/4″ x 13¼″ x 40″. Each of these members has a 3/8″ x 3/8″ rabbet cut along the rear edge to take the back panels as shown in Fig. 7. The end members have a 3/8″ x 3/4″ rabbet cut along the inner face at each end to take the bottom and top mem-

bers. The center cabinet partition members have a tongue at each end as shown in Fig. 7. To provide for the adjustable shelves, a series of 1/4″ holes is located and bored to a depth of 3/8″ as indicated in the same figure. When these members have been prepared, the end cabinet partitions are glued to the center cabinet partitions as noted in sketch.

The back panels will require two pieces of 3/8″ stock 17⅜″ wide and 39¼″ long and one piece 3/8″ x 35¼″ x 39¼″. Use plywood other than fir.

The upper cabinet is assembled by joining the partitions to the top and bottom members, then applying the end members. Bar clamps should be used to hold the various members in place while the glue is given time to set. The assembled work should be immediately checked for squareness, then the back panels secured in their rabbets with glue and brads.

The crown molding shown in Figs. 8 and 9 is built up of a number of pieces. The various members, after being molded on the shaper, are joined together with glue and flathead wood screws. About 12 lineal feet of each piece will be required. Member E is a piece of mahogany $\frac{13}{32}''$ x 2" with the front edge molded. Member G is a piece $\frac{5}{16}''$ x $1\frac{1}{8}''$ with its front edge molded. Piece F is made from $\frac{7}{8}''$ x $2\frac{5}{16}''$ stock.

After these three moldings have been prepared, they should be cut to size and assembled to the top. The best procedure to follow is to join molding E and G to F, using glue and wood screws as indicated in Fig. 8. Before applying the screws, mark off the approximate length of each piece, then place the screws accordingly. The approximate lengths can be obtained by

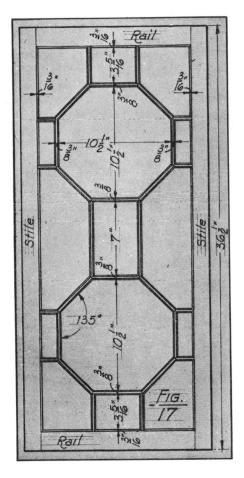

FIG. 17

laying out the location of piece E on the cabinet top and taking the actual measurements from this layout. Keep in mind all butting ends of the molding must be mitered. When the three moldings have been assembled, the exact lengths are marked off and the pieces cut to the required size. This section of the molding is secured to the cabinet top with glue and screws.

Brackets shown in Fig. 9 are cut, fitted and secured behind the molding. Crotch veneer is cut and glued to F.

Molding H requires $1\frac{1}{2}''$ x $1\frac{3}{4}''$ stock. It is cut and fitted to the top of G, then secured with glue and 2" No. 9

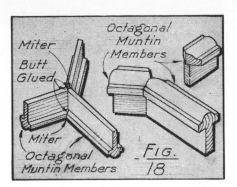

FIG. 18

flathead screws. The dentils J require $\frac{1}{8}''$ x $\frac{19}{32}''$ stock. The slots that form the dentils can be made with a dado head set to cut $\frac{1}{4}''$ wide. The dentil strips are glued to member H as shown in Fig. 8. Molding K requires $\frac{23}{32}''$ x $1\frac{7}{8}''$ stock. It is fastened to H with glue and $1\frac{1}{4}''$ No. 7 flathead screws. Molding L is made of 1" x $2\frac{1}{4}''$ stock and is fastened to K with glue and $1\frac{1}{2}''$ No. 8 flathead screws. As shown in Fig. 9, this member of the crown molding is left out of the center section. To complete this center section, the pediment and pediment molding will have to be prepared.

The pediment shown in Fig. 10 and in graph squares on the main drawing will require the preparation of a full-size pattern. The pediment is to rest on the top of molding K and its forward face is to be located flush with the forward edge of this molding as shown in Fig. 8. It is to be supported and secured by means of glue and the brackets shown in Fig. 9.

A piece of $\frac{5}{8}''$ x $10\frac{1}{4}''$ x $39\frac{3}{4}''$ stock, faced with crotch veneer as shown in the main drawing, is required for the pediment. The pattern is traced on the stock; then the wood is cut to shape on the band or jig saw. Each boss, made of $\frac{7}{8}''$ stock, and its rosette of $\frac{3}{8}''$ stock are the same diameter as that section of the pediment to which they are joined. These are glued in place. Fitting of the pediment to the crown molding will require the mitering of the ends.

The pediment molding requires two pieces of $\frac{7}{8}''$ x 5" x 27" stock. The outer contour of this molding is taken directly from the pediment; then this edge of the stock is cut to shape on the band or jig saw and finished on the sanding drum. The width of this molding is to be 1". It is marked off so as to follow the contour of the edge already cut, then shaped on the band saw. Molding of this stock will require the preparation of a fixture as shown in Fig. 10. The upper end of the molding is coped around the boss, then the lower

end mitered to fit against member L of the crown molding. The pediment molding is glued in place.

All shelves are made of $\frac{5}{8}''$ stock. Those that are to be placed in the end cupboards and end cabinets are to be $9\frac{5}{8}''$ wide and $16\frac{5}{8}''$ long while those for the center cabinet and center cupboard are to be $12\frac{3}{8}''$ wide and $34\frac{1}{2}''$ long. If shelf supports as shown in Fig. 2 are used, the ends of each shelf will have to be cut as shown in Fig. 11.

The doors for the lower cupboard are shown in Figs. 12 and 13. The stiles and rails are made of solid stock while the panels may be made of $\frac{3}{4}''$ plywood faced with mahogany. A $\frac{1}{4}''$ groove $\frac{1}{2}''$ deep is cut along the inside edges of the stiles and rails to take the panel. The panel has $\frac{1}{4}''$ x $\frac{1}{2}''$ rabbets cut along the edges and ends on both faces to produce $\frac{1}{4}''$ x $\frac{1}{2}''$ tongues to fit the grooves in the rails and stiles. The ends of the rails have $\frac{1}{4}''$ x $\frac{1}{2}''$ tongues cut to fit the grooves in the stiles. The stiles and rails are glued to the panel. Be sure to check the work for squareness.

As shown in Fig. 14, a mahogany inlay quadrant is set into each corner of the panel. The grain of the quadrant is parallel to the rails. The recess should be cut slightly less than the thickness

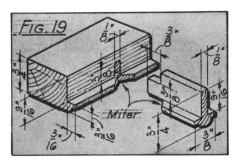

FIG. 19

of the inlay; then after they are glued in place, they may be sanded flush. The applied molding that is flush with the joint formed by the panel meeting the rails, stiles and quadrant is shown in section at D on the main drawing. The molding, following the contour of the quadrant, will have to be cut circular in shape before molding on the shaper. The moldings are applied with glue, using veneer pins to hold them in position while the glue is setting.

The completed doors are fitted to the cabinet allowing sufficient clearance between the upper rail and the molding and the lower rail and the base so that there will be no danger of the doors' striking or rubbing against these parts. The doors are hung with $1\frac{1}{2}''$ brass butts. Gains are cut into the doors and cupboard sides to take the hinges. The key escutcheons and locks are applied to the stiles as in the main drawing.

The cabinet doors are made of ¾" stock and are shown in Figs. 15 and 16. After the various pieces of stock have been cut to the dimensions shown in these sketches, the molding and the rabbet for the glass are cut along the inside edge of each member. The rails are joined to the stiles with mortise-and-tenon joints. The moldings are mitered at the corners. The muntins are made of ¾" x ⅜" stock with ⅛" x $\frac{9}{16}$" rabbets cut in the faces and with the edge molded as shown in Fig. 19 and at C on the main drawing. The muntin stock is cut on the shaper.

Laying out and cutting the muntins to size will require the preparation of a full-size layout as shown in Fig. 17. The light octagonal shaped frames are first prepared from the muntin stock. These pieces are cut to size, having their ends mitered at an angle of 67½°. They are butt-glued as shown in Fig. 18 and held together temporarily with bank pins or veneer pins. The as-sembling of the frames should be done directly on the full-size layout.

The vertical muntins connecting the two octagonal frames are joined to the frames as shown in Fig. 18. Cutting the miter in the molding of the octagonal frame will have to be done with great care. It is advisable to pre-pare a fixture to hold the frame when doing this work. The muntins are butt-glued to the octagonal frame. The vertical muntins connecting the octago-nal frames to the upper and lower rails are identical for all doors. They are mitered and butt-glued to the octagons, but are mortised into the rails as shown in Fig. 19. The horizontal muntins that connect the octagon frames to the stiles will vary in length for the outer cabinet doors and the center cabinet door. By measuring these frames it will be noted that the latter measures 14$\frac{13}{16}$" between the glass rabbets in the stiles while the former measures 15⅛". The muntins are cut accordingly to be mitered to the octagon as shown in Fig. 18 and joined to the stiles as shown in Fig. 19.

With the completion of the various parts, the assembly can be undertaken. The stiles and rails are joined together, making certain they are square. The muntins that join the octagons to the stiles and rails are set in their respective mortises, then the octagons joined to these muntins. After the glue has set, the frames are fitted to the cabinet and hung with 1½" brass butts.

Cardboard patterns of the various pieces of glass should be prepared. The cutting of the glass may be done di-rectly from these patterns. The glass is held in place by means of ⅛" x ¼" quarter-round glass bead. The glass bead should be fastened to the muntins with ¼" No. 1 flathead screws.

Finishing the completed cabinet will require a coat of stain followed by a wash coat of shellac, then an applica-tion of paste wood filler of the same color as the stain. Several coats of white shellac or clear lacquer should be applied and the work rubbed down with pumice stone and rottenstone. Be-fore finishing, all hardware and glass should be removed.

New England
ROCKER

Bedroom chair by courtesy of the Brooklyn Museum. It is from the historic Schenck House, erected in Canarsie before 1775

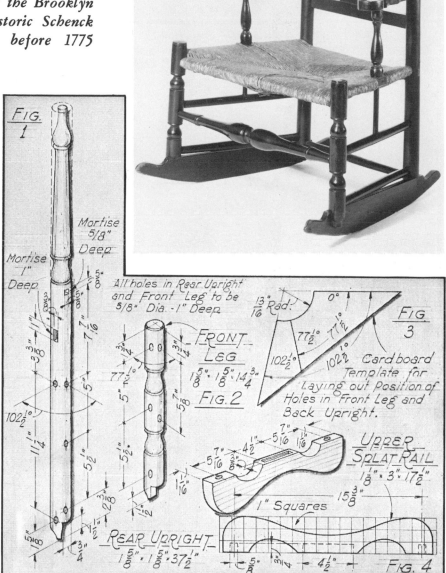

ROCKING chairs are an essential and authentic part of the Colonial setting. They bring back fond memories of a mother rocking her baby to sleep and suggest the soft, sweet lullabies sung by the pioneer women who helped build our country.

Here is a beautifully fashioned small bedroom rocker, painted black. It is a fine model for reproduction, not too difficult to construct and well worth all the work put into it. The measured drawings were made by courtesy of the Brooklyn (N. Y.) Museum. The rocker is exhibited in a bedroom from the Schenck House, which was built in Canarsie before 1775.

Construction may be started with the rear uprights. These will require two pieces 1¾" square and at least 38" long. A center mark is established on each end; then the live and dead centers of the lathe are driven into them. The piece is set in the lathe and turned to a finished diameter of 1⅝" with gouge and skew chisels.

The locations of the various beads, coves and shoulders are marked. With the round-nose, skew and gouge, these are turned to shape. The turning should then be sanded smooth.

The various holes and mortises as shown in Fig. 1 should be marked while the stock is still in the lathe. The holes for one set of rails must be bored at an angle of 102½° to the other set. One method is to lock the stock in the lathe; then with the aid of the tool rest, draw a line from one end to the other of the 1⅝" section of the turning. Next prepare a cardboard template as shown in Fig. 3, marking off the degree points with a protractor. Place the template against the turning

so that the "0" mark is on the horizontal line. The location of the line that establishes the 102½° point can now be carried over from the template to the stock and the work is revolved in the lathe so that this point is in line with the tool rest. The tool rest can now be used to draw a horizontal line through the location point.

With the aid of the tool rest, the lines establishing the widths of the

mortises that are to take the arm and lower splat rails can be laid out. The shoulder at the lower end of the upright, shown in Fig. 1 and the main drawing, should also be laid out before the waste at each end of the stock has been removed.

The holes are bored with a ⅝" bit to a depth of 1". If a large V-block is available, there should be no trouble boring these holes at the proper angle.

131

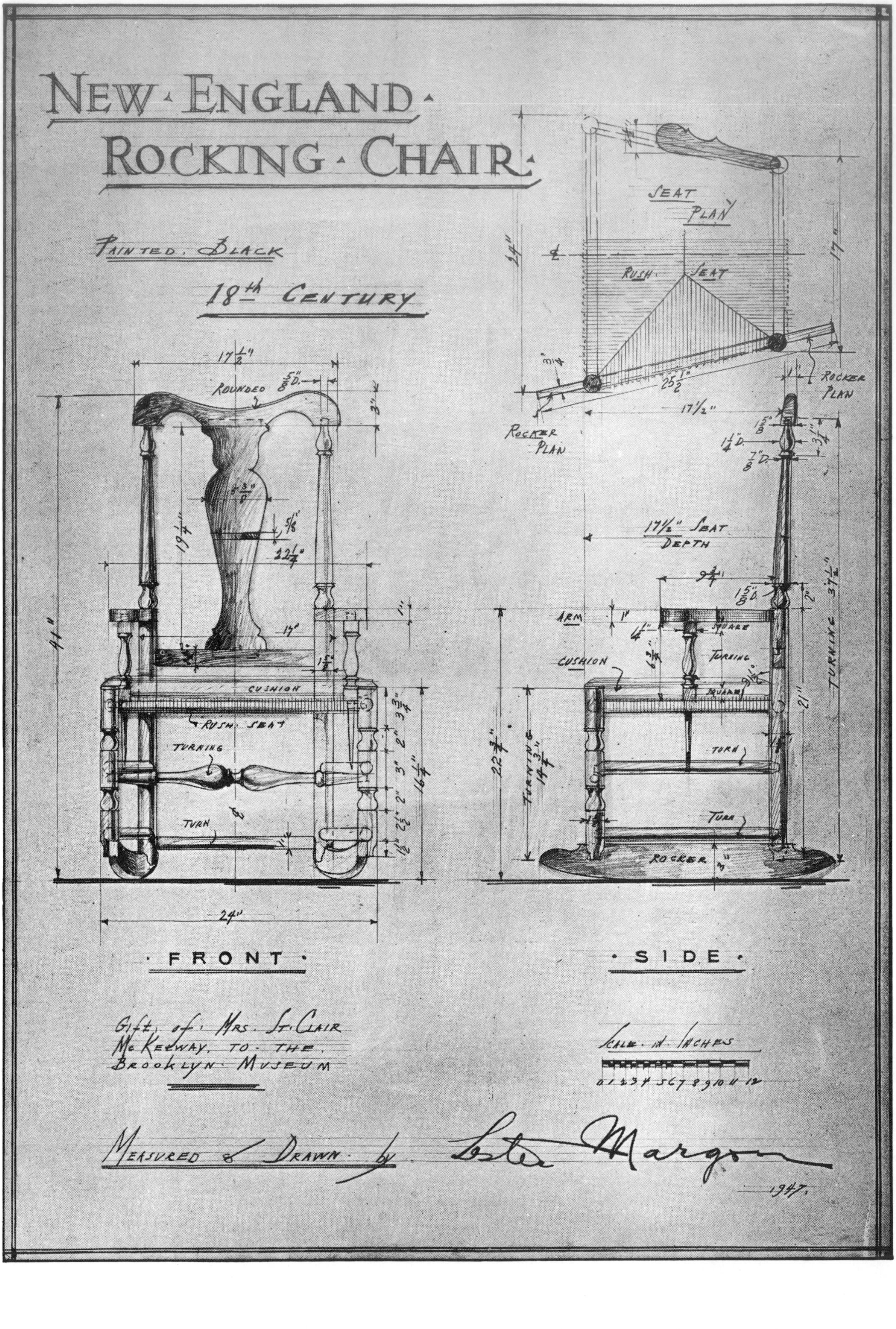

NEW·ENGLAND·
ROCKING·CHAIR·

PAINTED·BLACK

18ᵗʰ CENTURY

SEAT
PLAN

RUSH SEAT

ROCKER
PLAN

ROCKER
PLAN

17½"

25½"

3¾"

FRONT

17½"
ROUNDED ⅝"D
3¼"

19½"

⅝"D

⅝"D

22¼"

4'1"

14"

1½"

CUSHION

RUSH·SEAT

TURNING

TURN

3¾"
3" 2" 2"
16¼"

⅛" 2⅝" 2" 3" 2⅛"

24"

SIDE

ROCKER
PLAN

1¼"D
⅝"D

1⅝"
3"

17½" SEAT
DEPTH

9¾"
1⅝"D
2"

ARM
1"
CUSHION
6¾"

SQUARE
TURNING
SQUARE

TURNING 37½"

21"

TURN

TURN

ROCKER

22¾"

TURNING 14¾"

SCALE IN INCHES
0 1 2 3 4 5 6 7 8 9 10 11 12

MEASURED & DRAWN BY   Lester Margon

1947.

The three holes for the side rails as well as the mortise that is to take the arm must be bored 1½° off square because of the slight splay of the rear upright. By tilting the drill-press table to the required angle, these holes can be bored correctly. The holes for the back rails and mortise that is to take the lower splat rail are bored at 90° to the stock. Clean out the mortises with a chisel.

For the front legs, two pieces 1¾" square and 15¾" long are turned between centers. After the holes are located, in this case 77½° apart, they are bored to the required depth with a ⅝" bit. All holes in these members are to be square to the stock as the front legs do not splay.

The side rails as shown in Fig. 11 require six pieces of 1⅛" square stock 17" long. Each is turned to a diameter of 1" with a ⅝" x 1" tenon turned on both ends to fit the holes previously bored in the rear upright and the front legs. Because of the splay of the back upright, the finished overall lengths of these rails vary as shown in Fig. 11. The seat rail is to be 16 9/16" long, the intermediate rail 16½", and the bottom rail 16⅜", including the

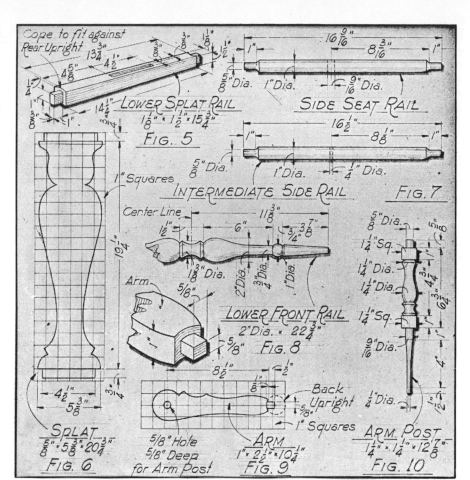

tenons. As shown in Fig. 7, the seat rail and the intermediate side rails are to be bored for holes that will take the arm post. The dimensions are from the end of the rear tenon. The variation of 1/16" is due to the splay of the back upright.

The rear seat rail and the lower back rail require two pieces 1⅛" square and 17" long. These are turned to a diameter of 1" and their overall length is marked—the seat rail 15¾" and the lower back rail 15½". Tenons ⅝" in diameter are turned on both ends of each. As shown in Fig. 11, the tenons on the lower rail should be ⅞" long while those on the seat rail are 1".

The front seat rail requires 1⅛" square stock 24" long, turned to a diameter of 1". Its overall length is 22¾". Tenons ⅝" in diameter and 1" long are turned on each end.

The lower front rail requires a piece 2¼" square and 24" long, turned to a diameter of 2". The overall length of 22¾" should be marked off and the tenons and various turned components located as in Fig. 8. This rail is then turned.

The upper splat rail, Fig. 4, will require a piece 1⅛" x 3" x 17½". A mortise to take the splat is located and cut. Holes to take the ends of the rear uprights are bored as indicated.

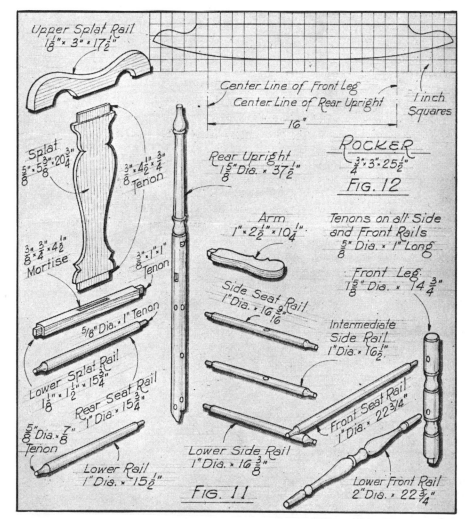

Prepare and trace a pattern on the stock. The wood can be cut on band saw or jig saw, then finished with a spokeshave. The rail tapers to 1" at the top, the wood being removed from the front face only. After tapering, the upper edge is rounded.

The lower splat rail, Fig. 5, will require a piece of stock 1⅛" x 1½" x 15¾". A ⅜" x 4½" mortise is cut to a depth of ¾" in the upper edge to take the tenon on the end of the splat. The rail is to be joined to the rear uprights by means of tenons that fit into the mortises previously cut. As shown in Fig. 5, the shoulders of these tenons must be coped to fit around the uprights. When laying out

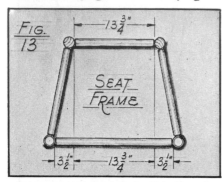

the tenons, do so on the assumption that the tenon is to be ¾" long. After cutting the tenons to this length, the coping can be done with a gouge and chisel. Cut to a scribed arc.

The splat, Fig. 6, will require a piece ⅝" x 5⅜" x 20¾". A full-size pattern will have to be prepared and traced on the stock. The tenons at each end should be laid out and cut to fit their respective mortises. The contour of the splat can be cut on band saw or jig saw, then finished with a spokeshave, chisel and sandpaper. Don't dull the crisp contour.

The assembling of the back and front units can now be undertaken. It will be noted that when the side and front seat rails are placed in the front leg, the corner of one interferes with the corner of the other, so the corner of each will have to be mitered. The same holds true when the side seat rail and rear seat rail are placed in the back upright. After mitering these members, the front unit consisting of the two legs, the front seat rail and the lower front rail is glued together and clamps are applied.

The back unit has the lower seat rail and lower splat rail glued to one upright; then the other upright is placed on the opposite ends of these members. The splat is glued in the lower splat rail, and the upper splat

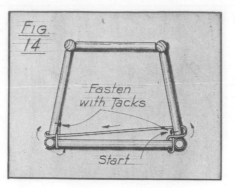

rail is placed over the ends of the uprights and splat. Clamps should be applied and the work checked for squareness before the glue sets.

As shown in Fig. 10, the arm posts require two pieces of 1¼" square stock 14" long. These are turned to a diameter of 1¼", then the various coves and beads are turned.

The arms require two pieces 1" x 2½" x 10¼". A full-size pattern will have to be prepared and traced on the stock. The wood is cut on band saw or jig saw, then finished with a spokeshave, chisel and sandpaper. The location of the ⅝" hole that is to take the pin on the end of the arm uprights should be bored ⅝" deep. The tenon on the end is cut to fit the mortise provided for it and coped around the turned upright.

The various rails are glued to the front legs, and the arm post is set in place. The arm is glued to the end of the arm post; then the back unit is placed on the opposite ends of the rails and arms.

The rockers are made of two pieces of ¾" stock 3" wide and 25½" long. A pattern is prepared and traced on the wood, after which it is cut to shape. As shown in Figs. 1, 2 and 11, notches are cut in the lower end of the front legs and rear uprights to take the rockers. The rockers are glued to these members, using ¼" dowels as pins to reinforce the joint. These dowels pass through the rocker and leg members and are finished flush.

The work should be finished before weaving the seat. A coat of shellac sanded with No. 2/0 paper after it has dried will seal the wood. A coat of flat black paint is then applied. A finish coat, either flat or semigloss, will complete the work.

The seat may be woven with rush if it is available, or imitation rush known as art cord can be used. As shown in Fig. 13, marks should be made on the front seat rail, 3½" from the legs. The space between the marks is equal to the exposed length of the

rear seat rail. The wedge-shaped sections as shown in Fig. 13 will have to be woven first. These sections are filled as shown in Fig. 14. With a length of rush about three feet long, tack one end to the inside surface of the side seat rail, then bring the loose end over and around the front rail. Pass it over and around the side rail, then across the opening. It is passed over and around the other side rail, then over and around the front rail. The end is brought back along the inside of the side rail and secured with a tack. This operation is continued with other lengths until the wedge-shaped sections are filled in as shown in Fig. 15.

To complete the weaving, a length should be rolled on a stick which is to be used as a shuttle. The end of the rush is tacked against the side rail; then the shuttle is brought forward around the front rail, over and around the side rail, across the opening of the seat, around the other side rail, around the front rail, then across the seat to the back rail where it is passed around the rail, then around the side rail, across the seat at the back, around the side rail and around the back rail. This is continued until the weaving appears as in Fig. 16. Filling in this section is done by working back and forth with the rush.

To attach an additional length of rush, use a square knot, but be sure that the knot is tied at such a point as to have it on the underside of the woven chair seat.

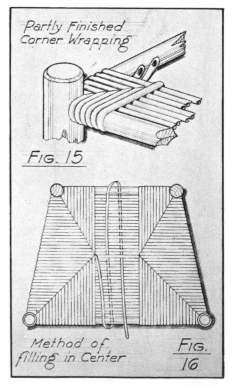

18*th Century American*

Hepplewhite Sideboard

The Baltimore Museum of Art where the sideboard is on display

THIS American Hepplewhite sideboard is one of the finest examples of American furniture design in existence. It was made by John Shaw, a cabinetmaker of Annapolis, Md., in 1797, and is one of the treasures in the furniture collection of the Baltimore Museum of Art. The museum authorities, in permitting measured drawings to be prepared, have conferred a favor on furniture lovers, particularly those who are craftsmen enough to undertake the reproduction of so magnificent a piece.

Because of the choice of richly figured woods, the oval inlays, the borders and other enrichment, the sideboard front is particularly colorful. In contrast, the top and sides are of plain, straight-grained mahogany.

Making the borders and inlays would be a considerable task; but fortunately stock borders and inlays are available that are almost, if not precisely, similar to the originals. An effort should be made to select veneers, too, that approximate the original in beauty of figure. So far as the interior drawer and cabinet divisions are concerned, however, the reproduction can be constructed to suit the particular needs of the maker. Above all, the finish of this piece is important because it must blend the various woods in a rich tapestry.

The sideboard requires the preparation of six legs made of 1⅞" square stock, each of which should be finished to a length of 37⅛". Each of these pieces, after being cut to size, should be arranged in its relative position, then labeled to indicate the position as well as numbered on the upper end as shown in Fig. 1 for future reference. Before any attempt is made to shape these members, all mortises and dovetail pins that are to take the various rails and other members should be laid out and cut.

As shown in Fig. 2, the end member is to be joined to the front corner leg by means of a mortise-and-tenon joint. The mortise should be laid out as indicated, then cut to a depth of ⅝". A dovetail is used to join the cupboard rail to the corner leg. The dovetail pins are laid out and cut in the upper

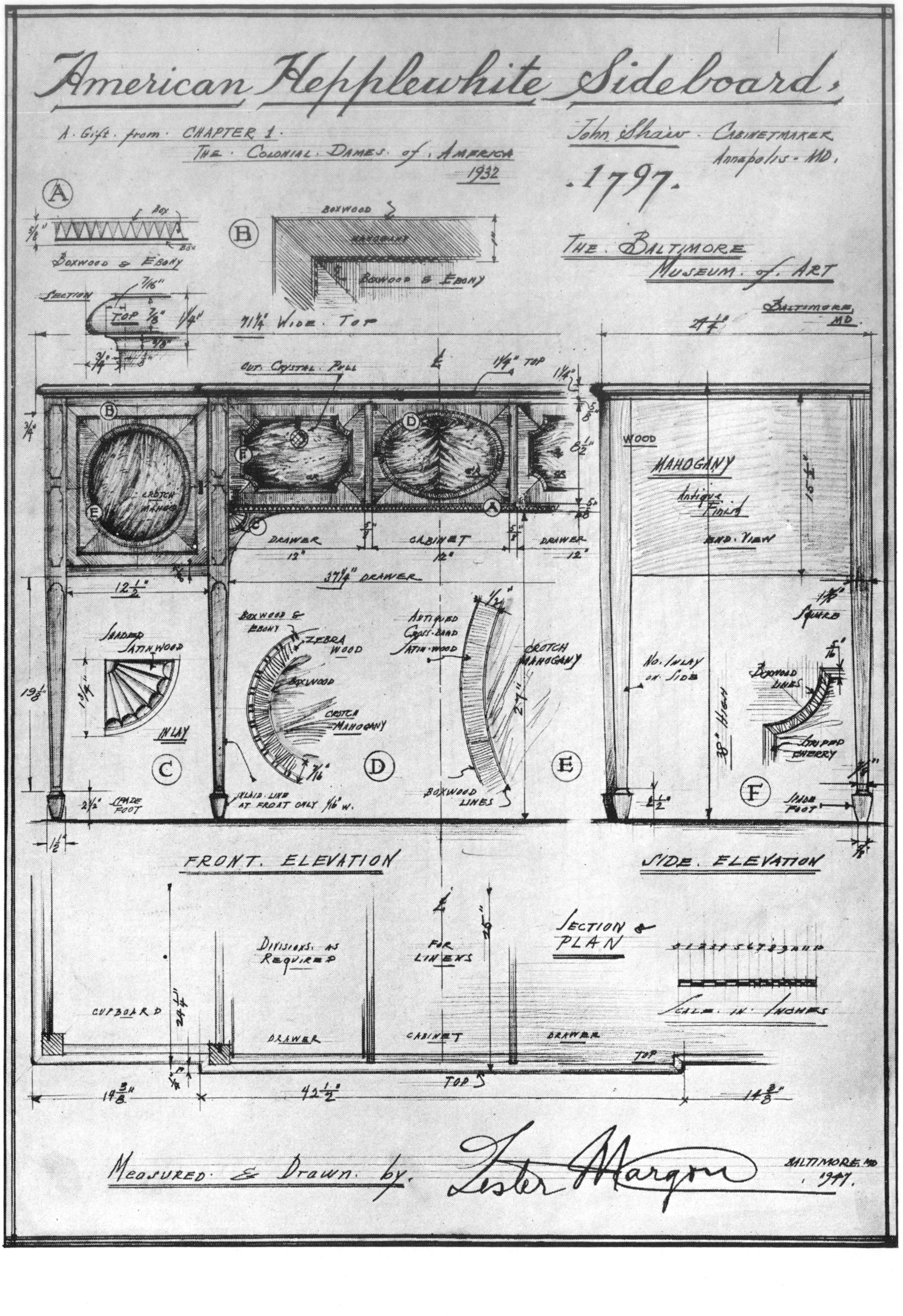

American Hepplewhite Sideboard.

A Gift from CHAPTER 1.
THE COLONIAL DAMES of AMERICA
1932

John Shaw. Cabinetmaker
Annapolis. MD.

.1797.

THE BALTIMORE
MUSEUM of ART

BALTIMORE,
MD.

(A) Boxwood & Ebony
SECTION

(B) BOXWOOD
MAHOGANY
BOXWOOD & EBONY
91¾" WIDE TOP

TOP

CUT CRYSTAL PULL
1¼" TOP

WOOD
MAHOGANY
Antique Finish
END VIEW

CROTCH MAHOG

DRAWER 12"   CABINET 12"   DRAWER 12"
37½" DRAWER

SANDED SATINWOOD
INLAY
(C)
SPADE FOOT
12½"
19⅝"
2½"
1½"

BOXWOOD & EBONY
ZEBRA WOOD
BOXWOOD
CROTCH MAHOGANY
(D)
INLAID LINE AT FRONT ONLY 1/16" W.

ANTIQUED CROSS-BAND SATIN-WOOD
CROTCH MAHOGANY
27"
BOXWOOD LINES
(E)

NO INLAY ON SIDE
38" HIGH

SQUARE
BOXWOOD LINES
STRIPED CHERRY
(F)
SIDE FOOT

FRONT. ELEVATION

SIDE. ELEVATION

CUPBOARD

DIVISIONS AS REQUIRED

FOR LINENS

SECTION & PLAN

DRAWER   CABINET   DRAWER
TOP
TOP

SCALE IN INCHES

19¾"   42½"   14⅜"

Measured & Drawn by   *Lester Margon*   BALTIMORE MD
1947.

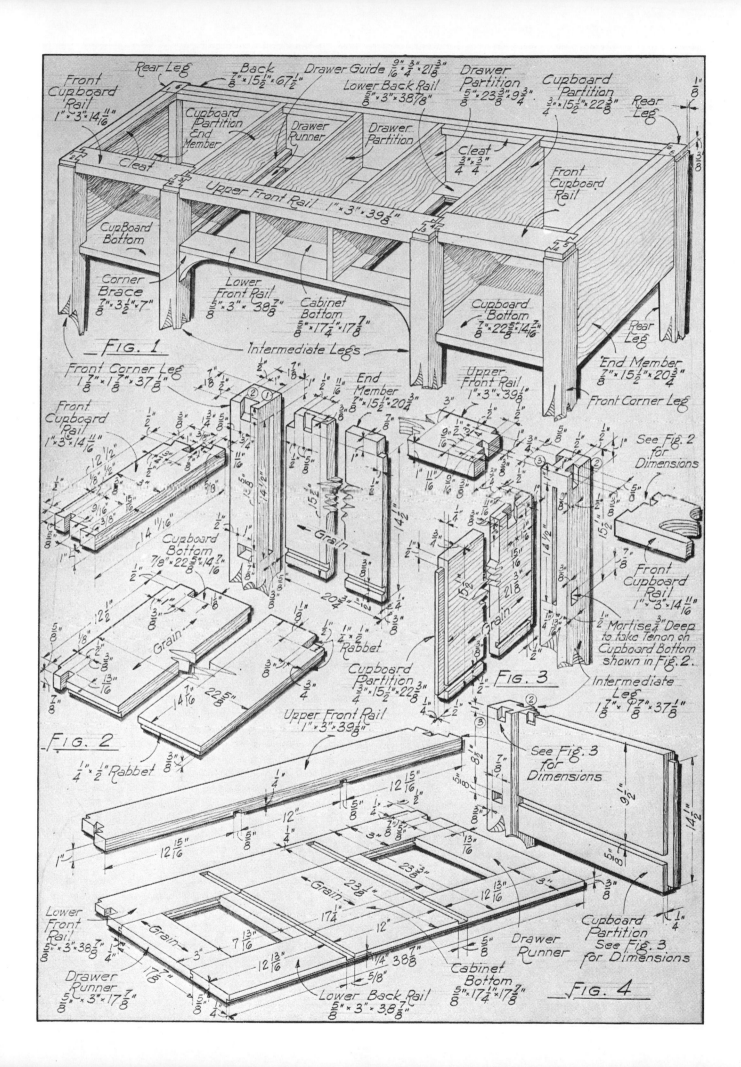

FIG. 1

FIG. 2

FIG. 3

FIG. 4

end of the leg member as shown in this sketch. The cupboard bottom is joined to the leg by means of a mortise-and-tenon joint, the mortise being laid out on the leg and cut to a depth of ⅝″. The other corner leg having the numbers 4 and 5 on the end requires a similar layout.

The intermediate legs shown in Figs. 3 and 4 are to have dovetail pins laid out and cut on the upper end to take the front cupboard rail and the upper front rail. The cupboard partition is to set into a mortise cut in the inside surface of each intermediate leg as shown in Fig. 3. The depth of this mortise is to be ⅝″. The cupboard bottom is to be joined to this leg by means of a mortise-and-tenon joint, with the mortise located and cut as shown in Fig. 3. On the opposite surface of the leg a mortise is located and cut to a depth of ⅝″ to take the lower front rail as shown in Fig. 4.

The rear legs, as shown in Fig. 6, are to have mortises laid out and cut

in adjacent sides to take the end and back members. The mortise that is to take the end member should be cut to a depth of ½″ while the one that is to take the back member should be ⅞″ deep. The rear edge of the cupboard bottom, as shown in Fig. 2, is to have a tenon cut on the end of it. A mortise in the rear leg is laid out and cut as in Fig. 6 to take this tenon.

With the completion of the various mortises and dovetail pins in the leg members, the legs can now be shaped. The contour of each leg is laid out either by means of a pattern or as individual layouts, following the dimensions as given in the main drawing. They are cut to shape on the band or jig saw, and then finished.

The end members are cut to the size given in Fig. 1. Tenons are cut on each end as shown in Fig. 2 to fit their respective tenons. A groove is cut along the inside face near the lower edge as shown in the same figure to take the cupboard bottom. The laying

out and cutting of the recess that is to take the dovetail on the cupboard rail completes this member.

The cupboard partitions, finished to the dimensions given in Fig. 1, have tenons cut on each end as shown in Figs. 3 and 4, with grooves cut on each face as shown in the same sketches to take the cupboard bottom and center section frame. On the upper edge, the dovetail pins that take the cupboard front and upper front rails are laid out and cut as shown in Fig. 3.

The back member, the size and shape of which is given in Fig. 6, is cut to size. The tenons are laid out and cut on each end as shown. The various dadoes and grooves are laid out as indicated and cut, finishing this part.

The cupboard bottom members shown in Figs. 1 and 2 are finished to the size given in the sketches. Tenons are cut in each end at the forward edge to fit the mortises previously cut in the front legs. At the rear edge, a tenon is cut at one end to fit the mortise

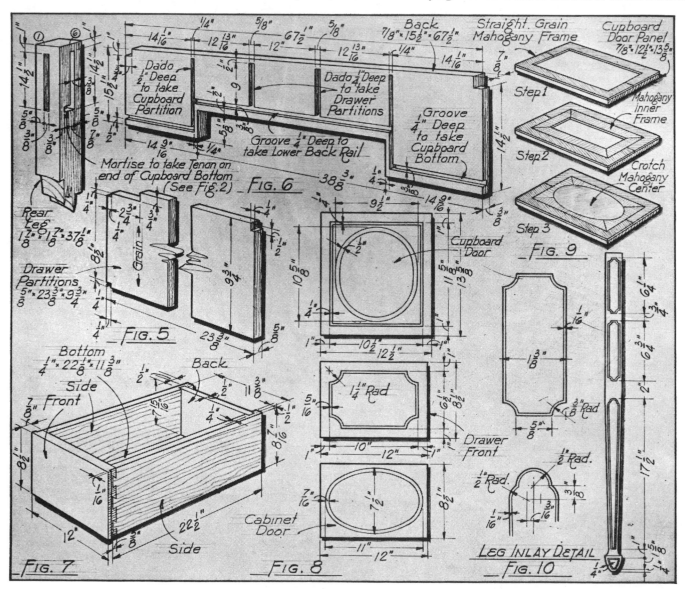

in the rear leg. A ¼″ x ½″ rabbet is cut along both ends and the rear edge to produce a ¼″ x ⅜″ tongue that fits into the grooves already cut.

The framework for the center section is shown in Fig. 4. The rails, drawer runners and cabinet bottom are cut to the sizes shown. The runners and cabinet bottom are joined to the rails by means of tongue-and-groove joints. The frame is glued together, then a tenon is cut at each end of the front rail to fit the mortises in the intermediate legs. A long gain is cut across the upper face of the frame as shown in Fig. 4 to take the drawer partitions. A rabbet is cut along the underface of the back rail to produce a tongue for the back member groove.

The front cupboard rails are cut to the size shown in Fig. 2. The ends of each member have dovetails laid out and cut as shown. To fit these in place, it will be necessary to place the end members and cupboard partitions in their respective legs. The upper front rail shown in Fig. 4 is handled in the same manner. A pair of gains will have to be cut across the underface of the front rail as shown in the same sketch to take the drawer partitions. The gains should extend to within ¼″ of the forward edge.

The drawer partitions shown in Fig. 5 are dressed to size, then cut as indicated to fit the various gains and dadoes provided for them in the front rail, lower frame member and back.

At this point, it is advisable to inlay the legs as shown in the main drawing and Fig. 10. The groove for the inlay is laid out and cut with a knife and chisel. If properly shaped gouges are available, they may be used for out-lining the curves. The inlay is glued in place; then after the glue has set, the projecting portion of the inlay is dressed flush with the leg. All members are sandpapered before assembly.

It is necessary that all assembling should be done without the use of glue at first to check the work, which is then taken apart and reassembled with glue applied to all butting surfaces. The cupboard partitions are joined to the intermediate leg members, then the lower center frame section is glued to the intermediate legs. The drawer partitions are glued to the lower frame section and the upper front rail is set in place. The back is placed over the ends of the partitions and lower back rail. Clamps should be applied to hold these members in place while the glue is given time to set. Be sure to check the corners for squareness. After the clamps have been removed, the cupboard bottoms are glued to the intermediate legs, partition and back. The end member is glued to the front corner and rear legs, then this assembled unit is set on the cupboard bottom and the end of the back member. The front cupboard rails are joined to the legs. The necessary clamps are applied and the work checked for squareness.

As shown in Fig. 1, shoulders are cut at the upper end of each leg to take the cove molding. This is done with a fine-toothed saw and a chisel. The corner braces shown in the same sketch are cut to shape and glued in place. The necessary cleats required to secure the top are cut to size and fastened with 1¼″ No. 8 flathead screws. The drawer runners are cut to size and glued in place.

A cove molding, as shown in section on the main drawing, is cut to shape from ⅜″ x ⅜″ stock and glued in place. All corners should be mitered. The inlays A and C on the main drawing are applied. The top is cut to the required size and shape and the forward edge and ends are molded. The top is applied with 1¼″ No. 8 flathead screws driven through the cleats into the top and 1½″ No. 8 screws driven through the front rails and into the top.

The drawers require stock as shown in Fig. 7. The sides are dovetailed to the front member while the back member is glued in dadoes cut on the inside face of the side members. The bottom is set into a ¼″ x ¼″ groove cut along the front and side members.

The cabinet and cupboard doors are made of ⅞″ stock cut to the sizes given in Fig. 8. The dimensions for the various inlays are shown in this same series of sketches. Figure 9 shows how the veneers are applied. After all veneers are applied, the grooves are cut for the inlays. When all inlaying has been completed, the doors are fitted, then the hinges and locks applied.

The finish should be natural if a dark mahogany was used. Staining of a piece with light inlays is a difficult operation. If staining is to be done, all inlays should have a coat of white shellac applied to them so that they will not be affected by the stain. Filling is done by applying a number of coats of white shellac and rubbing each one down with No. 4/0 sandpaper. The final coat of shellac should be rubbed down with No. FFF pumice stone and rubbing oil, followed by rubbing with rottenstone and oil.

Oak, mahogany and maple are blended in this chest to form an antique mosaic. The inlays are of a type that can be duplicated without difficulty.

Inlaid Chest of Drawers Craftsmen Can Copy

IN EARLY Colonial times the chest was one of the principal objects of furniture. Because of its great utility a chest, with or without drawers, assumed a place of importance in nearly every room in the house. Chests of many varieties brought over from England served as models for American cabinetmakers. These pieces were always of simple rectangular construction but were often richly adorned on the outer surface.

The fanciful small chest of drawers, which is constructed of oak, mahogany and maple as illustrated in the photograph and measured drawing, embodies the Elizabethan tradition of sturdy, rectangular construction. The use of simple geometric inlay as its chief source of decoration and the application of molding on the drawers and the use of fielded panels at the sides, all create a distinctively rich form of embellishment. But its decoration does not end with these features. The extra quality of color is added in the combined use of oak, mahogany and maple blended to give the effect of an antique mosaic.

The carcase of the chest is made of two side units joined together by the front and back rails as shown in Fig. 9.

Construction is started with the side units which consist of the posts, upper and lower side rails and side panels. Four posts made of oak and finished to an overall size of 1½" x 2½" x 30 9/16" are required. The upper side rails, also of oak, are made of stock 1⅛" x 3¾" x 19¼". The lower side rails measure 1⅛" x 3" x 19¼". The mahogany side panels require stock 15/16" thick, 18¾" wide and 20 9/16" long. In order to obtain a panel of this width it will be necessary to glue together several pieces of narrow stock. The panels should be made oversize so they can be cut down and squared

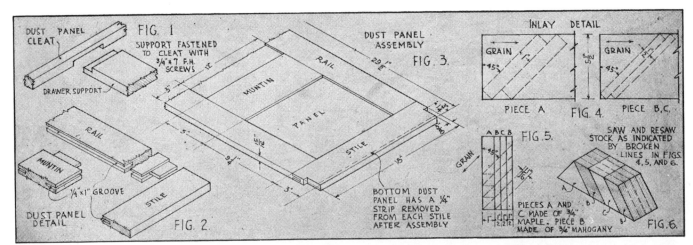

Note to Reprint Edition: This piece is now the property of Trent House, Trenton, New Jersey.

140

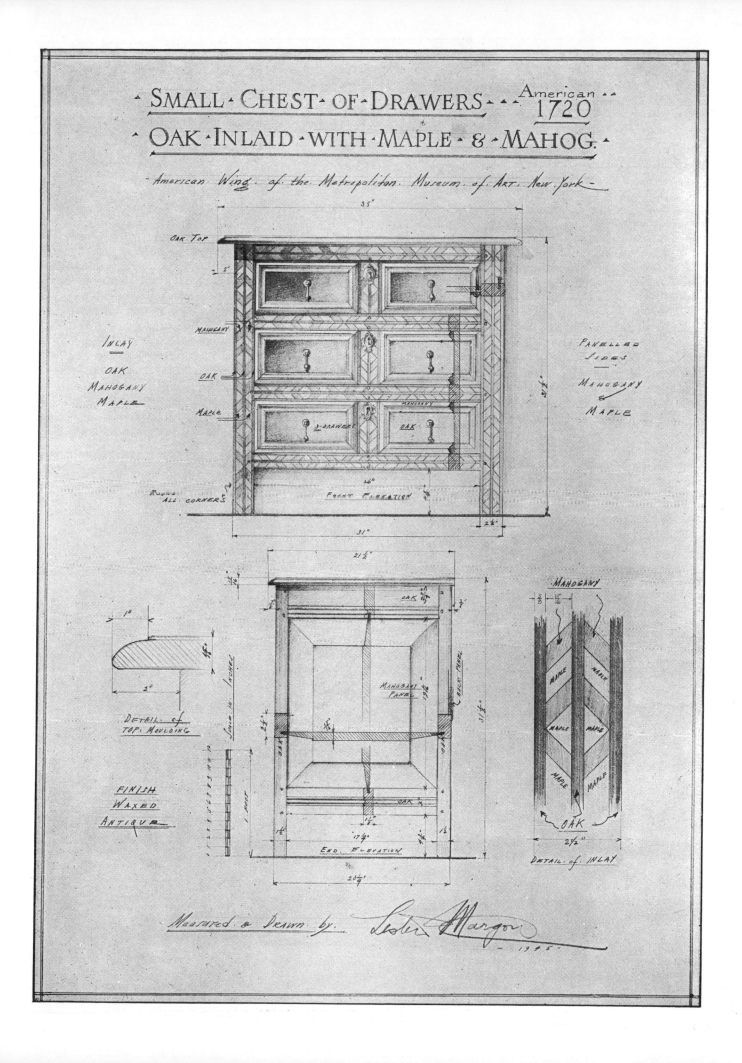

SMALL · CHEST · OF · DRAWERS · ·· American ·· 1720
OAK · INLAID · WITH · MAPLE · & · MAHOG.

·American· Wing· of· the· Metropolitan· Museum· of· Art· New York·

INLAY

OAK
MAHOGANY
MAPLE

PANELLED
SIDES

MAHOGANY
&
MAPLE

DETAIL of
TOP MOULDING

FINISH
WAXED
ANTIQUE

END ELEVATION

MAHOGANY

DETAIL of INLAY

Measured & Drawn by. Lester Margon

- 1945 -

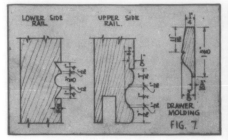

FIG. 7

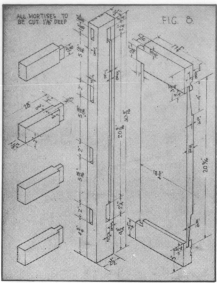

FIG. 8

to the proper size later.

As shown in Fig. 8 the front and side rails are joined to the post by means of mortise and tenon joints, while the side panel is set in a groove cut in the post. The back rails are joined to the back post in the same manner. After the posts have been cut to size they should be arranged in their relative positions and marked on each face for future identification. The mortises to take the side rails, shown in Fig. 8, are laid out on the inside face of each post. The groove for the side panel is laid out on the same face. Mortises for the front and back rails are laid out next.

The cutting of mortises will be made considerably easier if a hollow mortising attachment for the drill press is available. All the mortises in the posts are $\frac{1}{2}$" wide and are cut to a depth of $1\frac{1}{8}$". The groove that is to take the side panel may be cut on the bench saw with a dado head set for a $\frac{3}{8}$" kerf. Care will have to be taken so that the bench saw will not cut beyond the limits of the groove. The ends of the groove must be cleaned out with a chisel. If a $\frac{3}{8}$" router bit is available for use on the drill press the cutting of this groove will be made easier. The groove should be cut to a depth of $\frac{3}{4}$".

Upper and lower side rails have barefaced tenons, dimensioned in Fig. 8, cut on the ends to fit the mortises. Tenons also are cut on the ends of the front and back rails.

The groove on the inside edge of upper and lower side rails can now be laid out for the panels. To check the correctness of the layout, the rails should be assembled to the posts. If these grooves line up with those previously cut in the post, the pieces may be taken apart so the cutting can be done on the bench saw.

The outside face of upper and lower side rails has a molding cut into it as shown in the end elevation of the main drawing. The detail of these moldings is shown in Fig. 7. The molding on the lower rail is cut along the center, while the one on the upper rail is cut along the lower edge. A combination

of small molding cutters set up in the drill press or in the spindle shaper is used to cut the molding. In the absence of the necessary cutters, the molding may be cut by hand.

The cutting of the fielded panels can now be undertaken. As shown in Fig.

8 the beveled edges and ends extend 4" in from the outside. The center of the panel is raised $\frac{3}{16}$" above the bevel. Outer edges and ends taper to a thickness of $\frac{5}{16}$". In order to lay out the panel, first the raised center section is marked on the face. A saw cut is made to a depth of $\frac{3}{16}$" on each of these lines. The required thickness of the panel along the edges and the ends is marked off next. Cutting of the bevel between the outside edge and the saw cut may be done by hand with the aid of a rabbet plane, or it may be done on the jointer. As the work progresses the panel should be tried in the grooves from time to time to check the fit.

The outside face of each front rail and each post is to be inlaid as shown in the photograph and drawing. Grooves measuring $\frac{1}{16}$" deep and $1\frac{1}{16}$" wide must be cut in these members to take the inlay strips. The grooves on the posts are located $\frac{3}{8}$" from the edges, while the grooves on the front rails are placed

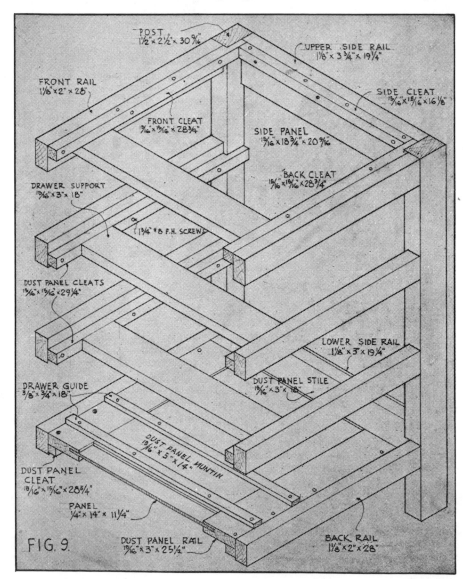

FIG. 9

$\frac{3}{32}''$ from the edges. They may be cut in one of several ways. The bench saw fitted with a dado head may be used; a router bit set up in the drill press may be employed; or a straight-faced cutter set up in the spindle shaper; or any electric hand router may be used.

Preparation of the inlay is shown in Figs. 4, 5, 6. It calls for a combination of maple and mahogany and is made of stock measuring $\frac{3}{4}''$ thick. Each piece should be $5\frac{1}{2}''$ wide and of sufficient length to produce 8 (A) pieces and 8 (C) pieces of maple and 16 (B) pieces of mahogany as shown in Fig. 4. The strips that go to make up the inlay are cut at an angle of 45° across the face of the wood. Pieces marked (A) are to be cut 1" wide, while the strips (B) and (C) are cut $\frac{1}{2}''$ wide. When sufficient strips are ready they are assembled.

As shown in Fig. 5 the strips call for a wide maple strip laid down first, then a narrow mahogany one followed by a narrow maple piece and a second narrow mahogany piece laid down last. These four pieces are glued and set in clamps. The other seven units of the inlay stock are glued up in the same manner. All excess glue forced from the joints by clamps should be wiped off with a damp cloth. After the glue has set and the clamps have been removed, the bench saw is used to cut the stock as indicated by the broken lines in Fig. 5. The final operation of preparing the inlay is that of resawing the pieces as shown by the broken lines in Fig. 6. Resawing should be done on a bench saw which is fitted with a hollow-ground combination blade that will produce a finished cut. It should be possible to obtain four pieces of inlay from each block, as the inlay need be only a little thicker than $\frac{1}{16}''$. Sanding is done after inlaying.

Application of the inlay to the rails and posts is the next step. A study of the photograph and the main drawing will show how these pieces are arranged in the grooves. Glue is applied to the groove as well as to the back of the inlay. Placement of the pieces should be started at the center. After the inlay has been set in place, a strip of paper is placed over the work, then a heavy piece of scrap stock is placed on the paper. Clamps are applied to force out excess glue and to hold the inlay in position. After the clamps have been removed, the inlay is dressed flush.

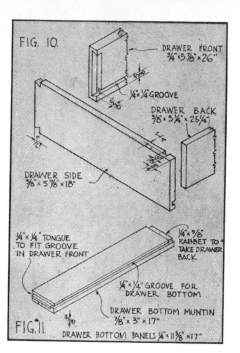

FIG. 10.

FIG. 11.

Before the carcase can be assembled, all members must be sandpapered thoroughly. The end rails are glued to one of the posts, and the end panel is slipped in place. Glue is not to be used on any part of the panel, as this member should be free to expand in order to prevent splitting. The opposite post can now be joined to the posts. Clamps should be applied.

The dust panel cleats and the cleats required to fasten the top in place can now be applied. Fig. 9 shows the sizes of each of these members as well as their locations. The front and back top cleats and the dust panel cleats must have rabbets cut at each end to fit around the posts. The drawer support cleats must have a dado cut across the center, as shown in Fig. 1, to take the drawer support. The cleats are fastened with $1\frac{3}{4}''$ No. 8 flathead screws.

Four drawer supports are cut to the size shown in Fig. 9. These members, with the exception of the top support, have rabbets cut across both ends as shown in Fig. 1 to fit the dadoes previously cut in the dust panel cleats. The three lower drawer supports are fastened in place with $\frac{7}{8}''$ No. 6 flathead screws, but the top support requires use of $1\frac{3}{4}''$ No. 8.

Each dust panel shown in Figs. 3 and 9 is made of the two rails, two stiles, a muntin and two panels cut to sizes given in Fig. 9. Rails, stiles and muntin are grooved as in Fig. 2 to take the panels. Tongues are cut on the ends of the rails and the muntins to fit the grooves. After the dust pan-

els have been assembled, rabbets are cut at the corners of the stiles as shown in Fig. 3 to fit the panels around the posts. The bottom panel must have a $\frac{1}{4}''$ strip removed from each stile as shown in Fig. 3 to allow for the projecting lower side rail. The panels are fastened in place with $1\frac{1}{2}''$ No. 8 flathead screws. Drawer guides are made up and fastened to the dust panels as shown in Fig. 9. These guides are placed equidistant from the center and are spaced 3" apart.

Drawer members are made of stock specified in Fig. 10. The sides are joined to the front by means of a single dovetail. The back is set into a dado cut across the side member. To take the drawer bottom a $\frac{1}{4}''$ x $\frac{1}{4}''$ groove is cut along the side and front members. The drawer bottom is made of two panels and a muntin as shown in Fig. 11. The muntin acts as a support for the drawer bottom and also as a drawer guide; it is made to fit between the guide strips previously fastened to the dust panels. The muntin has a tongue cut on one end to fit the groove in the drawer front and a rabbet cut on the other end to fit around the drawer back. When the muntin is being set in place it must be centered to line up with the drawer guides.

A piece of stock $\frac{3}{8}''$ thick, $2\frac{1}{2}''$ wide and $5\frac{7}{8}''$ long, inlaid in the same manner as the posts, is prepared and glued to the center of each drawer front as shown in the photograph and main drawing. Drawer molding shown in Fig. 7 is applied to the drawer fronts with glue and brads.

The back of the chest is made of four panels, each being $\frac{5}{8}''$ thick, $7\frac{15}{16}''$ wide and 28" long. A $\frac{1}{4}''$ x 1" rabbet is cut on all four sides. The panels are fastened to back rails and to posts with brads.

The top is made of $\frac{15}{16}''$ stock, $21\frac{1}{2}''$ wide and 35" long. The two ends and front edge are molded as shown by the detail in the main drawing. The top is fastened to the chest with $1\frac{3}{4}''$ No. 8 flathead screws driven through the cleat and into the top.

Drawer pulls and escutcheons should be applied, but should then be removed for greater freedom in finishing the chest. The finish should be natural, achieved preferably by the application of several coats of wax to seal the grain. Stain should not be applied unless the inlays are first protected by a coat of shellac. If stain is to be used, it is followed by wax.

18th Century Mahogany Cellarette

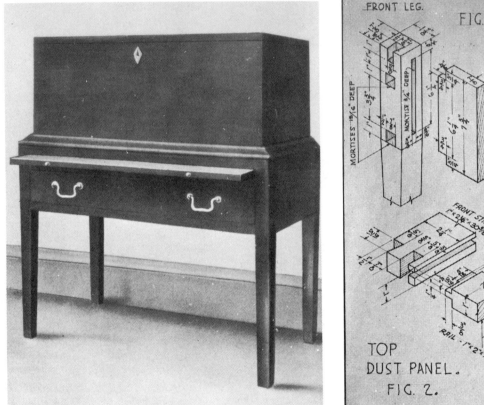

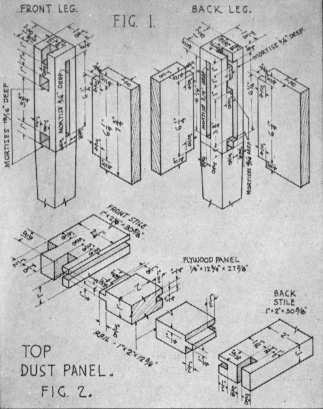

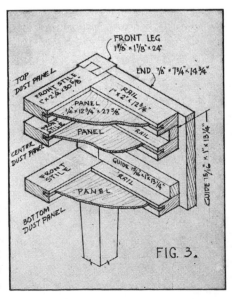

This piece, now in the historic Ford Mansion, Morristown, N. J., is used by permission of Mrs. Paul Moore, the donor, and Mr. Francis S. Ronalds, the co-ordinating superintendent

IN COLONIAL days boxes were made for everything. There were silver chests, sewing cabinets, cupboards and cabinets for pewter, chests for blankets, but most unusual of all were the cellarettes to hold wines and liquors. Many of these chests were low with handles at each side so they could be transported from room to room, but others were built on stands and became permanent fixtures in the dining room.

The mahogany cellarette selected for presentation here is a chest on a stand and it was found in the Ford Mansion at Morristown. The gift of Mrs. Paul Moore of Convent, N. J., to the Morristown National Historical Park, this

cellarette is of particular interest because of its simplicity, fineness of line and proportions and because of its complete utilitarian aspect. In reproduction the interiors of the cellarette should be planned according to individual needs. Below the cellarette proper you will notice a sliding shelf and below that a drawer in which to put all the necessary paraphernalia for graceful hospitality.

One of the great historical shrines of America now under the direction of the National Park Service of the U. S. Department of Interior is the Ford Mansion in the National Historical Park at Morristown, New Jersey. In this house the antique cellarette is now sheltered,

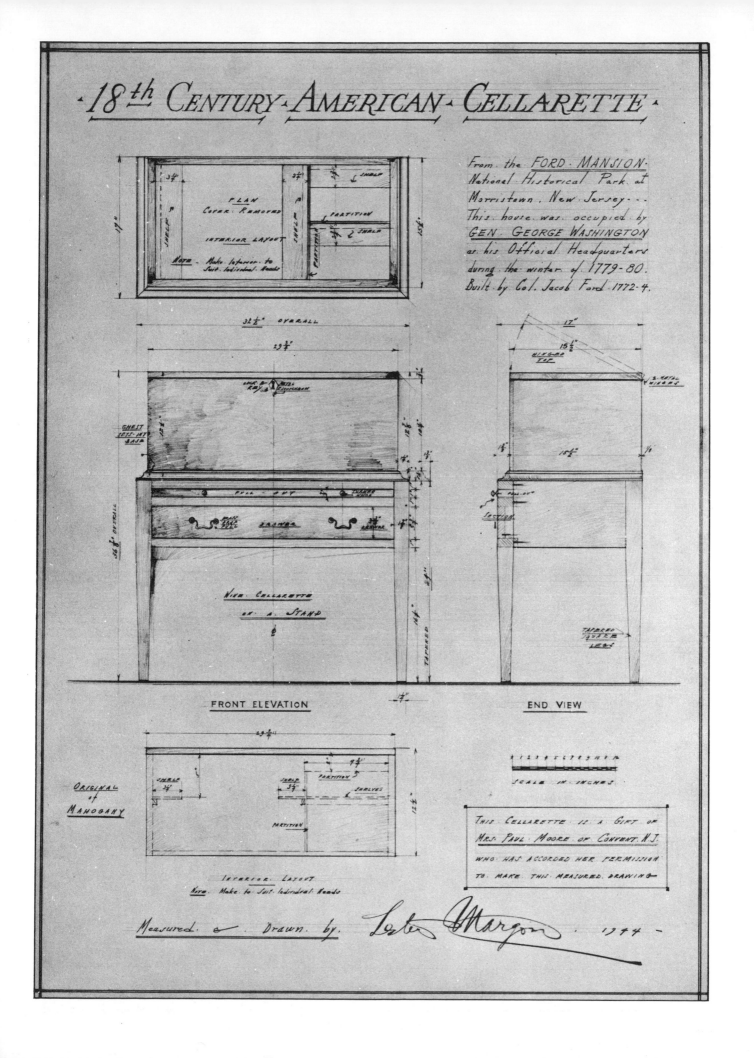

18th Century American Cellarette

and here General George Washington set up his official headquarters during the winter of 1779-80. The house was built by Col. Jacob Ford between 1772 and 1774.

With its magnificent Palladian entrance, this mansion is a splendid example of late Colonial architecture. It was here that Lafayette was received when he brought word that the King of France was sending a fleet of ships and 6,000 troops to the grateful assistance of the American ally.

Craftsmen who plan to reproduce the cellarette should consider it as two separate units, these being the table and the chest. The completed chest will be set on the table and will fit in the rabbet of the molding. Construction should be started with the table, as the chest must be fitted to this unit. While the original was built of mahogany any cabinet wood such as walnut, birch or maple can be substituted.

The legs are made of four pieces of 1⅞" square stock 24" long. The relative position of each leg should be established and marked in some manner so that the mortises and dovetail sockets that are to take the tenons and dovetail pins of the aprons and stiles can be located and laid out. As shown in Fig. 1 the front legs have a ⅜" x 6¼" mortise located on one surface to take the

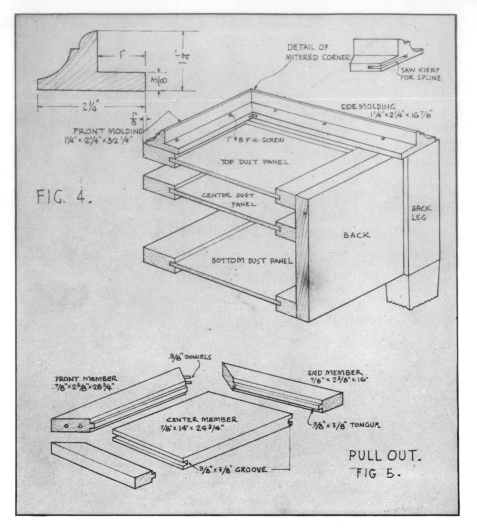

FIG. 4.

PULL OUT.
FIG 5.

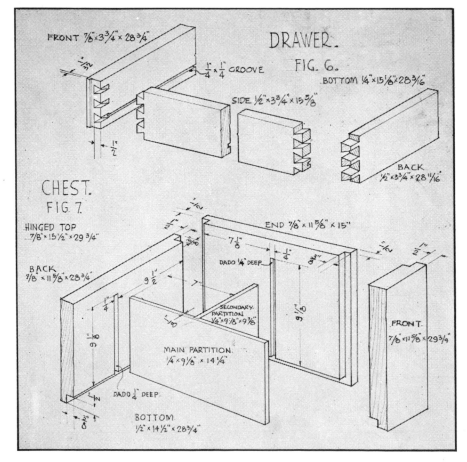

DRAWER.
FIG. 6.

CHEST.
FIG. 7.

side aprons. These mortises are cut to a depth of ¾". On the adjacent surface of these legs, a dovetail socket is laid out and cut on the upper end to take the front stile of the top dust panel. Two mortises measuring ⅞" wide, 1" long and 15/16" deep are laid out and cut on the same surface to take the tenons on the ends of the center and bottom dust panel stiles.

The back legs as shown in Fig. 1 have mortises ⅜" wide, 6¼" long and ¾" deep laid out and cut on adjacent surfaces to take the side and back aprons. At the upper end of each leg a dovetail socket is located to take the dovetail pin on the end of the back stile of the top dust panel. Two mortises ⅝" wide, 1" long and 15/16" deep are laid out below the dovetail socket to take the tenons on the ends of the back stile of the center and bottom dust panels. The locations of these cuts are in Fig. 1.

Each of the four legs is tapered from a point 7¾" from the upper end down to the lower end. The tapering is done on all four surfaces to bring the leg measurement to 1¼" at the lower end. A tapering jig used on the bench saw will simplify the cutting of the taper. If this method is used, some allowance should be made for dressing the sawed surfaces smooth either with a hand plane or on a jointer.

The side aprons, or ends, require two pieces of 7/8" stock 7¾" wide and 14¾" long. The back apron is made of a piece of 7/8" stock 7¾" wide and 30¼" long. As each of these aprons must have tenons of identical size laid out and cut at each end, the pieces should be worked together. Each tenon is 3/8" thick, 6¼" wide and 3/4" long. They have a 3/4" shoulder at each edge and a 1/2" shoulder on the outside face. After the tenons have been cut and fitted to their respective mortises the work should be assembled temporarily for checking.

The three dust panels are identical in size and construction except that the ends of the top dust panel stiles are to have dovetail pins cut on them rather than tenons. Each dust panel requires two stiles, a front stile measuring 1" x 2¼" x 30 5/8" and a back stile measuring 1" x 2" x 30 5/8"; two rails measuring 1" x 2" x 12¾" and one plywood panel ¼" x 12¾" x 27 5/8".

The first step in preparing the stock for the panels is to cut a ¼" x ½" groove on the inside edge of each rail and stile to take the ¼" panel. The groove should be located ¼" from the upper face of each member. Tenons are cut on each end of the rails to fit the groove as shown in Fig. 2. The stiles of the top dust panel have dovetail pins cut as shown in Fig. 2, to fit the dovetail sockets on the ends of the four legs. The center and bottom dust panel stiles have tenons cut to fit the mortised legs.

The panels should be assembled temporarily and then the entire table should be assembled. If all units fit together properly the table can be taken apart so that all parts can be sanded. The dust panel members are glued and clamped. Assembly of the table is then started. Each side apron is glued to its two adjoining legs. As soon as clamps are applied the corners are checked with a try-square. Next, the bottom and center dust panels as

well as the back apron are jointed to one of the side units. The other side unit is then set in place. Before the top dust panel can be positioned, the two pull-out guides must be set in place as shown in Fig. 3. These guides measure 15/16" x 1" x 13¼" and are fastened to the end aprons with 1¼" No. 7 flathead screws which have been countersunk in the guides so that the screw heads will not interfere with the free movement of the pull-out. The final step is to place the top dust panel on the legs. Clamps should be applied to hold the various units together, and all corners should be checked for squareness. A section of the assembled work is shown in Fig. 3.

Around the top of the table, molding is to be applied as shown in Fig. 4. This is made of 1¼" stock 2¼" wide. A piece of stock six feet long will be sufficient to produce the front and side moldings. The outside edge is shaped on the spindle shaper to the common contour given in the drawing, Fig. 4. A rabbet measuring 7/8" x 1" is cut on the bench saw. The two side moldings are cut to a length of 16 7/8" while the front molding measures 32¼" long. The butting ends of the molding are mitered at an angle of 45° and a saw kerf is made in the stock slightly below the rabbet to accommodate a small spline. The spline is cut and driven in place. The molding is fastened in place with 1" No. 8 flathead wood screws as shown in the detail.

The pull-out shown in Fig. 5 is made of two end members that act as battens, a front member and a center member. The center member has a 3/8" x 3/8" groove cut on each end and on the outside edge. The end and front members have a 3/8" x 3/8" tongue cut on the edge to fit the groove. The butting ends of the front and end members are mitered at 45°. Dowels 3/8" in diameter are set into the mitered ends to join the end and front members together. The center member is slipped into place along the tongues. After the pull-out has been assembled it is sandpapered and fitted in place.

The drawer shown in Fig. 6 has

the front made of 7/8" stock 3¾" wide and 28¾" long; the sides are made of ½" stock 3¾" wide and 15 5/8" long and the back is made of ½" stock 3¾" x 28 11/16". A ¼" x ¼" groove is cut on the inside face of each member to take the bottom panel. The drawer ends are joined to the front and back members by means of dovetail joints. After the joints have been cut and the work has been fitted together for the purpose of checking the accuracy of construction, the drawer can be permanently assembled.

The chest shown in Fig. 7 is made up of 7/8" stock, 11 5/8" wide for the end, front and back members, while the bottom is made of ½" stock 14½" wide and the top calls for 7/8" stock 15½" wide. Each member is cut in the lengths given in the detail sketch. The ends of the front, back and end members are rabbeted as shown. The bottom edge of each member is rabbeted to receive the bottom panel.

Provisions have been made to divide the chest into three compartments, separating them with partitions made of ¼" stock. Dadoes ¼" x ¼" are laid out and cut as indicated to receive the partitions. The partitions themselves are joined together by means of a dado joint. After the dadoes have been cut the work can be assembled with glue. Clamps are applied to hold the side members while the glue is given time to set. Before the bottom piece is added, the partitions are slipped into position from the underside of the chest. A suggested shelf arrangement is shown in the interior layout and the plan of the chest. The shelves are made of ¼" stock and are supported by 3/8" x ½" cleats.

All necessary hardware should be applied but, with the exception of the hinges, it should be removed for the purpose of finishing. If open-grain wood has been used for construction, filler should be applied after the stain coat. Several coats of white shellac should be rubbed down when hard with No. 00 steel wool or with pumice stone. A coat of wax rubbed in well will complete the work unless the builder elects to add a coat of non-staining bakelite base varnish.

Antique Spinning Wheel for Flax

A spinning wheel is among the most decorative of furniture accessories. This one was measured for reproduction in the historic Old Barracks, Trenton, N. J.

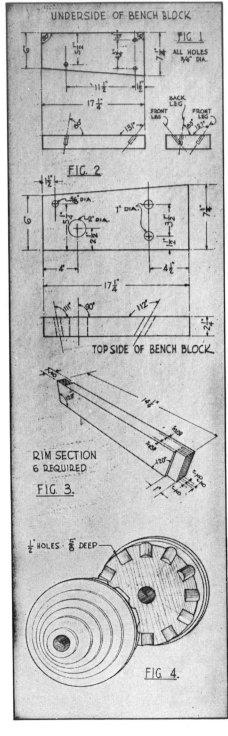

SPINNING wheels are practically never sold at auctions. Families cherish them and pass them along from generation to generation. They are among the rarest of household antiques.

At the Old Barracks built in 1758 in Trenton, N. J., the excellent old spinning wheel shown here was found and measured. The piece is on loan to the General George Washington Chapter of the Daughters of the American Revolution by Mrs. George B. Yard of Trenton.

Construction of the spinning wheel starts with the bench block. Holes are bored in the underside to take the legs as in Fig. 1 and on the top side for posts as shown in Fig. 2. While the original had tapered holes to take the posts, it is suggested that all holes be made with parallel sides and that the turnings be

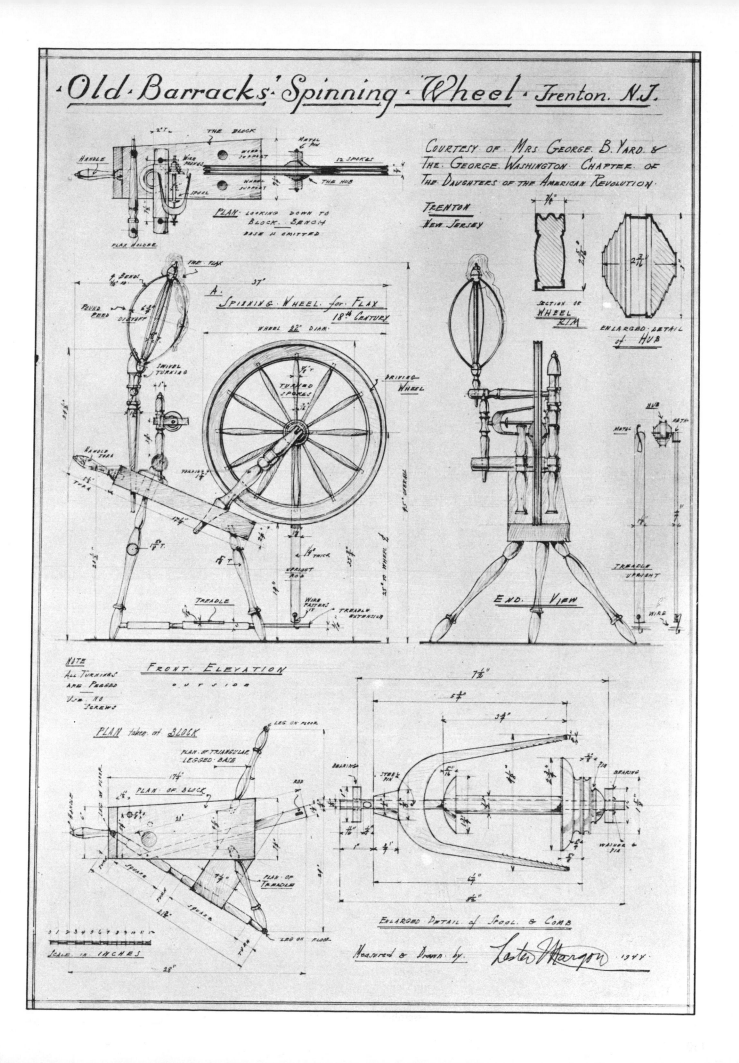

Old Barracks' Spinning Wheel · Trenton. N.J.

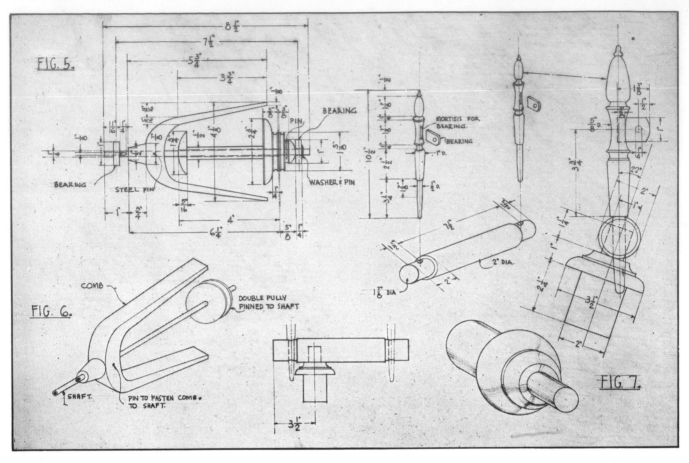

FIG. 5.

FIG. 6.

COMB

DOUBLE PULLY PINNED TO SHAFT

SHAFT.

PIN TO FASTEN COMB TO SHAFT.

FIG. 7.

shaped as shown in Fig. 7.

The back leg is a turning made of 1¾" square stock finished 18¾" long. The two front legs are made of the same stock, 20½" long. All three legs have tenons 1" long turned on the upper end to fit holes in the bench block. The turned legs are set in place temporarily while holes are located in front and back legs to take the treadle assembly. The center of these holes is 1¾" from the floor. The holes should be ½" in diameter and ¾" deep.

The treadle is made of three pieces in Fig. 8. The pivot member is 1" square stock shaped as shown and having a ½" pin at each end to fit freely in the leg holes. The arm, made of ⅜" stock and foot rest made of ⁵⁄₁₆" stock, are cut to shape and fastened with dowels and glue.

The treadle is now set in place in the legs and the legs are glued to the bench block. The handle in the end of the block is a turning made of 1¼" square stock with a ⅝" pin ¾" long.

The unit supporting the comb and spool is made of two posts with bearings, a crosspiece to carry the uprights and a base to join the crosspiece to the bench block. These are shown in Fig. 7. The crosspiece is a turning 2" in diameter and 10½" long. Two ½" holes are bored in the crosspiece to take uprights and a 1" hole is bored 3½" from one end to take the base turning. The angle at which holes are bored is shown. The base is a turning 3½" in diameter and 4½" long.

The posts are turnings made of 1¼" square stock finished to a length of 10½" and shaped as in Fig. 7. A mortise is cut in each post to take a bearing. The bearings are hardwood, ¼" thick, 1" wide and 1⅜" long with a ¼" hole bored in each to take the shaft of the comb and spool assembly. With the exception of the bearings these parts can be assembled and set up on the bench block.

The comb and spool assembly, the most important functioning part of the spinning wheel, is shown in Figs. 5 and 6. The shaft is a piece of ¼" rod with a ⅛" hole drilled in the end for a depth of ¹⁵⁄₁₆". An oval-shaped hole is cut through the shaft at right angles to the hole in the end in order to pass the flax through the shaft and onto the comb. The comb, made of ¾" stock, is fastened to the shaft by a steel pin. The small hooks placed on the arms of the comb over which flax passes on its way to the spool may be small L hooks or short lengths of wire. The two-step pulley is fastened to the shaft with a steel pin after the spool has been positioned.

The spool is a turning made of 3" stock finished to an overall length of 4". The single pulley at the end of the spool is shaped on the stock. The spool has a hole bored through the center to

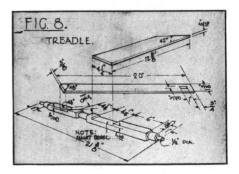

FIG. 8.

TREADLE.

NOTE:

permit its free rotation on the shaft.

After comb and pulley are assembled, the bearing on the far side is placed on the shaft and the washer and pin that hold this bearing on the shaft are added. The bearings are now added to the uprights.

The wheel is assembled from six rim sections cut as shown in Fig. 3. Shaping of the wheel to the section shown in the main drawing is done as an outboard operation on the lathe with an auxiliary faceplate made of wood and attached to the standard faceplate.

The hub is made of two pieces glued together for turning with paper inserted in the glue joint in order that they may be separated for assembling the spokes. Holes $\frac{1}{2}$" in diameter and $\frac{5}{8}$" deep are bored in the hub and rim to take spokes. Holes should not be located at the joints of the rim sections.

Spokes are turned with $\frac{1}{2}$" x $\frac{5}{8}$" pins at each end. The wheel is assembled by placing spokes in the rim and covering with hub sections at center.

Turnings that support the wheel are finished to a diameter of $1\frac{5}{8}$" and a length of $17\frac{3}{4}$". A $\frac{1}{4}$" slot 1" deep is cut in the upper end of each support to take the $\frac{3}{16}$" axle. The axle is made of $\frac{3}{16}$" rod 6" long with one end bent to form the crank. The axle hole in the hub should form a drive fit.

The post supporting the distaff is $19\frac{1}{2}$" long. The turned arm of this unit is $1\frac{1}{4}$" in diameter and $10\frac{1}{2}$" long. The distaff is a turning 18" long with 4 round reeds $\frac{3}{16}$" in diameter.

Construction of the treadle upright, or link, will complete the spinning wheel.

American Whatnot

This intriguing piece is in the Old Merchant's House, New York. Built in 1830 as a residence for Seabury Tredwell, it is now owned by the Historic Landmark Society

THE American whatnot was fashionable during the first half of the nineteenth century. It replaced the many brackets that had previously been used to hold bric-a-brac and china. With the revival of interest in the furnishings of that period—late Federal and Victorian—whatnots are now highly prized and sought after by collectors and decorators because they are without a peer for displaying china, glassware and small ornaments.

We are beginning to realize that many of the old whatnots are of excellent design and workmanship. This piece, which is reproduced by permission of the Historic Landmark Society, is an especially fine example.

The construction of the whatnot should be started with the shelves. These will require five pieces of ½" solid stock, each being 30" long. The top shelf should be 4½" wide, the third shelf 5⅞" in width, the second shelf 7¼", the first shelf 8⅝" and the bottom shelf 10".

After each piece has been cut to size, the holes that are to take the turned columns are located on the face of each as shown in Fig. 1. As illustrated in the photograph, the other columns are in line with one another from top to bottom, therefore the location of the holes in the shelves that are to take these must line up. The forward columns are stepped back between each shelf and finished with the finial. The finial is in line with the column below it, therefore the upper end of the column and the lower end of the finial are placed in the same hole. Before boring any of the holes, check the layout of them on one shelf against the one that is to be placed above it. The forward hole of the upper shelf must line up with the second hole in the shelf immediately below. Each hole is to be bored through the stock with a ½" bit.

The next step is to prepare a full-size pattern of each shelf contour by using the graph-squared drawing shown in Fig. 2 as an aid in laying out the patterns. All shelf contours can be traced on the stock with the aid of carbon paper. The shelves can be cut to shape on the band or jig saw; then the front edge and both ends can be molded on the shaper.

The columns are made of a number of turnings set between the shelves. There are to be five sets of columns, each set consisting of four identical turnings. Since the length and detail of the sets vary, it is advisable to lay out full-size patterns for each set of turnings. The detail of the turning shown on the main drawing applies to the columns between the bottom shelf and the first shelf.

The column between the first and second shelves has a turned section 12¼" long as shown in the front elevation. The overall lengths of the components are given in this elevation. The details of the components can be worked out, following the detail of the turning for the lower column. The patterns for the columns between the second and third shelves and the third and top shelves should be developed in a like manner.

The Old Merchant's House in New York

The upper end of each column is to have a ½" pin ¼" long turned on the end. The columns that are used at the front of the whatnot are to have ½" pins ½" long turned on the lower end while those that are used at the rear are to have ½" pins ¼" long turned on the lower end.

The lower set of columns will require four pieces of stock 1⅜" square and 16" long. The next set will take

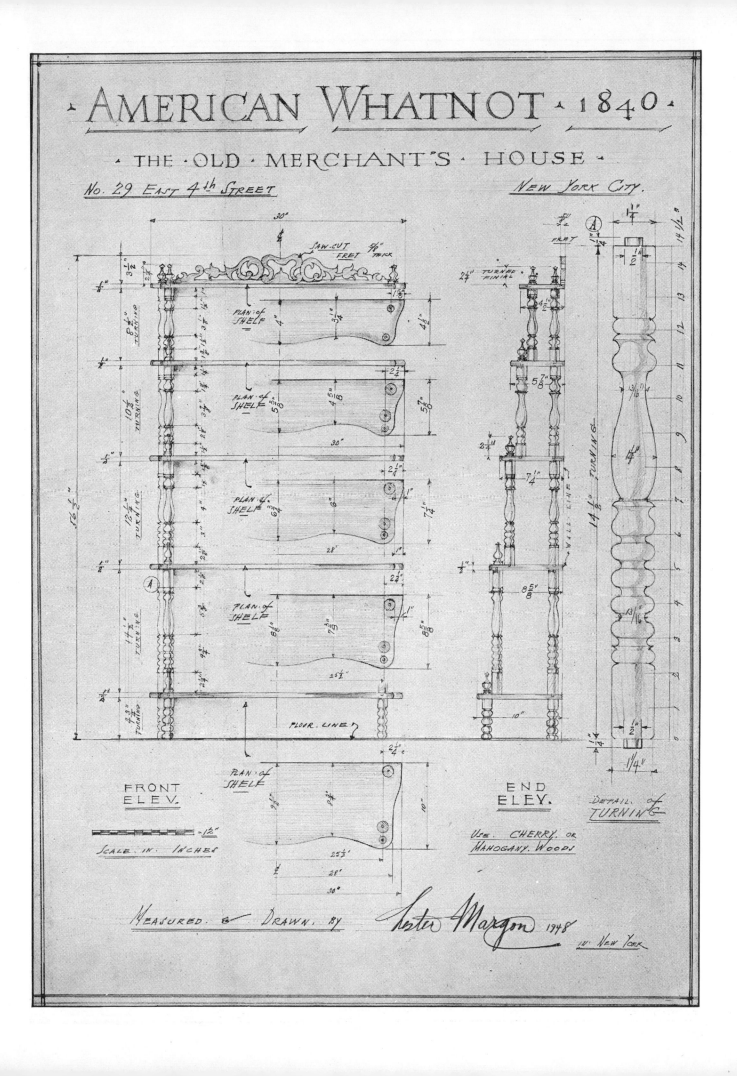

AMERICAN WHATNOT · 1840 ·

· THE · OLD · MERCHANT'S · HOUSE ·

No. 29 EAST 4th STREET   NEW YORK CITY.

SAW-CUT FRET ⅝" THICK

PLAN OF SHELF

FRONT ELEV.

SCALE IN INCHES

END ELEV.

USE CHERRY OR MAHOGANY WOODS

DETAIL OF TURNING

MEASURED & DRAWN BY   Lester Margon 1948

IN NEW YORK

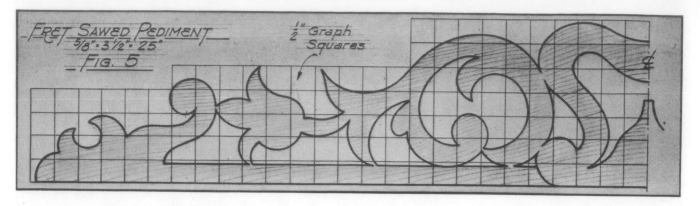

FRET SAWED PEDIMENT
5/8"·3 1/2"·25"
FIG. 5

1/2" Graph Squares

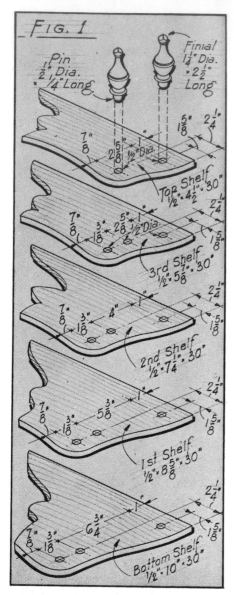

FIG. 1

Pin 1/2" Dia. × 1/4" Long

Finial 1 1/4" Dia. × 2 1/2" Long

Top Shelf 1/2" × 4 1/2" × 30"

3rd Shelf 1/2" × 5 5/8" × 30"

2nd Shelf 1/2" × 7 1/4" × 30"

1st Shelf 1/2" × 8 5/8" × 30"

Bottom Shelf 1/2" × 10" × 30"

four pieces 1 3/8" x 1 3/8" x 13 3/4". The third set takes four pieces 1 3/8" square and 12" long while the fourth set requires four pieces 1 3/8" x 1 3/8" x 10". Stock of the lengths specified allows for the pins at each end as well as for waste at the live and dead centers of the lathe.

When turning the stock for the columns, center each piece in the lathe, then turn the stock down to its largest rough diameter with a gouge. The finished outside diameter of 1 1/4" should be arrived at with the use of the skew chisel. The location of the various beads, coves and pins should be marked off on the cylinder. The ultimate depths of the beads and coves should be established with the aid of a parting tool and calipers. The turning of the pins at each end should not be undertaken until all other turning has been completed. The coves are turned to shape with a 1/4" gouge while the beads are shaped with the skew chisel. The work should be sandpapered with No. 1/2 and No. 2/0 sandpaper, then the pins turned at each end. Keep in mind that the pins on the lower end of the forward columns are to be 1/2" long while all others are to be 1/4" in length.

The feet shown in Fig. 3 will require four pieces of 1 3/8" square stock 6" long. These pieces are set up in the same manner as were the columns.

The finials, shown in Fig. 4, will require twelve pieces of 1 3/8" square stock 3 1/4" long. These are turned to

shape between centers in the lathe.

The feet are glued to the lower shelf; then the first set of columns is set in place. The first shelf is joined to the upper end of these columns, and the second shelf set in place. The third set of columns is placed in the second shelf, then the third shelf joined to the upper pins. The last set of columns is placed in position in the third shelf, and the top shelf set in place. The finials are applied as shown in the main drawing.

The pediment at the back of the top shelf will require a piece of 5/8" stock 3 1/2" x 25". A full-size pattern of this member should be prepared, using the graph-squared drawing shown in Fig. 5 as an aid in laying out the pattern. The pattern is traced on the stock, then the work cut to shape on the jig saw, using a fine-toothed blade to eliminate the need for excessive sanding. The completed pediment is fastened to the top shelf with 7/8" No. 5 flathead wood screws driven from underneath.

If mahogany has been used for the construction, a filler should be applied to close the grain. The filler used should be light mahogany if the work has not been stained. If cherry was used, the work need not be filled. In this case, all that is needed is an application of stain if it is desired to give color to the work. In either case, two coats of clear lacquer, preferably water clear, should be sprayed on it. When hard, the work should be rubbed down with pumice stone and water followed by rottenstone and water.

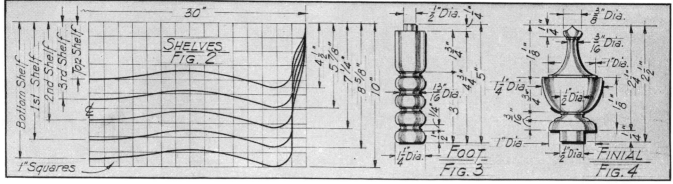

SHELVES FIG. 2

30"

1" Squares

Bottom Shelf
1st Shelf
2nd Shelf
3rd Shelf
Top Shelf

FOOT FIG. 3

FINIAL FIG. 4

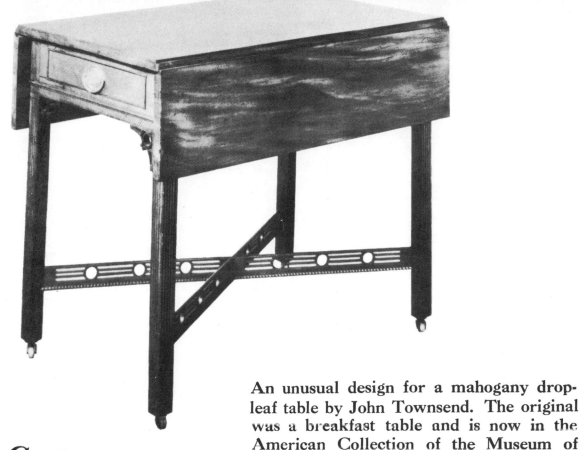

An unusual design for a mahogany drop-leaf table by John Townsend. The original was a breakfast table and is now in the American Collection of the Museum of Fine Arts, Boston, Mass.

18th Century
PEMBROKE TABLE

DETAILS of exceptional interest and variety mark this mahogany breakfast table. It was built by John Townsend, a cabinetmaker of Newport, R. I. Permission to reproduce the photograph and make the measured drawings was given by the Boston Museum of Fine Arts, where the piece is now part of the American Collection.

This type of small rectangular dropleaf table is known as a Pembroke table after the Earl of Pembroke. The leaves are supported by brackets in the frame. These so-called "fly brackets" are characteristic of American Pembroke tables and also appear in the English tables by Sheraton and Hepplewhite.

The Townsend version of the Pembroke table is noteworthy because of the pierced, crossed stretchers with a carved egg-and-dart lower molding, as well as the beautifully designed corner brackets and the leg ornamentation of flutes and filled-in flutes.

Construction of the table should be started with the leg members. These will require four pieces of stock dressed to 1 7/16″ square and 26½″ long. The legs should be arranged in their relative position and marked in some manner for future reference. The mortises that are to take the end apron frame and the side apron are laid out on adjacent sides of each leg member according to the dimensions given in Fig. 2. These mortises are cut to a depth of 11/16″, which allows for 1/16″ clearance for the tenon.

As shown in the end elevation, a small molding is to be applied above the incised diaper design. To take this molding, a groove ⅛″ x ¼″ is cut across the outer face of each leg member as shown in Fig. 2. The inner corner of the leg members is to be chamfered as shown in the front elevation of the main drawing and in Fig. 2. This is a stopped chamfer and may be cut on the jointer or by hand with a chisel and plane.

At this point it might be best to lay out and cut the mortises for the stretchers as shown in Fig. 7. The mortise is located 4½″ from the lower end of the leg and measures ¼″ wide and 1½″ long. As shown in the section, the vertical center of the mortise is along the center line of the chamfer. The angle at which the mortise is to be cut is 75° to the surface of the chamfer. If the mortise is to be cut on the drill press, the angle can be obtained by tilting the table to 15° off horizontal or by placing a wedge-shaped strip cut at an angle of 15° under the leg member.

The outer surfaces of each leg have flutes and reeds cut along them as shown in the leg detail of the main drawing. This ornamentation extends from the bottom of the leg to within 5½″ of the upper end. The lower section for a distance of 6¼″ is a filled-in flute as shown in the detail. This can be cut on the drill press or on the shaper with a reed cutter. The

155

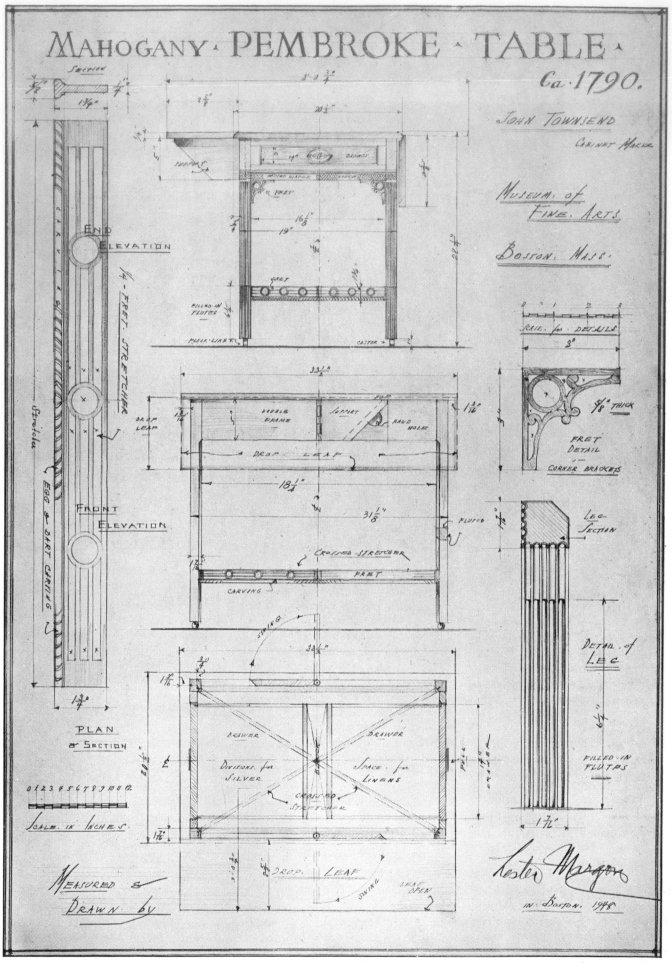

MAHOGANY · PEMBROKE · TABLE ·

Ca · 1790.

JOHN TOWNSEND
Cabinet Maker

MUSEUM · OF
FINE · ARTS

BOSTON · MASS ·

END ELEVATION

FRONT ELEVATION

PLAN & SECTION

SCALE IN INCHES.

MEASURED &
DRAWN by

SCALE for DETAILS

FRET DETAIL
or
CORNER BRACKETS

LEG SECTION

DETAIL OF LEG

FILLED-IN FLUTES

IN BOSTON · 1948

remaining portion of the ornamentation is done with a flute cutter. The upper end of each reed will have to be finished off by hand with a wood carver's gouge.

The end aprons are frames as shown in Figs. 1 and 4. Each frame will require a bottom rail, a top rail and two stiles, the dimensions of which are given in Fig. 3. The stiles are joined to the rails by means of mortise-and-tenon joints. The mortises are laid out on the rails following the dimensions given in Fig. 3 and cut to a depth of 9/16". Tenons are laid out on both ends of each stile member; then the tenons are cut to fit their respective mortises.

After the stiles have been fitted to the rails, the members are glued together. Clamps should be applied and allowed to remain on the assembled work while the glue is given time to set. It is of the utmost importance to check the assembled frames for squareness immediately after the clamps have been applied. If the frame is not square, this condition can be corrected by a slight shift of the clamps. Failure to check the frame may result in its being out of square permanently.

When the clamps have been removed, work on these frames can be

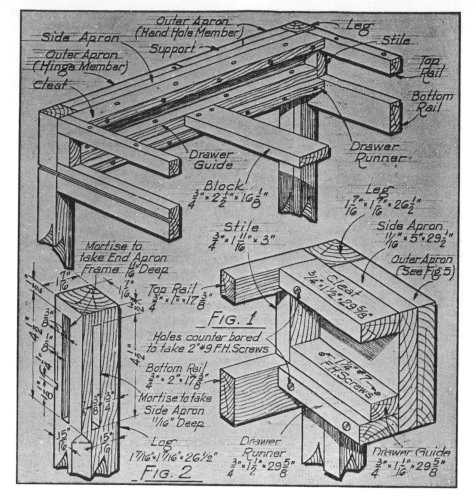

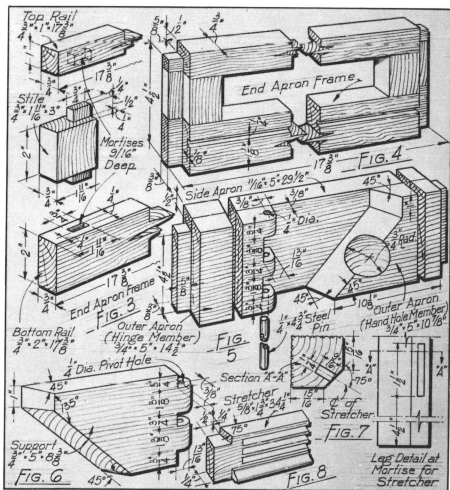

continued. Tenons must be laid out on each end of the frames as shown in Fig. 4; then the tenons are cut to fit their respective mortises that were previously cut in the leg members. The outer face of the frame member has a ⅛" x ¼" groove cut along the bottom rail as shown in Fig. 4 to take the applied molding. Before the groove is cut, it should be laid out and the frame member then set in place between the legs to make certain that this groove will line up with those that were cut in the leg members.

The end apron frames are now joined to the legs. Apply glue to all butting surfaces before assembling. Clamps should be applied to hold the members together. Check the measurement between the legs at the top and bottom to make certain they are parallel. The corner formed by the joining of the apron and leg must be checked for squareness.

The incised diaper design shown in the end elevation consists of a series of diagonal cuts made with a wood carver's parting tool. The cuts are spaced about ⅜" between centers and are made on a slant of 45°.

The molding shown in Fig. 10 may be cut on the shaper, if cutters small enough are available. Otherwise it

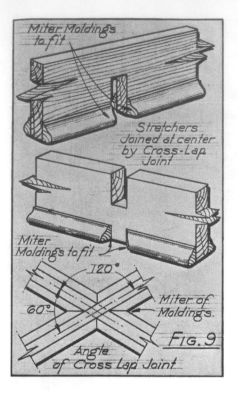

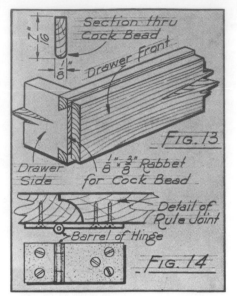

is best to prepare this molding with a scratch beader. Two pieces of such molding will be required, each being about 20″ long. The pieces are fitted in the groove that extends across the lower rail of the apron frame and across the legs. Each piece should be cut to length and dressed to fit from the outside of one leg to the outside of the other. The molding, when completed, is glued in place.

Each side apron as shown in Fig. 5 actually consists of two aprons, one being the apron that joins the legs together while the other consists of three pieces of wood, two of which are glued to the full-length apron and one acts as the support for the drop leaf.

The full-length apron is cut to the size shown in Fig. 5, having a tenon on each end to fit the mortise in the leg. The hinge member of the outer apron is cut to the size shown in the same figure, then the slots that form one half of the hinge are laid out and cut. A ¼″ hole to take the ¼″ x 4¾″ steel pin is bored through the knuckle member to within ¼″ of the lower edge. The hand-hole member of the outer apron is cut to the size and shape given in the same figure. The opening for the hand hole is shaped with a gouge. When completed, these outer apron members are glued to the main apron.

The support shown in Fig. 6 is cut to the size and shape given in the sketch. The completed piece is fitted in place between the outer aprons that were applied to the main apron; then the ¼″ pivot rod hole is bored through the support knuckles while this member is in position.

The stretchers will require two pieces of stock, the size of each being given in Fig. 8. The detail of the pierced work is shown in the main drawing and should be laid out on the stock. The circular openings may be made with a bit; the slots are cut to shape on the jig saw. After the piercing has been done, the members are shaped as shown in section on the main drawing. The molded lower edge is cut on the shaper, while the upper portion, which has a finished thickness of ¼″, is cut to thickness on the jointer.

As shown in Fig. 8, a tenon is cut on the ends of each stretcher member to fit the mortises in the leg. It should be noted that the shoulder of the tenon is cut at an angle of 75°. Figure 9 shows the layout of the cross-lap joint at the center of each stretcher. It will be seen that the molding at the lower edge of the stretchers must be mitered to fit at the joint.

Assembling the side aprons and stretchers with the end units can now be undertaken. The two stretcher members are joined together, then inserted in the leg of one end unit. The aprons are also joined to this same unit. The second end unit can now be placed on the other ends of the aprons and stretchers. It will be necessary to

spring the stretchers slightly to get them into the mortises. Clamps should be applied and the work checked for squareness.

The ornamental brackets shown in Fig. 11 are cut to shape on the jig saw, then glued in place. The drop-leaf supports are set in place and the pivot pins inserted.

The various members that are required for the drawer runners, guides, block and cleat as shown in Fig. 1 are cut to the sizes given, then fastened in place with screws. Figure 12 shows the drawer construction along with the dimensions of the various members. After the drawer has been assembled, the rabbet for the cock bead as shown in Fig. 13 is cut. The cock bead is made up and applied to the rabbet using glue to secure it in place.

The table top and drop-leaf members are finished to the sizes given on the main drawing. The rule joint shown in Fig. 14 is cut on the shaper by using appropriate cutters. The top is fastened in place with 1¼″ No. 7 flathead screws and the drop leaves hinged as shown in Fig. 14. Drawer pulls and casters are applied, completing the work. Casters, of course, are optional and may not be desired by the craftsman who is copying this piece.

In order to finish the piece, it will be necessary to remove the hardware. The work should be stained and filled with a paste filler. This is followed with a shellac or a clear lacquer finish, either of which should be rubbed down with pumice stone and rottenstone to produce a satin finish.

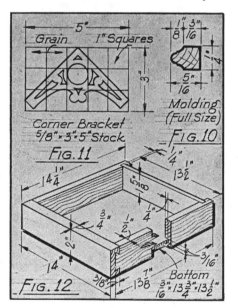

American
FIRE SCREEN

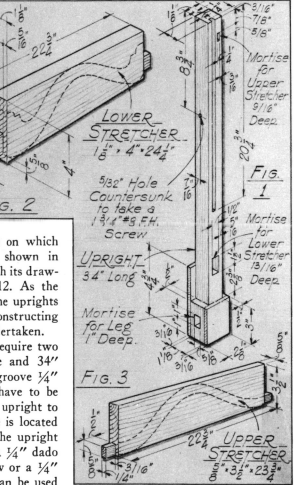

I N SIZE and character, this late 18th Century mahogany fire screen recommends itself for reproduction as a very graceful and fitting adjunct in any period-furnished room of today.

The original was made by a New York cabinetmaker. The shield, which slides up and down, is covered with part of a remarkable old English print on linen called "The Apotheosis of Franklin." This has red decorations on a white ground.

Of special interest is the extended shelf containing two small drawers for miscellaneous small objects. A candlestick was often set on the shelf to provide light for reading or sewing. The design of the cabriole feet is of exceptional elegance and true to the best traditions of the Queen Anne style.

The fire screen is a purchase of the Rogers Fund and is on display in the American Wing of the Metropolitan Museum of Art, New York, by permission of which the photograph above is reproduced here.

The construction of the fire screen should be broken into three main units, these being the upright or stand, the parts of which are shown in Figs. 1 to

5, the screen with its frame on which the cloth is stretched and shown in Figs. 6 to 9, and the shelf with its drawers, shown in Figs. 10 to 12. As the sliding screen is to fit into the uprights of the stand, the work of constructing the stand should be first undertaken.

The stand uprights will require two pieces of stock 1⅛" square and 34" long. As shown in Fig. 1 a groove ¼" wide and 3/16" deep will have to be made along one face of each upright to take the screen. This groove is located ¼" from the rear edge of the upright and should be 20¾" long. A ¼" dado head set up on the bench saw or a ¼" router bit in the drill press can be used to cut the groove. In either case, the lower end of the groove will have to be cut square by hand with a chisel.

The upper and lower stretchers which separate the uprights are joined to them by means of mortise-and-tenon joints. Mortises to take the tenons on the ends of the upper and lower stretchers are laid out on the face of each upright as shown in Fig. 1. The cutting of these mortises may be done on the drill press set up as a hollow mortiser or they may be cut by hand

by boring a series of holes to the required depth with an auger bit, then cleaning out the excess wood with a chisel. The mortise for the upper stretcher should be cut to a depth of 9/16" while the mortise to take the lower stretcher is to be cut to a depth of 13/16".

The shelf is to be secured to the uprights with 1¾" No. 8 flathead screws. A hole to take the screws is to be located and bored in each upright as

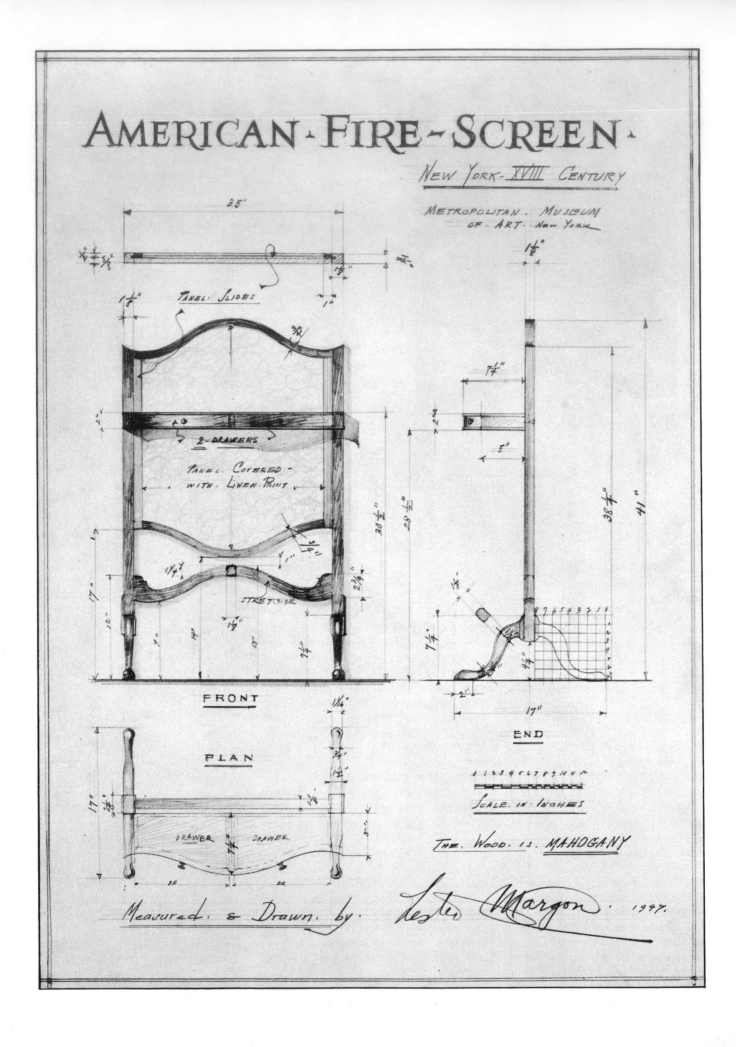

AMERICAN · FIRE ~ SCREEN ·

NEW YORK - XVIII CENTURY

METROPOLITAN · MUSEUM
OF · ART · NEW YORK

PANEL · SLIDES

2 · DRAWERS

PANEL · COVERED ·
WITH · LINEN · PRINT

STRETCHER

FRONT

PLAN

DRAWER   DRAWER

DR   DR

END

SCALE · IN · INCHES

THE · WOOD · IS · MAHOGANY

Measured · & · Drawn · by · Lester Margon · 1947.

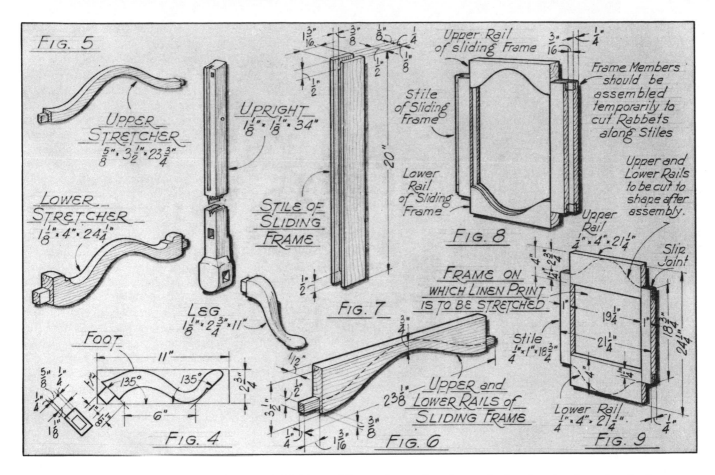

FIG. 5

UPPER STRETCHER
$\frac{5}{8}$" × $3\frac{1}{2}$" × $23\frac{3}{4}$"

LOWER STRETCHER
$1\frac{1}{8}$" × 4" × $24\frac{1}{4}$"

UPRIGHT
$1\frac{1}{8}$" × $1\frac{1}{8}$" × 34"

STILE OF SLIDING FRAME

LEG
$1\frac{1}{8}$" × $2\frac{3}{4}$" × 11"

FOOT

FIG. 4

FIG. 7

Upper Rail of sliding Frame

Stile of Sliding Frame

Lower Rail of Sliding Frame

FIG. 8

Frame Members should be assembled temporarily to cut Rabbets along Stiles

Upper and Lower Rails to be cut to shape after assembly.

Upper Rail $\frac{1}{4}$" × 4" × $21\frac{1}{4}$"

Slip Joint

Lower Rail $\frac{1}{4}$" × 4" × $21\frac{1}{4}$"

FIG. 9

Stile $\frac{1}{4}$" × 1" × $18\frac{3}{4}$"

FRAME ON WHICH LINEN PRINT IS TO BE STRETCHED

UPPER and LOWER RAILS of SLIDING FRAME

FIG. 6

shown in Fig. 1. These holes are to be countersunk on the rear edge in order that the head of the screw will be flush with the surface of the wood.

The lower end of each upright is to be shaped as shown in the main drawing, Fig. 5 and the photograph. In order to do this, it will be necessary to glue pieces to each side of the post as shown in Fig. 1. A piece $\frac{1}{2}$" × $1\frac{1}{8}$" × 3" is to be glued to each edge of each upright at the lower end. It is best to cut these pieces $1\frac{1}{4}$" wide before gluing them; then, after the glue has set and the clamps have been removed, the edges can be dressed flush with the faces of the uprights. To the inside face of each upright, a piece of 3/16" stock $2\frac{1}{8}$" wide and 3" long should be glued, while against the outer face, a piece 3/16" × $2\frac{1}{8}$" × $4\frac{3}{4}$" should be glued as shown in Fig. 1.

The feet of the stand are to be joined to the uprights by means of mortise and tenon joints. The mortises that are to take the tenons on the end of each foot are to be laid out and cut in each edge of the upright as shown in Fig. 1. The mortises are cut in the same manner as were those in the upright which are to take the stretchers. With the completion of the mortises the preparation of the feet can be undertaken.

The feet, as shown in Fig. 4, will **require** four pieces of $1\frac{1}{8}$" × $2\frac{3}{4}$"

stock 11" long. The angle cuts locating the bottom of the foot and the shoulder of the tenon should be laid out first with the aid of a bevel. The length, width and location of the tenon are laid out next, using the T-bevel. Preparing a full-size pattern of the foot, then tracing it on the stock within the limits of the layout lines is the last layout operation on the face of the stock. Cutting out the tenon to fit the mortise will require making the first cut at the end of the tenon. On this sawn end should be laid out the thickness of the tenon. The shoulders of the tenon are cut on

the bench saw, then the cheek cuts are made. The cheeks of the tenons should be trimmed by hand with a chisel to fit them to their respective mortises. The cutting of the foot to its required shape can be done on the band or jig saw.

Shaping of the foot and the lower end of the uprights can now be started. The foot is worked to shape with a spokeshave, rasp and file, then set into the upright in order to carry the contour line in an even flow to the blocks of the upright. The shaping of these blocks is done with the same tools. The work is sandpapered with coarse and

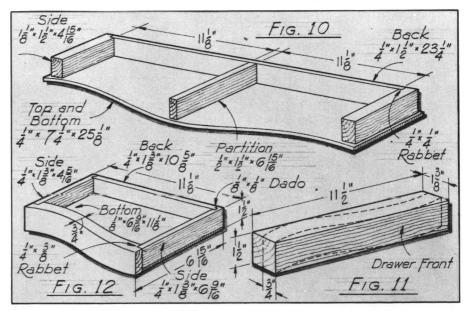

FIG. 10

Side $1\frac{1}{8}$" × $1\frac{1}{2}$" × $4\frac{15}{16}$"

Back $\frac{1}{4}$" × $1\frac{1}{2}$" × $23\frac{1}{4}$"

Top and Bottom $\frac{1}{4}$" × $7\frac{1}{4}$" × $25\frac{1}{8}$"

Back $\frac{1}{4}$" × $1\frac{3}{8}$" × $10\frac{5}{8}$"

Partition $\frac{1}{2}$" × $1\frac{1}{2}$" × $6\frac{15}{16}$"

Rabbet $\frac{1}{4}$" × $\frac{1}{4}$"

Side $\frac{1}{4}$" × $1\frac{3}{8}$" × $4\frac{5}{8}$"

$\frac{1}{8}$" × $\frac{1}{8}$" Dado

Bottom $\frac{1}{4}$" × $6\frac{9}{16}$" × $1\frac{1}{8}$"

Rabbet $\frac{1}{4}$" × $\frac{3}{4}$"

Side $\frac{1}{4}$" × $1\frac{3}{8}$" × $6\frac{9}{16}$"

FIG. 12

Drawer Front

FIG. 11

fine sandpaper to remove all tool marks.

The lower stretcher is made of 1⅛″ stock 4″ wide and 24¼″ long. Tenons are laid out on each end as shown in Fig. 2; then they are cut to fit their respective mortises. A full-size pattern of the lower stretcher contour is prepared and traced on the stock. The wood is cut to shape on the band or jig saw and the corners rounded.

The upper stretcher will require a piece of ⅝″ stock 3½″ wide and 23¾″ long. Tenons are laid out on each end as shown in Fig. 3, then cut to fit their respective mortises. A full-size pattern of this member is laid out and traced on the stock and the wood cut to shape on the band or jig saw. The complete upper stretcher is set in place so that the sweep of the upper end of the uprights may be laid out. The cutting to shape and finishing of the upper end of each upright completes the construction of this unit.

Each member should be sanded thoroughly with No. 1/2 and No. 2/0 sandpaper preparatory to assembling. The feet are glued to the uprights, then the uprights joined to the stretchers. The clamps should be left on until the glue has had time to set.

The construction of the sliding frame is the next unit to be undertaken. This consists of two rails shown in Fig. 6 and two stiles shown in Fig. 7. The stiles will require two pieces of stock ½″ x 1 3/16″ x 20″. A ¼″ groove is cut along the center of the inside edge and along the center of both ends as shown in Fig. 7. The groove along the edge is to be ⅜″ deep while those on the ends are to be ½″ deep. The end grooves are to take the tenons of the ends of the rails while the groove along the edge is to take the frame over which the cloth is stretched.

The upper and lower rails will require two pieces of ½″ stock 3½″ wide and 23⅛″ long. Tenons are laid out on each end as shown in Fig 6, then cut to fit snugly into the grooves of the stiles. It is important that this fit be snug because the cutting of the rabbets along the stiles as shown in Fig. 8 will have to be done before the members are assembled permanently. A full-size pattern of this member should be prepared and traced on the stock. The inside contour only is cut to shape on the band or jig saw. With the aid of a ¼″ straight-face cutter set up in the drill press or the spindle shaper and using a depth collar as a guide, a ¼″ x ⅜″ groove is cut along the inner edge of each rail member. The frame members are assembled temporarily and the rabbets cut along the stiles as shown in Fig. 8. The contour of the outer edge of the upper and lower frame members can now be cut and finished. Permanent assembly of this unit cannot be done until after the work is finished.

The linen frame as shown in Fig. 9 is made of ¼″ stock. The stiles require two pieces 1″ x 18¾″ while the rails take two pieces 4″ x 21¼″. The rails are joined to the stiles by means of slip joints. The frame is assembled and the members secured by glue. The upper and lower rails are to be shaped in order to fit into the grooves in the sliding frame. This fit should be fairly loose as the linen and the tacks that secure the linen to the frame must be allowed for. When completed, both sides of the frame should be covered, securing the material with small tacks driven into the outer edges of the frame members.

The shelf requires two pieces of ¼″ x 7¼″ x 25⅛″ stock for the top and bottom. These pieces are cut to the shape shown in Fig. 10 and on the main drawing. The ends and forward edges are molded by hand with a spokeshave and sandpaper. The location of the sides and partition are established on the inside face of both members. The stock for the sides and partition is cut to size and shape as shown in Fig. 10. A ¼″ x ¼″ rabbet is cut along the back end of the side members to take the back members. The side and partition members are joined to the back member with glue and small brads; then these assembled parts are joined to the bottom member in the same manner. The top member is immediately placed in position. Apply glue to the upper edges of the partition, side and back members and place the assembled work in clamps. After the clamps have been removed, the shelf is secured to the uprights with 1¾″ No. 8 flathead screws.

The drawer fronts are cut from 1⅜″ stock 1½″ wide and 11½″ long as shown in Fig. 11. The sweep of the curve on these members should follow that of the top and bottom shelf members. The drawer fronts can be cut to shape on the band or jig saw, then dressed smooth with a spokeshave and sandpaper. As shown in Fig. 12, a ¼″ x ⅜″ rabbet is cut along each end to take the side members while a ⅛″ x ⅜″ rabbet is cut along the lower inside edge to take the bottom member. The drawer side and back members are cut to the sizes given in Fig. 12, then the dadoes and rabbets are cut as indicated to join these members together. Glue and brads secure the front, back and side members together. The bottom member is cut to fit in the rabbet of the front member, then secured with glue. Suitable drawer pulls should be provided. The original has brass pulls.

The completed work is finished by applying stain and paste filler, then several coats of orange shellac, rubbing varnish or clear lacquer. The finish should be rubbed down with No. 3/0 steel wool or No. 4/0 sandpaper. The frame to which the linen was secured can now be placed in the sliding frame and the sliding frame assembled. The sliding frame is slipped in the grooves of the uprights, completing the work.

BILL OF MATERIALS

Pcs	Th	W	L	Part
		Stand		
2	1⅛	1⅛	34	Uprights
2	3/16	2⅛	3	Blocks
2	3/16	2⅛	4¾	Blocks
4	½	1⅛	3	Blocks
4	1⅛	2¾	11	Feet
1	⅝	3½	23¾	Upper stretcher
1	1⅛	4	24¼	Lower stretcher
		Sliding Frame		
2	½	3½	23⅛	Rails
2	½	1 3/16	20	Stiles
		Linen Frame		
2	¼	1	18¾	Stiles
2	¼	4	21¼	Rails
		Shelf		
2	¼	7¼	25⅛	Top and bottom
2	1⅛	1½	4 15/16	Sides
1	½	1½	6 15/16	Partition
1	¼	1½	23¼	Back
		Drawers		
2	1⅜	1½	11½	Front
2	¼	1⅜	6 9/16	Side
2	¼	1⅜	4 5/16	Side
2	¼	1⅜	10⅝	Back
2	⅛	6 9/16	11⅛	Bottom

All dimensions in inches

Paneled Setting for Colonial Furniture

Furniture as distinguished in quality as that described in the preceding pages deserves a fine setting such as provided by pine paneling like that in this room, which is used by courtesy of the Brooklyn Museum

COLONIAL furniture without an authentic background often loses much of its inherent quality and charm. It therefore is the purpose of this article to provide measured drawings of a typical setting for the fine period furniture the craftsman may have built.

The Bliss House chosen for presentation formerly stood at the corner of Montpelier and Main Streets in Springfield, Mass., and was built in 1754. It is a typical, moderate-size dwelling of the colonial period without much distinction in its architectural exterior.

The interior, however, is very good and has been selected for reproduction. The mantel elevation of a bedroom proved best because of its simplicity, restraint and excellent proportions. Of special interest is the setback of the mantel that is in itself so unusual and intriguing. The chaste brick fireplace, the slate hearth and the classical wood molding surrounding the brick opening as well as the picture panel above are features worthy of reproduction.

Pine rooms are noticeably in vogue today in many of the finest homes; yet paneling of this type is not very expensive. In the modern manner only one wall needs to be paneled, and the mantel elevation is generally the wall selected; the other walls are then painted or papered. In order to hold the room together, from a decorative viewpoint, the cornice molding is carried around the room, a pine chair rail and a wood baseboard are added. Stock moldings, of course, can be substituted for the shapes shown.

The photo is particularly interesting because of its paneled ceiling, but this feature is obsolete and should not be used. Either a plaster ceiling or a very simple beamed ceiling is advisable.

After the craftsman has paneled a room in wood, additional pieces of the finest colonial furniture will be desired.

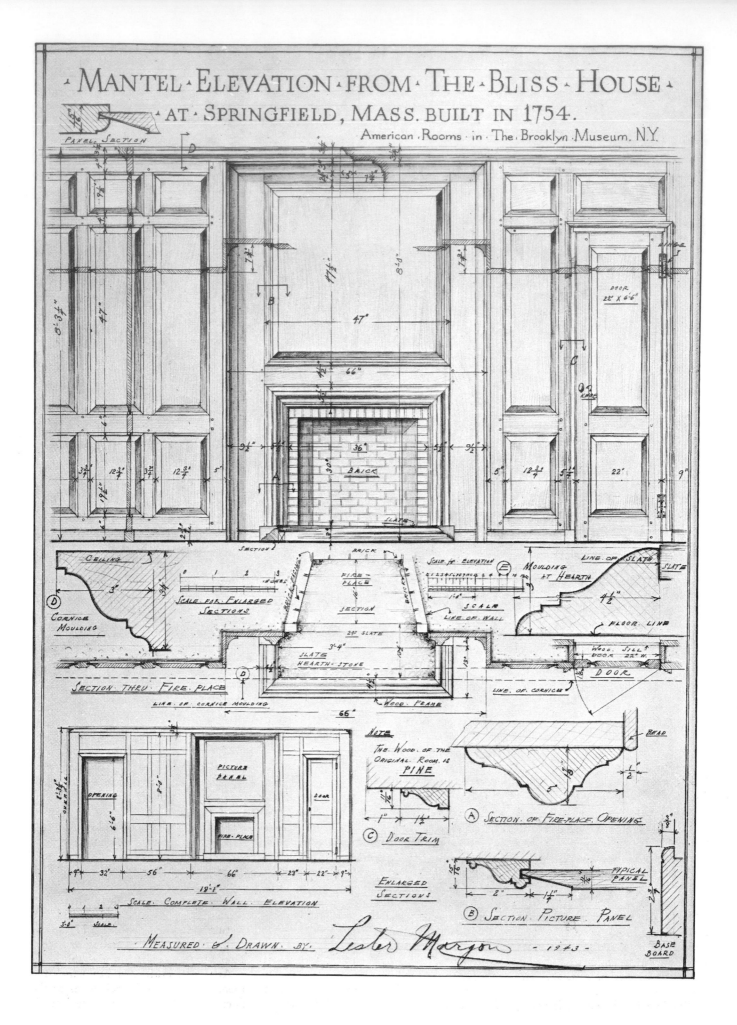

· MANTEL · ELEVATION · FROM · THE · BLISS · HOUSE ·
· AT · SPRINGFIELD, MASS. BUILT IN 1754.

American · Rooms · in · The · Brooklyn · Museum · N.Y.

PANEL SECTION

DOOR 22" X 6'-6"

BRICK

36"

SLATE

SECTION

CEILING

CORNICE MOULDING

D

SCALE FOR ENLARGED SECTIONS

SECTION · THRU · FIRE · PLACE

LINE OF CORNICE MOULDING

BRICK

FIRE PLACE

SECTION

SLATE HEARTH-STONE

WOOD FRAME

66"

SCALE FOR ELEVATION

SCALE

LINE OF WALL

MOULDING AT HEARTH

LINE OF SLATE

SLATE

FLOOR LINE

WOOD SILL DOOR 22" W.

DOOR

LINE OF CORNICES

OPENING

PICTURE PANEL

FIRE PLACE

DOOR

9" 32" 56" 66" 23" 22" 9"

19'-1"

SCALE · COMPLETE · WALL · ELEVATION

SCALE

NOTE

THE WOOD OF THE ORIGINAL ROOM IS PINE

C DOOR TRIM

ENLARGED SECTIONS

BEAD

A SECTION · OF · FIRE · PLACE · OPENING

TYPICAL PANEL

B SECTION · PICTURE · PANEL

BASE BOARD

MEASURED & DRAWN BY Lester Morgan - 1943 -

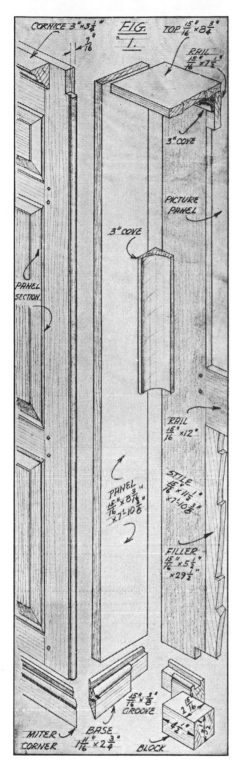

eling into the space. Any required change should be made in the lengths of the rails or the paneling rather than in the widths of the various stiles.

Before construction can be undertaken the location of the units should be marked off on the floor; from the dimensions obtained along these lines, the panel sizes can be established. The layout of the wall elevation shows the paneling broken up into five main units consisting of a connecting door, closet door, wide panel section, narrow panel section and fireplace unit. The particular layout adaptable to the room that is to be paneled may consist of of any combination of these units or any variation of the size of the units that can be fitted along the wall.

After the panel arrangement has been determined it will be necessary to lay out the sizes of the various members that go into the construction of each unit. From this layout the bill of materials is made up. It is important to take into consideration the method used in joining the various members that make up each unit so that allowance is made for joints when the stock is being cut to size.

As shown in Figs. 1 and 3, the units when completed are set into base members fastened to the floor with nails. When making up the stiles for the various units, the builder must deduct the height of the base members from the floor-to-ceiling measurement in order that the units fit in place.

The fireplace unit is made of two stiles and two rails as shown in Fig. 1. The rails are joined to the stiles by means of pinned mortise and tenon joints. The filler at each side of the fireplace opening is doweled into the rail first and is then joined to the stile with dowels at the same time the rail is put in place. The picture panel is set in molding as shown in detail (B) of the main drawing. This molding is fastened to the stiles and rails with finishing nails. The molding shown in detail (A) is fastened to the fillers at each side of the fireplace opening as well as to the rail above the opening. When the unit is complete, the base is fastened to the floor and the unit is set in the groove. The side panels that form the recess are fastened to the fireplace unit with finishing nails, before the top is put in place. The large cove molding is applied as shown.

The wide and narrow panel sections as well as the door sections are made as shown in Fig. 2. The rails are mortised into the stiles, while the molding on the edges of the rails is coped.

The stile that butts against the side panels of the recessed fireplace unit is rabbeted and beaded as shown in Fig. 1. The door stiles are notched as shown in Fig. 3 so that the base block and door trim can be set in place.

When these completed units are being set up the baseboard is first fastened to the floor to receive panels and stiles, while a nailing strip is fastened to the ceiling to provide a means of securing the upper ends of the panels.

They can be built from time to time. Eventually it will be the most friendly room in the house. All members of the household will naturally migrate into that room. It will prove to be a greater sanctuary for rest than you have ever hoped for.

In all probability the wall that the craftsman wishes to panel is such that the overall dimensions of the various units shown in the drawing will not fit. It may be necessary to increase or decrease the widths of the panels or the fireplace section in order to fit the pan-

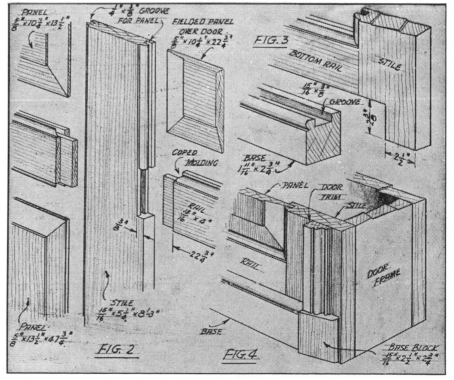

INDEX

Dover Books on Art

ART ANATOMY, Dr. William Rimmer. One of the few books on art anatomy that are themselves works of art, this is a faithful reproduction (rearranged for handy use) of the extremely rare masterpiece of the famous 19th century anatomist, sculptor, and art teacher. Beautiful, clear line drawings show every part of the body—bony structure, muscles, features, etc. Unusual are the sections on falling bodies, foreshortenings, muscles in tension, grotesque personalities, and Rimmer's remarkable interpretation of emotions and personalities as expressed by facial features. It will supplement every other book on art anatomy you are likely to have. Reproduced clearer than the lithographic original (which sells for $500 on up on the rare book market.) Over 1,200 illustrations. xiii + 153pp. 7¾ x 10¾.

20908-3 Paperbound $2.50

THE CRAFTSMAN'S HANDBOOK, Cennino Cennini. The finest English translation of IL LIBRO DELL' ARTE, the 15th century introduction to art technique that is both a mirror of Quatrocento life and a source of many useful but nearly forgotten facets of the painter's art. 4 illustrations. xxvii + 142pp. D. V. Thompson, translator. 5⅜ x 8.

20054-X Paperbound $2.00

THE BROWN DECADES, Lewis Mumford. A picture of the "buried renaissance" of the post-Civil War period, and the founding of modern architecture (Sullivan, Richardson, Root, Roebling), landscape development (Marsh, Olmstead, Eliot), and the graphic arts (Homer, Eakins, Ryder). 2nd revised, enlarged edition. Bibliography. 12 illustrations. xiv + 266 pp. 5⅜ x 8.

20200-3 Paperbound $2.00

THE STYLES OF ORNAMENT, A. Speltz. The largest collection of line ornament in print, with 3750 numbered illustrations arranged chronologically from Egypt, Assyria, Greeks, Romans, Etruscans, through Medieval, Renaissance, 18th century, and Victorian. No permissions, no fees needed to use or reproduce illustrations. 400 plates with 3750 illustrations. Bibliography. Index. 640pp. 6 x 9.

20577-6 Paperbound $3.75

THE ART OF ETCHING, E. S. Lumsden. Every step of the etching process from essential materials to completed proof is carefully and clearly explained, with 24 annotated plates exemplifying every technique and approach discussed. The book also features a rich survey of the art, with 105 annotated plates by masters. Invaluable for beginner to advanced etcher. 374pp. 5⅜ x 8.

20049-3 Paperbound $3.00

OF THE JUST SHAPING OF LETTERS, Albrecht Dürer. This remarkable volume reveals Albrecht Dürer's rules for the geometric construction of Roman capitals and the formation of Gothic lower case and capital letters, complete with construction diagrams and directions. Of considerable practical interest to the contemporary illustrator, artist, and designer. Translated from the Latin text of the edition of 1535 by R. T. Nichol. Numerous letterform designs, construction diagrams, illustrations. iv + 43pp. 7⅞ x 10¾.

21306-4 Paperbound $2.00

Dover Books on Art

LANDSCAPE GARDENING IN JAPAN, Josiah Conder. A detailed picture of Japanese gardening techniques and ideas, the artistic principles incorporated in the Japanese garden, and the religious and ethical concepts at the heart of those principles. Preface. 92 illustrations, plus all 40 full-page plates from the Supplement. Index. xv + 299pp. 8⅜ x 11¼.

21216-5   Paperbound $4.50

DESIGN AND FIGURE CARVING, E. J. Tangerman. "Anyone who can peel a potato can carve," states the author, and in this unusual book he shows you how, covering every stage in detail from very simple exercises working up to museum-quality pieces. Terrific aid for hobbyists, arts and crafts counselors, teachers, those who wish to make reproductions for the commercial market. Appendix: How to Enlarge a Design. Brief bibliography. Index. 1298 figures. x + 289pp. 5⅜ x 8½.

21209-2   Paperbound $3.00

THE STANDARD BOOK OF QUILT MAKING AND COLLECTING, M. Ickis. Even if you are a beginner, you will soon find yourself quilting like an expert, by following these clearly drawn patterns, photographs, and step-by-step instructions. Learn how to plan the quilt, to select the pattern to harmonize with the design and color of the room, to choose materials. Over 40 full-size patterns. Index. 483 illustrations. One color plate. xi + 276pp. 6¾ x 9½.   20582-7   Paperbound $3.50

LOST EXAMPLES OF COLONIAL ARCHITECTURE, J. M. Howells. This book offers a unique guided tour through America's architectural past, all of which is either no longer in existence or so changed that its original beauty has been destroyed. More than 275 clear photos of old churches, dwelling houses, public buildings, business structures, etc. 245 plates, containing 281 photos and 9 drawings, floorplans, etc. New Index. xvii + 248pp. 7⅞ x 10¾.   21143-6   Paperbound $3.50

A HISTORY OF COSTUME, Carl Köhler. The most reliable and authentic account of the development of dress from ancient times through the 19th century. Based on actual pieces of clothing that have survived, using paintings, statues and other reproductions only where originals no longer exist. Hundreds of illustrations, including detailed patterns for many articles. Highly useful for theatre and movie directors, fashion designers, illustrators, teachers. Edited and augmented by Emma von Sichart. Translated by Alexander K. Dallas. 594 illustrations. 464pp. 5⅛ x 7⅛.

21030-8   Paperbound $3.50

Dover publishes books on commercial art, art history, crafts, design, art classics; also books on music, literature, science, mathematics, puzzles and entertainments, chess, engineering, biology, philosophy, psychology, languages, history, and other fields. For free circulars write to Dept. DA, Dover Publications, Inc., 180 Varick St., New York, N.Y. 10014.